THE
HOUSE LURCHER

THE
HOUSE LURCHER

Jackie Drakeford

SWAN·HILL
PRESS

First published in the UK in 2003
by Swan Hill Press, an imprint of Quiller Publishing Ltd

Reprinted 2007

British Library Cataloguing-in-Publication Data
A catalogue record for this book
is available from the British Library

ISBN 978 1 904057 34 5

Printed in Great Britain by Biddles Ltd, King's Lynn, Norfolk

Swan Hill Press

an imprint of Quiller Publishing Ltd
Wykey House, Wykey, Shrewsbury, SY4 1JA, England
E-mail: info@quillerbooks.com
Website: www.countrybooksdirect.com

Especially for Irene and 'Witch'

Saluki lurcher (E. Dearden)

CONTENTS

Acknowledgements

With special thanks to Linda Thurlow, and the helpers at the Mid-Sussex
Happy Breed Dog Rescue

1 IN THE BEGINNING

Here you are, with a lurcher in the family. Perhaps you set out to get a completely different sort of dog, but were waylaid by the huge beguiling eyes. Perhaps you had already met other lurchers, and decided that this streamlined, gentle dog was for you. Or perhaps you aren't quite sure how it happened, but she is here anyway. In order to understand your lurcher better, it is necessary to know a little about how lurchers came to exist in the first place.

In essence, the lurcher is a cross between a running dog, also known as a sighthound or gazehound, and a working dog, most usually a border collie or a terrier. Sometimes the dog before you is the result of a cross between two or more sighthounds, such as a saluki/greyhound. Purists call these 'longdogs'. In this book, you will notice I use the term 'longdogs' to cover both lurchers and sighthound to sighthound crosses, as they are all 'long dogs'. This length of back is significant, and we will return to it presently. Sometimes, lurchers are the product of very mixed ancestry, having been bred lurcher to lurcher for generations, their work being the selection process used when deciding what to breed to whom, but the basics are unchanged. No matter how many breeds are involved, there are only running dogs and working dogs in the mixture.

The purpose of the lurcher was to put meat upon the table, in the days when meat was hunted as much as reared. In the old days, it was difficult to overwinter domestic livestock, and most were killed at the end of autumn and preserved by pickling and salting, as well as consumed with glee at the great feasts that were held at this time. Only the best of breeding stock was kept back. The only way to get fresh meat through the winter was to hunt it, and this was done with hawks and with hounds. There is a great hunting tradition within the British Isles, which were once famous throughout the known world for their hunting dogs: running mastiffs, holding mastiffs, scenting hounds, and the ones we are interested in, which are the gazehounds. You can see these tucked away in the old paintings, embroidered on tapestries, carved into furniture, adorning gateposts, coats of arms and statuary, and featured in the old legends. They were collectively knows as 'greyhounds', and like today's lurchers, came in all shapes, sizes and colours, as well as rough or smooth coated. They hunted by sight, (hence the terms 'gazehounds' and 'sighthounds') and were sprinters rather than stayers; high-couraged, they could course and catch any animal that was suitable for food. They lived in their owners' homes, and were most highly regarded.

Then came the Norman Conquest, and different kings, who wanted all the hunting for themselves. I come from the New Forest, in which the Game Laws have been a thorn in the side of the natives (who proudly refer to themselves as 'Commoners' and hold ancient Forest Rights) ever since. Even the Romans were happy to allow the locals to continue with their hunting tradition, but not the Normans, who imposed draconian penalties both on dogs that looked capable of running down game, and the people who owned them. Certain social orders were exempt, for instance the clergy. Remember Chaucer's Prioresse?

> 'Of smale houndes (small hounds) hadde she, that she fedde
> On rosted flesh (roasted flesh), and milk, and wastrel bread (fine white bread)'.

Or indeed, his Monk?

> 'Greihoundes he hadde, as swift as foule (birds) of flighte.'

The common man could no longer hunt for food with his dog. In the New Forest, there is a pub called 'The Crown and Stirrup' to commemorate the practice of testing dogs by seeing if they could pass through the King's stirrup. Those that were too large were deemed capable of catching hares and deer (the rabbit had not established in the wild at that time) and were 'lawed' a procedure which crippled them either by cutting off two toes on the forefoot, or, more rarely, by severing a tendon above either the wrist or hock. Penalties for poaching were even more severe: people caught so doing were apt either to have hands cut off, or to be executed, depending on the nature or frequency of the crime, and the mood of the lawgiver.

The peasantry did not give up so easily; while the Forest Laws were not so simple to defy, in other areas it was a matter of crossbreeding the running dog with another sort of cur, one which would hide its racy lines under a shaggy coat. Initially, the herding dogs in their various forms were ideal for this, being easily available, and of course it was quite justifiable to own such a dog. How milord's greyhound was induced to serve the droving cur when she came on heat is a matter for conjecture, but it certainly happened, and many a nondescript mutt hid a secret or two under her unkempt hair. Even nowadays, there are lurchers bred so, and not for all that different a reason.

So the lurcher came into being, and its reputation went before it. The gypsy dog, the poaching dog, the mouching cur, possessed of great intelligence and cunning, rarely caught in the act (and dead as a result if it was) and the bane of the keeper. If there was trouble with poaching, the gamekeepers made sure to shoot the dogs involved, if they could not catch the men, for a good dog took time to replace.

Nowadays, the lurcher has come in from the cold, and has no more need to hide its shape, the result being that it is easily recognisable. However, nothing else has changed about it. The lurcher is still used by many people to put meat upon the table, and all the instincts that made her invaluable to the poacher or the hungry cottager remain unchanged. She is still silent, clever, swift, and suspicious of going near strangers. She has a strong drive to steal food. She needs to run. She makes the most wonderful companion, if you can only understand her. She has a lot of advantages: she is clean, loving, easy with other dogs, good with children as long as they are not allowed to hurt or frighten her, can be trained to a high standard, and only makes a noise when it is necessary. After her exercise, she will happily sleep all day until the next walk. She does not hassle or yap or ricochet off the walls with excitement. She is not dominant, and likes the security of her place in the family pack. Lurchers have no inherited physical defects; they live for a long time, commonly into their teens, and will stay healthy with no more than good common-sense care. And when the world is dark for you, she will put her head on your lap and offer the most perfect, uncritical friendship and comfort. In return, there are just a few matters in which you will have to meet her half-way.

In order to understand how her mind works, you need to have a rough idea of how she is bred. A lurcher is like a fruit cake (some would say a complete fruit cake) in that there are differences in the basic recipe to suit everybody, and how you train your lurcher will depend on whether she has more sultanas than cherries. It is a wise dog that knows its own father, but even for dogs that have been lurcher to lurcher bred for generations, it is possible to have sufficient knowledge of what breeds made up the mixture just by looking at her. Let's have a look at what you can get.

The Main Base Breeds
The Greyhound

There are some lurchers that seem almost indistinguishable from greyhounds. The greyhound is a tall, well-muscled dog with a gentle disposition, and she is built for short bursts of incredible speed. Every registered greyhound in the world today traces its pedigree back to Lord Orford's Czarina, bred in the 1770s and which was never beaten in a course. Lord Orford rescued the breed, which was losing its 'fire', by crossing in bulldog blood, not the wheezing bow-legged travesties that are the modern KC registered bulldog, but an animal with the speed, agility and courage to drive and hold a bull. Similar animals are seen today in the American bulldog and the Victorian bulldog, which are the result of different breeders trying to re-create the original bulldog. The experiment was a resounding success, and a few generations later, Czarina swept all before her in her working life and produced several litters, from which every registered greyhound is now descended.

Very greyhoundy lurchers do not need a lot of exercise in terms of time, but they do need to be able to run freely at least twice a day. They soon get the fidgets out of their feet, but if they are not allowed to run, they become very unhappy. They have little hair underneath them in order to dissipate the heat caused by running, which means that they can feel the cold, and they appreciate a coat while they are leadwalking in winter. They also need somewhere to sleep that is warm; your sofa will do nicely. Because of their physique, they can rub themselves bald or even sore if they do not have somewhere soft to sleep. Lurchers can survive any amount of comfort. They are also sensitive to some anaesthetics and sedatives because of their lack of body fat. No lurcher should be allowed to become fat; it is not good for any dog, but especially not for the long slender limbs of the running dog. The greyhound type has catlike, well-knuckled feet, and the whole impression is of grace and elegance. However, these dogs are strong and tough, and do not need to be wrapped in cotton wool. They might cry if they tread on a nettle, tiptoe round puddles and have a severe allergy to rain, but they need to be out in the fresh air and feel the wind in their ears. They are a proper hound, and should be treated like one – but don't forget to dry them thoroughly when you get indoors again! Because of their speed – greyhounds are the second fastest sprinters in the world, after the cheetah – they can injure themselves, particularly their feet, if they run on hard, rutted or flinty ground. Often these dogs have to retire early because of foot or tendon injuries, and in extreme cases have a toe amputated. They can still last for years, much as ex-racehorses can still lead long and useful lives, and be the most delightful companions, but they won't be fast enough for competition any more. Greyhound is the baseline of most lurchers, and is added for speed, silence and kind nature.

How do you know that your lurcher isn't a greyhound? Almost all greyhounds are registered and ear-tattooed at birth, one ear being tattooed for

Greyhound lurcher

an English registered greyhound, both for an Irish dog. Baby greyhounds are very expensive, and destined for a working life either racing or coursing. Very occasionally, a litter is not tattooed and registered, and the resulting pups sold as pets or as lurchers, but this is extremely rare and usually the result of an accidental mating, or (in the case of one such that I know) a situation where, due to a momentary lapse, an on-heat bitch was turned out with several male dogs and probably mated all of them. In such a case, she could have carried pups by different sires (see Chapter 11: Breeding Lurchers) and so those pups could not be accurately pedigreed. Some breeders would have just crossed their fingers and put one sire on the paperwork, but this one was honest; the pups sold as pets at £100 each instead of racing greyhounds at well over £1000. Therefore, if your smooth-coated very greyhoundy lurcher is not tattooed, she most likely to be a genuine lurcher, although there is an outside chance, a very small one, that she is a greyhound.

Just a few words about the show greyhound: you do get greyhound classes in lurcher shows, but there is a totally different type of greyhound that is bred solely for Kennel Club showing, and is registered with this august body. These are never used for lurcher breeding, because they are such an exaggerated

13

shape that they cannot run, and would not remain sound if anyone tried to work them. If you are ever able to see some of these at close quarters, it is interesting, if rather sad, to compare the different conformation with that of a working greyhound.

The Whippet

The whippet is much more than a diminutive greyhound, being a separate breed in its own right. Whippets are fast and fiery, possessed of lightning take-off speed, and extraordinary turning ability. There are slight differences in type: some have pricked ears, some rose ears, some are roach or wheel-backed, some are the same shape as a greyhound. Like greyhounds, they are fastidious in their personal habits, like and need warmth and comfort, and have to have free-galloping exercise. They have more stamina than greyhounds, although whippets are in essence speed dogs rather than the endurance type. They are clever dogs, sweet-natured, and very trainable. Although the whippet tends to be a silent dog, she is possessed of an ear-splitting scream which she will use when excited, such as when she sees the lure on a racetrack. The whippet is one of the few breeds where the same dog can show at Kennel Club events, race and course, so true has the type been kept. Whippet is added to the lurcher mix to bring down the size, and add courage and agility. Whippets are

Racing whippet

Saluki lurcher

often crossed with greyhounds to create what is sometimes referred to as a 'grew'. These dogs are much in demand as lurchers, being of a good size, generally 23 to 24 inches high, very fast and game for anything. Grews and racing whippets are flatter in the back than the show whippet, but still have a distinctive curve over the quarters. The whippet and the grew both, like the greyhound, have very tight, well-knuckled feet.

The Saluki

The saluki is another dog that has kept its type, and can race, course, and show in Kennel Club events. The saluki originated as the desert dog, the hunting hound of the Bedouin, who even now jealously guard the pedigrees of their best hounds. The saluki is found all across the Middle East where the authorities still allow hunting; it comes in feathered and smooth versions, and is highly prized. Unlike other dogs, which are deemed 'unclean' and treated at best with contempt, the saluki has elevated status, and traditionally shares the tent and life of her Arab owners. Salukis are notoriously difficult to train, which is why the purebred is seldom worked as a lurcher, whereas purebred greyhounds or whippets will do the lurcher's job quite happily, though they

15

lack the stamina of a crossbred. However, it is perfectly possible to train the saluki, and lurchers with a proportion of this distinctive sighthound in them, but it does take a little more application, as salukis are both sensitive and stubborn. It is important to get the recall training done early, or else what you will see most of your saluki lurcher is her rear end disappearing over the horizon. Also she needs to be very thoroughly steadied to stock: she has been bred for thousands of years as a gazelle hound, and finds the thunder of galloping hooves tremendously exciting. Salukis seem to be aloof, but they are in fact very deeply loving, which is why they suffer so from change of ownership. If you have a saluki cross, she will repay your efforts in training and kindness a thousandfold, but first she must satisfy herself that you are worth the effort. Salukis blossom when they are kept close to their people, and they are not a dog that will give of their best if you don't give them enough of your time and company. They will not be your slave, but your companion. If you want a forgiving, clinging dog that hangs upon your every word, don't get a saluki cross. If, however, you are willing to understand her and work with her personality not against it, you will have a quite exceptional dog.

Saluki blood is easy to define in the lurcher. First, there are the ears, which are large, dropped, and often tasselled. The saluki profile is distinctive, with a very long snout and a huge nose on the end, though the head is narrow and with a distinctive occipital bump. The body is narrow, too, and you will be able to span her 'waist', just before her hindlegs, quite easily with your hands. This characteristic is much valued by the Bedouin. The pin-bones of her hips are very prominent: this is correct and not a sign that the dog is underweight. Her feet are extraordinary: long-toed and often feathered, with thick nails. These are all-terrain feet, suitable for galloping across the sand and rocks of the desert. With her slender limbs she often looks as if she is wearing snowshoes. Her toes are very flexible, and she can hold your hand with a front foot just as easily as a human can. The narrow chest is very deep; some people think that a wide chest denotes heartroom, but in a running dog, the lungs and heart – which are, as you would expect, huge – are contained in the depth of the brisket, not the width of the chest. So this slender dog, that often looks like Kipling's 'a rag, a bone and a hank of hair' has tremendous depth, and therefore tremendous stamina. Your saluki cross can gallop for far longer than the greyhound or whippet, though she is not as fast, and lacks the whippet's explosive starting 'kick'. She has a strong guarding instinct, bred in from the days when the sheik's tent was her responsibility, and care must be taken not to underestimate this. Strangers who approach the saluki-bred hound without

Typical saluki profile (E. Dearden)

introduction, or even try to reach into her car, are liable to wish that they had not. One of your responsibilities as the owner of such a hound is never to put her in the position where she feels justified in using her teeth, and so signing her own death warrant by simply doing her job. The saluki is a strong-minded dog with definite ideas about where she fits into the family, but she is never anything other than pleasant and easy to live with. The saluki tail is long, often but not always feathered, and the feather can take a year to arrive in a young dog. Not infrequently, these tails are curly, and this should not be considered a fault, but very much a part of this most distinctive dog. The coat is soft, and not weather-proof; your saluki cross can cope with heat and cold to extremes, but wet is not good for her. Saluki is used in the lurcher for stamina and toughness.

The Deerhound

The Scottish deerhound most closely resembles the ancient wolfhound, and is probably bred from the same stock. She is a gentle soul, but nobody's fool. Easy to train and live with, she has tremendous stamina as well as a ground-eating stride that is as effective up or downhill as it is on the flat. She is fast

17

Deerhound pup 14 months

Deerhound/greyhound second cross

and strong enough to catch and kill a red deer; because this is the original purpose of the breed, her shoulder and neck articulation is that of a dog bred to reach up, rather than down, to her quarry. Like the saluki, she has all-terrain feet, with long toes heavily furred, and exceptionally thick strong nails. Her coat is dense and wiry, and turns the weather well, far better than that of any other sighthound. Deerhounds are slow to mature, and may be well into their third year before they stop growing, and the purebreds are not long-lived, twelve being a good achievement. The hybrids – the lurchers – can live well into their teens, but great care must be taken in the early part of their lives, because they are large-framed dogs that need proper feeding, adequate but not over-exercising, and enormous patience while they mature physically and mentally. There is ample reward for this little bit of extra trouble, the deerhound cross being one of the easiest hounds to live with. Deerhound is added to the lurcher mix to give biddability, courage, stamina, and a weatherproof coat.

Irish Wolfhound

Lurchers, especially rescued ones, are frequently described as Irish wolfhound crosses, but this is almost always incorrect. The modern Irish wolfhound is a re-created breed, in which the baseline incorporated those few that were remaining when the breed almost died out, and which may well not have been purebred. To these was added the Scottish deerhound, and several examples of large shaggy hound that conformed more or less to the type. All went well, and the animal levelled out at a useful size, and in theory able to do its original job, until the usual regrettable desire in the showing world to get the size up resulted in extensive addition of great dane blood. This proved disastrous, the show standard great dane already being a short-lived oversized dog which passed its numerous health problems on to the reinvented wolfhound. As a consequence, the modern Irish wolfhound is lucky to live in health beyond its sixth year, and is so heavily built that it would have trouble sustaining a canter, never mind pursuing and catching a creature as athletic as a wolf. As such, it is quite unsuitable for inclusion in a lurcher breeding programme. Additionally, being a rare breed of dog, very expensive to buy and breed, it is highly unlikely that any owners would be willing to allow their hound to be used on a greyhound or lurcher. I once, in many years of lurcher judging, came across a supposed Irish wolfhound cross Scottish deerhound at a lurcher show in the West Country, and I believe that it was genuine: a magnificent beast 30 inches tall but lean and elegant. It looked capable of slaying anything from wolves to invading warriors. Certainly, the present breed of Irish wolfhound is in urgent

Purebred Irish wolfhound

need of an outcross if it is to return to type, and this would be a useful way to do it. From the lurcher side of things, if you are told a lurcher is an Irish wolfhound cross, you may safely disbelieve it.

Borzoi

The same applies if you are told a lurcher is a borzoi cross. This graceful Russian wolfhound is also rather expensive and not easily found; it is doubtful if many lurcher breeders could find a borzoi breeder willing to allow his or her precious stud dog to be used to produce crossbreds, and the stud fee would be immense compared to the selling price of lurcher pups. I knew of a purebred borzoi that was used with deadly effect on foxes, but she was aggressive with other dogs and not too friendly with people, either. There is always the risk that this temperament will come through if a borzoi is used; the lurcher is by definition a gentle, biddable dog capable of agility as well as speed, and in all honesty, there is little positive that borzois could contribute to the mixture, being large hounds that need a lot of space to turn in, heavy-coated for our climate, and too often uncertain of temper. This is exceptional in the sighthound breeds and may be due to one of two things. The best borzoi bloodlines were wiped out in the Russian Revolution, and it could be that the stock which escaped had to be very closely bred, in which circumstances unsoundnesses of mind and body are more easily set into the breed. Or it could be that, whereas by tradition, other sighthound breeds lived in the homes of their owners and therefore a good temperament was essential, borzois were kept kennelled, often in huge numbers, and so their relationship with the human race was more professional than personal. Borzois and their crosses are still used in America, (see Chapter 9) chiefly for hunting coyotes and jackrabbits, at which they evidently excel, and my contacts in the USA tell me that they have not experienced much in the way of temperament problems in these hounds. Possibly this is due to a larger or different gene pool, as the American borzois came over with the early settlers, long before the Russian Revolution.

Sometimes rough collie ('Lassie' collie) is used in lurcher breeding and the results claimed to be Borzoi crosses, the heavy coat and distinctive profile being similar enough to give rise to rumours that the one has been crossed into the other at some time in the distant past. Apart from looks, there is little to recommend the rough collie's use in a lurcher breeding programme, the modern 'Lassie' having far too heavy a coat and not enough in the way of brains. A litter of supposedly genuine Borzoi crosses appeared in the Midlands a short while ago, but of their subsequent lives, I know nothing.

Border Collie

The border collie cross greyhound is probably the most popular and easily found lurcher type, and for many, the true classic. Good collies are strong, intelligent, easily trained and very versatile. They have excellent coats, tough round feet of the 'cat' type, as distinct from the 'hare' type of the saluki or deerhound, are quick to mature, and very long lived, sometimes getting to twenty and beyond. The use of the border collie in the lurcher goes back to when the sheepdog was the most easily found type of dog; thus there was usually an in-season bitch about when the greyhound was available, and also the offspring do not look particularly 'sighthoundy' and so did not attract too much attention. Many people reckon the border collie cross to be the best; while I am not one of them, I am certainly an admirer of its talents. There is little that a border collie cross cannot do, and if obedience competitions are what you like, the border collie lurcher is one of the easiest dogs to bring up to standard. The first cross, i.e. the collie/greyhound, always has a smooth, dense coat, and is sometimes quite heavily built. As you would expect, black and white colouring predominates, and sometimes the mottling, known as 'merle', which is usually accompanied by one or both eyes being blue or ticked. The

Purebred merle border collie

Greyhound/border collie first cross

border collie throws a wide skull and a broad chest, often with a characteristic neck ruff. Many people favour a second cross back to greyhound or whippet, called a 'threequarter bred' which gives a smooth short coat and a hound that, at first glance, seems to be a small stocky greyhound, until you take in the width of head and chest. One of the other popular crosses is to take the first cross, i.e. collie/greyhound back to the collie, which is known as a 'reverse threequarter bred'. These dogs are usually collie-coated, though there may be one or two smooth coats in the litter, and look like lightly-built border collies. As you would expect, the collie temperament is stronger in the reverse threequarter than the first cross, and so you have a dog that needs to be kept busy. Border collie is added to the lurcher for stamina, coat and trainability.

The Bearded Collie

The 'beardie' is a popular little dog that has not been used in lurcher crosses for as long as the border collie, but is increasingly gaining favour, not least for the variety of pretty colours that it produces as well as an appealing 'scruffy' look. A happy dog with an engaging temperament, she is not as busy as the border, and is a little more stubborn. Quick to mature and very long-lived, the beardie cross

Bearded collie cross – Hancock bred

trains on well, and waxes fat on rations that would starve a greyhound. The coat is harsh, thick and double, and may need a little attention as it gathers mud and ice in winter, and benefits from clipping in the summer – the old shepherds used to shear their beardies along with the sheep. Beardie feet are round and wide, heavily furred and usually seem a size too big. The beardie skull is big and broad, especially if the dog is show rather than working bred. These dogs are wide at chest and quarters, strong and tough, cheap to maintain, and will live happily indoors or out. They can handle the worst weather, and are always ready to accompany you for as much exercise as you want to take. As well as the straight beardie cross, a very popular type is created by crossing a bearded collie with a border collie, and then using the result on a greyhound. This gives the typical beardie wide head and rough coat, but not quite such a thick coat as the first cross. It is an attractive and versatile animal, straightforward to train and easy on the eye. David Hancock of Sutton Coldfield specialises in beardie, border, and beardie/border crosses, and if you have ever heard of a lurcher referred to as a 'Hancock' it means that it is one of his breeding. Bearded collie is added to the lurcher for coat, toughness and looks.

The Australian Kelpie

The kelpie cross is a relative newcomer to the lurcher world, and already has a staunch following. Brought to fame by professional lurcher trainer Dave Sleight* whose display team is a popular feature at shows all over the country, the kelpie cross is a strong contender in obedience and field trial competitions. At first glance, these dogs do not look particularly of lurcher type, especially those crossed to whippet rather than greyhound, but they are deceptively fast, and quick on the turn. Less manic than the border collie, the kelpie is a clever and yet biddable dog, and its lurcher descendants are smooth-coated, broad of chest and skull, and muscular for their size. Easily mistaken for a bull terrier cross, the difference is most readily seen in the feet, which, in the case of the kelpie, are extremely well cushioned and tight. The kelpie cross is still quite rare, and not often seen in rescue homes, but should you take one on, be prepared to give her a lot of mental stimulation and work as well as plenty of exercise. Kelpie is added to the lurcher mix for toughness and trainability.

Australian Cattle Dog

Not the commonest of lurchers, these, but a few come into rescue centres.

*Dave Sleight, OutBack Productions, 19 Hoober Street, West Melton, Rotherham, S.Yorkshire S63 6AX

L to R – beardie lurcher, kelpie/collie/whippet, kelpie/greyhound

Purebred Australian cattle dog

They are clever dogs that bond strongly with their owners, and so suffer very much when they change hands. The cattle dog has a strong guarding instinct, which is difficult to contain, her concerns being directed to people and animals alike. She is a special dog with the right owner and the right environment, needing to live somewhere fairly remote, where she is not constantly meeting strangers. Cattle dogs are very hardy and brave. The cattle dog lurcher is not recommended as a pet except for very experienced dog owners who are able to offer a securely-fenced environment and plenty of exercise as well as diligent training. They are working dogs, and the best belong to people who work them full time. Hampshire pest controller Phil Lloyd is a cattle dog lurcher specialist, and his video *Dances with Dingoes** is very informative about the origins of the cattle dog, and the working ability of the lurcher so derived.

The Staffordshire Bull Terrier

Another very popular cross in some parts of the country, this type has the typical Staffie broad skull, prominent eyes, smooth coat and muscular body. Once, pit bull crosses were used, but now that is not legally possible, (pit bull terriers by law must not be allowed to breed, and it is compulsory to neuter them; anyone offering 'genuine pit bull terrier lurchers ' is either breeding illegally or telling lies) the Staffie has taken over. There is a sub-type known as the 'Irish Stafford'(not KC recognised) which is a leggier and more athletic-looking animal than the show Stafford, and is the preferred option for lurcher breeding. Staffordshire feet are wide with a tendency to splay as the dog gets older, which gives the Staffie lurcher as distinctive a look as the wide grin beneath the wide head. Purebred Staffords are known for being family dogs, and are fiercely loyal and protective; as you would expect, this comes across in the lurcher. From time to time, the Staffie lurcher inherits a level rather than scissor 'bite', sometimes even slightly undershot, but this should not be seen as a problem. The second cross back to greyhound produces a lovely animal with slightly prominent cheeks, flat wide skull, and an athletic body that takes very little compared to some sighthounds in the way of keeping fit. They hold their weight well, and are economical to feed. They can be noisier than you would expect from a lurcher, not necessarily from barking, but with the typical Staffie yell in moments of excitement. These are high-couraged dogs which are not quarrelsome but will not back down if attacked. Easy to train, clean and sweet-smelling, the Staffie cross will fit easily into most households. Staffordshire bull terrier is used to give courage.

---

*Phil Lloyd, Moucher Productions, PO Box 372, Southampton SO14 OTA

Bull terrier cross

The English Bull Terrier

Though this will give courage as well, the English bull terrier is too much of a cripple nowadays to use in the makeup of a working dog. The huge head and comparatively weak quarters, plus a character that is genial but not the sharpest tool in the box, would add nothing of value to the lurcher. I have seen only one of these: a sweet-natured bitch that could not run, and did not survive beyond her first birthday.

The Bedlington Terrier

Bedlingtons are spirited terriers, and used more often than other terriers in lurcher mixes because they are naturally silent. This does not mean that they make no noise at all, but rather that they only do so when it is necessary; the excited constant yapping of other terrier breeds is a world away from the Bedlington. The first cross is always rough coated, and either blue or fawn; sometimes the linty coat of the show Bedlington comes through, which means that the lurcher soaks through very quickly in the rain; sometimes the coat is coarse and weatherproof as it should be. Bedlington blood is very prepotent, and even a fourth generation cross will have an unmistakeable look to it. The skull is middling broad, with a distinctive occipital bump at the back and very

27

Bedlington/whippet

Airedale lurcher

strong jaws with big teeth – the Bedlington was expected to kill a fox with one bite. Eyes are usually oval and slanting, and a light eye is not a fault. Ears can throw to either parent, but the rose ear of the sighthound is more usual than the drop ear of the Bedlington. The back of the Bedlington is arched, sometimes wheelbacked, sometimes roached, and the gait has a distinctive roll at a trot. Feet are small, neat and tight, and the tail is usually carried high. The Beddy cross is easy to train and quiet, but is quick to take offence if another dog attempts to bully her, and she bears a long grudge. They are fast and agile, very brave and feisty, and extremely loyal. One of the classic crosses is the Bedlington/whippet, a deceptively frail-looking hound that is, in reality, anything but frail. The combined intelligence and agility can sometimes mean that you find your Beddy cross on the worktop, window-sill or even, as we have done, the mantelpiece. The Bedlington/greyhound is less apt to do this, but is otherwise just like its smaller cousin, just a few sizes larger. Bedlington is added to lurchers to bring the size down as well as contributing intelligence, agility and a quality known as 'fire'.

Other Terriers

Every other terrier breed has been crossed into the lurcher at some time or another, mostly to add coat, the only feature in which the Bedlington is lacking. The terrier is usually crossed with whippet rather than greyhound, creating an attractive looking little dog with terrific acceleration, sometimes referred to in the working dog world as a 'whirrier'. Terriers that are too large to go to ground, for instance the Kerry blue or the Airedale, tend to be crossed with greyhound rather than whippet, and make useful lurchers. Any dog with terrier blood in it is going to be feisty, strong-minded and lively; the small ones retain the instinct to go to ground.

German Shepherd

This is quite a popular cross, the best being intelligent and biddable. The first cross looks like a leggy GSD, though the ears do not always remain erect. The black and tan colouring is very dominant, as is the thick heavy coat. German shepherd feet are very distinctive, being large and with a tendency to splay. Sometimes the over-articulated back legs of the GSD are inherited, but most often the better physique of the greyhound comes through. GSD crosses are heavy in the forelimbs, and can have loaded shoulders; for that reason, the first cross is usually put back to a greyhound and will then give a much better proportioned dog. The GSD can be noisy, and obviously has a good guarding instinct; it is very loyal, and can be trained to a high standard. The first cross needs to know its place in the pack being one of the few lurcher types that has a tendency to dominance, but this varies with the individual, and often the greyhound side comes through to give a softer nature.

German shepherd is added to the lurcher to give strength and trainability; how successful this is depends very much on the quality of the original GSD parent.

Labrador

This is a cross that makes a delightful dog, but is not that often seen, possibly because the Labrador cloddiness tends to overwhelm the greyhound gracefulness. In particular, the Labrador first cross tends to have a big head in proportion to its body, though this is not inevitable. Always smooth coated, with the Labrador colouring tending to dominate, these dogs are cheerful, biddable hounds with the Labrador love of water, retrieving and eating well established. The ears, otter tail and broad skull tend to give the game away, even in the second cross, but it is the love of water that will really tell you whether you have Labrador in your lurcher. Though almost all lurchers enjoy water on a hot day, it is only those bred for it that will slosh through icy ditches for fun in the middle of winter.

Labrador is added to the lurcher to give a strong retrieving instinct and a good nose.

Other Crosses

These are the lurcher types that you will come across most frequently, though

German wirehaired pointer lurcher

Mainly deerhound, but whippet, saluki and greyhound as well

there are the occasional more unusual ones. Other gundogs are crossed with greyhound from time to time, notably the German wirehaired pointer, which is a specialist working dog and would frankly make a nightmare pet. They are strong-minded and need an enormous amount of exercise and mental stimulus; though they can be trained to an exceptional standard, relatively few people are capable of doing so, and those who are might prefer not to. If you decide to take one of these on, be prepared to commit yourself to a huge amount of exercise in all weathers. Very occasionally, lurchers appear that are claimed to be composites of one of the rarer sighthounds, such as the pharaoh hound or the sloughi, but this is unlikely, given their scarcity. I have seen Rhodesian ridgeback crosses, which looked meaningful, poodle crosses which were attractive, stubborn and highly intelligent (the poodle was originally a gundog) and husky crosses which were a nightmare, being difficult to contain on their owner's property, and impossible to stockbreak. A life on the lead is no life for a running dog.

Lurcher Types

Given the foregoing, you should be able to have a reasonable idea of what breeds have gone into the makeup of your lurcher. As some have been bred lurcher to lurcher for generations (often referred to as 'bitza' lurchers because they contain bits of this and bits of that) this is not an exact science, more of an educated guess. So let us see what you can tell from the dog in front of you.

Appearance and Characteristics
Colour

Though a good dog is never a bad colour, some colours are rarer than others. If your lurcher is merle-coloured, then she has a good proportion of collie blood. The merle colouration does not exist in many breeds, corgi and great dane being two where it is found but which are not used for lurcher breeding. Merle is plentiful in border and bearded collies, and a merle lurcher almost always indicates one or both of these in her makeup. Black and tan is less common in lurchers, though a very dominant colour in dogs generally. Tan with a black saddle may well indicate GSD, so check the feet and ears next to confirm, and take a good look at the coat, shoulders and articulation of the back legs. Another contributor of black and tan, especially with a long soft coat, can be saluki, which is the only easily available sighthound that carries this colour: check feet, profile and tail, plus body width. Or else the black and tan could come from terrier origins, of which there are several possibilities, lakeland or Jack Russell being the more usual, other possibilities being from Airedale, Welsh, border or of course the good old mongrel terrier. Tricolour is found in collies, but less readily passed on; it is however common in the saluki. Red grizzle (red fawn overlaid with black hairs) is another colour that comes from the saluki; brindles usually indicate whippet, greyhound or bull terrier, especially when with a white shirt front, toes and tail-tip. There is certainly brindle in the desert-bred saluki, though I believe it is frowned upon in the KC showing world, and may not be accepted. The deerhound is most usually blue, but can be solid colour from oatmeal to red, though these are rare. A most beautiful deerhound colour that is making a welcome comeback is the heather brindle, a lovely tweedy colour of mixed browns with brindle striping. A brindled dog, like a tabby cat, has the brindling in individual hairs, which have multicoloured banding, rather than solid-coloured hairs being overlaid with hairs of a different colour. Therefore you can tell if a long-coated dog is a true brindle by examining single hairs. It is a very ancient colour, and only exists in very old established breeds. Another very ancient colour, much prized by the Celtic chieftains of old and recorded in their songs and legends, is white with red ears; this still occurs in lurchers, the ear colour varying from palest lemon to fox red, the rarest and most valued. This colour comes directly from the greyhound or the whippet. Black masks come from greyhound, saluki and

One of the most ancient colours – the red-eared white

whippet, usually extending to black-rimmed eyes as well, as if the lurcher has outlined them with kohl. Liver or chocolate is an uncommon colour, its presence generally pointing to Labrador or kelpie, though liver and white would argue a case for the German pointer.

Eyes

A blue, ticked or odd-coloured pair of eyes comes from one of the collie bases. It can also denote husky (which acquired it from the collie in the first place) but the husky cross is sufficiently unusual and distinctive that the lurcher before you is very unlikely to be bred so. Light amber eyes occur frequently in lurchers, and are seen in many of the breeds that make up a lurcher composite, so are not a good guide to origins, though eye shape can be. Prominent eyes can come from whippet or Staffordshire; the bigger the eye the more greyhound, saluki or whippet there is. A small eye in a large head can be from deerhound or Bedlington, especially if the eye is almond-shaped rather than round. The saluki has a large, long almond eye, slanted and with a wide field of vision. There is no eye shape or colour that should be considered a fault in a lurcher. The ticked eyes, known as 'moon-pie' in some areas, used to be a cause of superstitious dislike but I suspect this is more due to a dog with this feature being easily recognised and traceable than for any other reason. Certainly, there is no evidence of the sight being affected. Amber eyes were much prized by the ancient Greek and Roman hunters, and are still favoured in the desert saluki; curiously, the modern Kennel Club does not take this into account and marks the light eye down.

Ears

Drop or large ears are found in saluki, Bedlington and Labrador crosses, large half-erect or erect ears also being from the German shepherd or the whippet. Some strains of collie also pass on pricked ears. Sometimes a lurcher will be able to prick her ears right up at will, usually when she spies something that might need chasing. Over-large ears seldom continue to the second cross, though one individual in a litter may carry them – otherwise the tendency is to revert to the rose ear. If there is more than one large-eared dog in the makeup, this can combine to throw the occasional pup with large ears. For instance, I bred a litter from a bitch that had saluki three generations back, and a dog that was half Bedlington. One of the pups turned out very like a greyhound/whippet – in fact the new owner's vet swore that that was how he was bred – but if you looked again and knew what you were looking at, the

How is this pup bred? Look at the saluki ears!

lurcher had large drop ears and a shorter tail than one would expect, with a saluki profile. Tasselled ears can come from many sources, so are not a good guide by themselves, though a characteristic tuft at the back of the ear will shout 'border collie' or 'saluki'. If accompanied by a ruff around the neck, it is likely that collie is not far away; this is not, however, to be confused with the deerhound legacy of a fringe down either side of the neck.

Head

A hunting dog needs the head in balance with her quarters; a big-headed dog will fall as it strikes its quarry if the quarters do not match or exceed the strength of the head. I have heard it said that a wide skull denotes brain power and a narrow skull the lack of it, but this is nonsense; let us not forget that Einstein had a smaller than average brain for his size. The longest and narrowest skull comes from the saluki, a long narrow dog in her entirety; the head simply matches the body. Deerhound heads are long and narrow, too, for the same reason. It is a mistake to think that the narrow head lacks jaw power, for both the deerhound and the saluki were bred to take the largest of quarry, and if the length and strength of jaw is examined, along with the masseter muscles in the cheek that operate it, the ability of these dogs to open a huge gape and close it with great strength will be realised. The borzoi also has a long narrow skull, and is still used to catch wolves in parts of Russia; proof in itself that the long jaw is not one whit inferior. Broad skulls come from the Staffordshire, which also bequeathed them to the whippet, the bull outcross in the whippet being of more recent times, the first two-thirds of the last century in fact, than Lord Orford's bull outcross in the greyhound. Collies of both sorts give a broad skull, as do the Antipodean herding breeds. The Bedlington contributes a particularly strong jaw, generally with very big teeth in it, and the typical occipital ridge along the top of the skull, ending in a bump right at the back. The deerhound has this last feature too, but to a lesser extent. Bedlington/whippet crosses often have a head that seems too large for the frail body, but look again and you will see that those sloping quarters are strong and in balance.

Feet

Long feet come from the saluki and the deerhound. These long feet can continue through several generations, so even if they are hairless rather than well-furred, the long, strong foot has come from one of these two sources. A big splayed foot can come from the GSD, a smaller splayed foot from the Staffordshire, Labrador or the bearded collie, the latter throwing a more rounded foot shape. Neat, high-knuckled feet are from the greyhound and the whippet; catlike well-cushioned feet from the border collie. If they are exceptionally well-upholstered, you might be looking at kelpie or cattle dog. Of course, lurchers sustain foot injuries that can affect the shape of the foot, (see Chapter 10) but the above information is intended to apply to the uninjured foot.

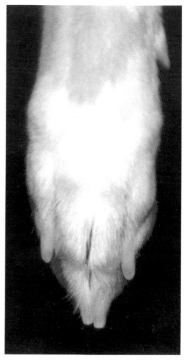

Long saluki forefoot (E. Dearden)

Body Shape

The saluki is very narrow, which characteristic is not easily lost even in a second cross. A very stocky dog denotes GSD, cattle dog, kelpie, Labrador or bull blood, slightly less so being a legacy of beardie or border collie. Topline is a good guide – that is, the contour of the back – Bedlington crosses and whippets giving an arched back, greyhound a slight rise towards the loins, saluki is flatter but still with a slight curve over the loins, the others being flat. As a dog ages, the topline levels and then sags, so this should be taken into account.

Neck and Shoulders

'A head like a snake and a neck like a drake' denotes the greyhound. The long, graceful neck will be there courtesy of the greyhound, whippet or saluki; the deerhound has a slightly shorter neck, and anything with herding blood in it, a shorter neck still, which increases correspondingly in girth. Likewise, the gazehound needs a very well laid-back shoulder, which becomes more upright as other breeds are added, unless working strains of those breeds are used.

Coat

The deerhound gives a harsh, broken coat with adequate undercoat, as against the beardie which throws a profuse coat which might need stripping. Collie coats are dense, smooth in the half-cross but coming through more like a true collie when crossed back to another long-coated dog. The saluki coat is silky and not profuse, the Bedlington coat often but not invariably soft and linty. No other cross gives this type of coat. The GSD coat comes through thickly, the density varying with the type of GSD. The more running dog that there is in the lurcher, the less hair you will find underneath, the most highly bred being quite naked there, which feature allows for rapid dissipation of heat.

Gait

Not an easy method of checking, but the rolling Bedlington gait is extremely distinctive, as is the mincing, high-stepping whippet; saluki can produce this feature, too. Don't be deceived by the prancing gait: it can turn at any time to the long, reaching gallop of the running dog. Any lurcher given to dropping on its belly and stalking something may safely be said to have a good amount of border or bearded collie in it. As a defensive posture, however, this can be seen in many other breeds of dog, though not, as a rule, in pure sighthounds. GSD and Labrador crosses have a heavier gait unless there is a lot of greyhound to lighten the shoulders. It is a characteristic of all lurchers to be able to trot leading with one shoulder in a slightly sideways motion: the movement looks ungainly but covers the ground like a wolf, while allowing the head free movement to increase the field of vision.

This information, applied to the dog in front of you, will give a surprisingly accurate picture of the breeds involved in her makeup, though this task becomes more difficult when many breeds have been involved through several generations. Observation of her general behaviour will tell you more as you get to know her better, but some elements of her origins will remain unknown. One is reminded of the apocryphal tale of the novice horse owner asking a dealer how a horse is bred. The answer? 'How would you like him to be bred?'

Age

If you have taken on a dog that is past her puppyhood, you can still take an educated guess at her age. There are several keys to this. Look at the teeth. A badly kept dog can have the most appalling teeth even when young, so you might have to wait until you have been able to clean them properly (see Chapter 10) but a very young dog has bright white teeth, and these gradually change to a more ivory colour as the dog ages. With proper care, even very old dogs can have a perfect set of teeth; as I write, there is a sixteen-year-old lurcher beside me, and her teeth are flawless. After the teeth, look at the growth plates on the wrists. If these seem to fit the dog, then she is fully grown and two years old or more. If they seem far too large for the legs, then there is still growing to do. Next, check the depth of the brisket. In an adult dog, this should be level with the elbows; bitches can have a little less depth than dogs. Now look at the topline, which starts to sag at about six or seven years old, and by ten or eleven has the spine standing clear of the muscle. As the dog ages, the wrists and hocks will lose their springiness and begin to sag, which again starts at seven or eight and is well-defined once the dog's age reaches double figures. Equally, the tendons in the paws start to stretch and sag until the foot flattens, the nails no longer touch the ground and have to be trimmed. Greying of the muzzle is not a reliable trend, as some dogs, especially black ones, grey there at an early age, but when the grey or white hairs extend to the cheeks and the legs, then you have a dog which is middle-aged. For the rest, again you have to rely on observation of the dog's general behaviour. Although they love to run right up into their teens, the mad tearing-about of the first five years gradually mellows during the next five, after which it only appears on special occasions.

Now that you have a reasonable idea of what ingredients have gone into your particular dog recipe, and of how old she is, you are in a much more positive position with regard to training her.

Greyhound/Labrador cross – note the large head

2 CHOOSING THE RIGHT LURCHER

It might at first seem difficult to choose the right lurcher for your own circumstances, given that they are crossbreds, and pedigree dog breeders will be quick to point out that, with one of their dogs, you have an exact blueprint of what it will grow up into. In fact, the issue is nowhere near so cut and dried, for there are marked differences in size and temperament even among pedigree dogs. Where show and work types exist within a breed, such as with the Labrador, even the shape can be different. The lurcher is always the same shape, and the colour is self-evident, so what you need to think about is size at maturity, temperament and coat type.

Puppies

Size is easy if you know the parents, and if not (it is a wise dog that knows its own father!) you can make a pretty accurate guestimate from looking at the

How big will they grow? Deerhound and whippet pups, 14 weeks

Note the growth plates on the forelegs of this beardie/collie lurcher

growth plates on the hocks and wrists, the size of the paws, and the age of the hound. When lurcher saplings grow, they are rather untidy about it: bits get left behind for a few weeks and then catch up rather suddenly. For instance, legs appear early on while the back is still short, so you have what appears to be a pup on stilts. The head will seem out of proportion one day, just before the milk teeth are cast, which occurs at around four to six months of age. The new teeth need a big muzzle to grow into, which is why the head will appear so large. The tail will be a source of exasperation for both of you, far too long to keep tidy, and always in the way. Your pup will grow more at the back end, then more at the front, so will seem forever either uphill or downhill, and during this spell, the spine will lengthen into the true longdog shape before the brisket drops, so your lurcher will look like a pipe-cleaner. When hormones flood the system and sexual development takes its turn, all the other growing will stop; after a while, the hormones will settle and the outer framework will have a growth spurt. While she is forever changing shape and proportion, she may seem uncoordinated, but don't worry, she is only temporarily clumsy because her centre of gravity is constantly having to be adjusted, and her young limbs do not yet have their adult strength. Just ignore it all, for one day everything will fit, and you will be mesmerised by her beauty.

Mentally, too, your lurcher will take her time, one day being very forward, full of lurcher intelligence, another day not connecting with the world at all. She will be a great, gangly, loopy, manic thing, all arms and legs, bending her back into a prawn shape and scooting about, charging up to you with her jaws agape in a huge grin, swerving round you and taking the whole world on in a curve. This is a lovely time, so enjoy it. Some days she will be doing serious growing, and only want to sleep in various attitudes of abandon, one moment curled up so tightly that she takes up less room than a terrier, and the next, draped over her bed (or yours) like a Salvador Dali watch. This is puppyhood: you cannot rush it and nor should you want to. Every day brings her nearer to the dog that she is destined to be. 'The first year they grow up, the second, out' is the maxim, meaning that although she will reach her adult height as a yearling, she will spend the following year broadening her frame and gaining in strength. At two years old she will be fully grown. Pups from the same litter can mature at different heights because of the different breeds involved; some may be rough and some may be smooth-coated, depending on the recipe. If coat is important to you, then pick a pup from breeding that ensures the coat type that you like. It is often difficult to predict how some pups will be coated if not specifically bred for a predictable coat type (a first cross greyhound/deerhound will always have a rough coat: a first cross greyhound/border collie will always have a smooth one). Multiple breeds in the cross add to the equation unless all are rough (Bedlington, deerhound) or smooth (whippet, greyhound); some pups are born fuzzy and will be long-coated, but a lot

Seven month old puppy on stilts — on window sill

41

of pups born smooth will end up with rough, broken or feathered coats, though they may be around a year old before the true coat type shows.

Temperament

Temperament is extremely important in a companion dog, which might have to meet all sorts of people and animals, stay in hotels, travel on public transport, and be in and out of other people's houses, all without a stain on either character or carpet. The lurcher temperament as a generalisation is laid-back and gentle; it is very, very rare to get anything else in the raw material, though bad treatment can bring anything out of any dog. They are polite but not effusive, except to their own people, and then only briefly; they are dignified and tolerant, quiet and refined. If you like a 'busy' dog, these are not for you. However, they are the sum of their parts, and whatever is in will come out, given the right stimulus. To be sure of the temperament, you need a good idea of what has been used in the cross, and the guidelines in Chapter 1 will be as accurate a measure as you will find. Then you need to think of what the base breeds are like, and given that all dogs are very much individuals, you will still have just as good an idea of how your young lurcher will turn out as you would with a pedigree pup.

The Working Type

Most lurchers are bred for work, and so their breeders choose working ability above all other aspects. As a working dog has to be intelligent and biddable, such dogs will still make first-class companions. I breed workers myself, but a good permanent home is more important to me than a working one, so some of mine do get placed as family dogs. All have been excellent in that role, and I never have to advertise my stock. If you want a lurcher as a pet, don't discount the working dog world as a source, but do be open with the breeder about your intentions. A minority may be frosty in response, but the more sensible will choose a pup out of the litter that would prefer being a family dog. No-one knows a litter better than the person who has been looking after it, so if the breeder steers you towards or away from a particular pup, heed his or her advice. The working instinct has not been bred out of the lurcher, so if you do not want yours to work, you will need to take certain precautions, which are covered in Chapter 7.

Show Dogs

A few breeders are concerned exclusively with show dogs. Most show dogs will work, given the opportunity, though not all working dogs have the

Working bred – up for anything (P. Blackman)

exquisite conformation of the show hound. As with pedigree dogs that are bred for showing, all else comes second to beauty, and for that reason, unless you are also committed to showing at a high level, I'd say be cautious about buying from show stock. Temperament, soundness and obedience is rarely tested, and there can be other unpleasant manifestations. One very well-known strain which wins all over the country is extremely noisy, and really only suitable for people who are far away from neighbours. Goodness knows where that attribute comes from, as the lurcher is normally known as much for its silence as its speed and sagacity. Breeders of show dogs may prefer to sell their pups out of the area where they live, to cut down on local competition; others are confident that they have chosen the pick of the litter, and will readily let you have a pup.

Obedience Dogs

There are also lurchers bred specifically for obedience competitions. These will usually have a high proportion of border collie, GSD or kelpie blood in them. There is no doubt that such dogs can be trained to extraordinarily high levels, and many are a revelation to see in action. Again, although I am a great admirer of such dogs and indeed know many personally, there is no doubt that a hound with the intelligence to win at the higher levels is going to be a lot of dog, and probably more than the average pet owner can cope with. She will certainly need a lot more stimulus, exercise and human interaction than many pet owners are capable of giving. If, however, you are confident that you can cope with this, then an obedience-bred lurcher will make a stunning companion, though she is unlikely to score in the show ring. Breeders of obedience strains will vet you very thoroughly before you are even allowed on the premises, and may decide not to let you have a pup. If this is the case, please do not feel offended, for few owners are truly suited to this type of lurcher. If, however, the breeder reckons that you are made of the right stuff, feel as if you have just been knighted, for there can be few greater compliments. Breeders of obedience dogs never have to advertise, and usually have long waiting lists, but if you attend obedience competitions and get to know the people involved, you will start to hear of litters being bred.

Racing Dogs

Although there is no money to be made in lurcher racing (there is no betting other than the odd private wager, and prizes if any are very small) it is a very popular sport, and many lurchers are bred specifically to race. These dogs are mostly greyhound and whippet bred, with only a very small amount of outside blood, and as a consequence look like purebreds. They run like them, too! If you like the idea of having a lurcher for racing, you will need one of these, because the more typical kind of lurcher very rarely wins at these events, though there are exceptions. Lurcher racing meetings also hold races for greyhounds, so you could bring your rescued greyhound as well.

Showing, obedience and racing competitions are covered in depth in Chapter 8.

Choosing A Puppy

Choosing a puppy from a litter can be quite daunting, especially when they all seem so appealing. Leave plenty of time for watching the litter, because this decision is very important: you hope to be together for the rest of her life, which will be longer than many marriages last. The breeder will let you know which pups are available, as some may already have been chosen, and you will have decided whether to have a dog or a bitch, and what colours you especially like or dislike. Though the colour does not affect the dog's personality, you will be looking at her for years, so you might as well pick a colour that you find pleasing. Sit where the puppies can see you and reach you, and take notice of what happens.

A well socialised puppy – six weeks. Look at those big paws

Old-fashioned advice was to choose the first pup that ran to you, but a bold pup grows into a bold dog, which may or may not suit your temperament. Equally, some pundits advise avoiding the shy pup, or the independent one that does not mix with her littermates. This is not necessarily bad advice, depending on whether you have the skill to train an independent pup, or the patience to bring on a shy one. I love a shy pup, they are my speciality; loners tend to be 'thinkers' which is very good in a working dog but can be rather a challenge in a pet – never take on a dog as clever as you are! I have one, and she is amazing, but she was very hard work as a youngster. I bred from her, and one of her pups was as smart as his mother: luckily a professional gundog trainer wanted a lurcher from me and I placed him there. I had every confidence that this man could bring out the best in what was going to be a quite remarkable dog.

Better advice is to let the puppy choose you. This does not mean that you pick the first pup to run up to you, but instead, the last one to leave you. I find with any litter I observe that the pups arrive in a bunch and jump all over me – the sign of a well-socialised litter – but presently they all toddle off to get on with their lives, except for one that will be asleep on my shoe, in my sleeve or on my lap. That is the puppy who wants to be my dog. If you do not like the one that chooses you, don't have her, but if you cannot choose between pups, this is a good way to decide.

45

Unusual sight – a litter at first birthday get-together. Dam with curly tail by sire, just behind

Obviously you want a healthy puppy. The litter should be bright-eyed and alert, with loose-fitting well-furred skins, plump but not obese bodies, sweet-smelling, and with no sign of dirty ears, eyes, noses or bottoms. If the litter that you see is lethargic, flat-bodied, or with weepy, crusted eyes, nose or ears, if pups smell rank or have signs of diarrhoea, tight-fitting skins or skin rashes, no matter how well bred they are or how far you have travelled to see them, leave them there. Better to have wasted your time and fuel than to waste a lot of money as well, not just in the purchase price or the immediate veterinary fees that it will take to get such a puppy to the stage that she should have been in when you went to see her, but for the unseen damage that she may carry in the form of ill-health for the rest of her life. You may be surprised that I recommend avoiding the obese puppy, but in fact these too can cost you a lot of money and break your heart at the end of it. It is rare to see obesity in lurcher puppies, but some breeders overfeed with high-protein food in order to get rapid growth. I have also seen obesity as the result of a very small litter. The pups not having to compete for food, they took little exercise compared to a normal litter, and fed extravagantly. When lurcher pups are too heavy, the weight can distort their growing limbs and joints, the result sometimes being turned-out feet, bent pasterns or hocks, or even hip dysplasia. Normally, there is not a whisper of hip dysplasia in lurchers, and I sometimes wonder if its prevalence in many breeds of pedigree dogs could be in part the result of overfeeding.

Sometimes a pup takes your eye from the moment you see the litter, and you hardly notice the others. If this is the case, then follow your intuition: any pup with that much charisma at such an early age is going to turn out to be something extra special. I chose my last pup from the litter at two days old, and never had the slightest inclination to change my mind. He was not the pick of the litter, but he was the best one for me personally, turning into the most delightful chap and a pleasure to have around.

Adult Dogs

You may decide to bypass the puppy stage and go for a fully-grown dog. Some really special hounds can be acquired this way, often beautifully trained and with years of life ahead of them. The most common reason for adult dogs becoming available is from working dogs who have either sustained injury or else developed some habit which precludes their continuing to work. Once recovered from injury, dogs that are not subjected to the stresses of field work will be quite sound enough to lead long, happy lives as pets. As far as working faults go, the dog may be hard-mouthed i.e. crushing her quarry when she catches instead of returning with it unharmed, or she may bark when chasing, a most undesirable trait known as 'opening up'. She may 'jack' or quit when she is chasing, or refuse to chase at all – a virtue in the pet owners' eyes! She may

A strong minded dog – could you cope

47

have refused to work the quarry that she has been bought for, or refuse to retrieve, or not get on with the owner's other dog. There are more serious crimes which *will* affect her desirability as a companion dog, such as being touchy with other dogs, noisy when left, or even attacking livestock. Most dogs can be trained out of these last, but it is as well to know exactly why she has become available. The working flaws, however, cannot be trained away, and so the dog must be moved on, though she has probably had a great deal of time, care and money spent on her. It is better to re-home a failed worker if the owner cannot live with the fault, as some can, because it is unfair for owner and dog to spend the rest of the dog's life resenting each other. Not everyone can afford to keep a kennel full of unsuitable dogs, and their failure might well be someone else's treasure. Racing dogs sometimes come up for re-homing as well, once they have lost their speed or if they become injured and cannot race any more. However, most owners tend to keep them in retirement, and maybe take a litter or two from them.

Many working dogs are kept in kennels, but that does not mean that they cannot adapt to house life. Most lurchers are naturally clean and will make the transfer gracefully with the minimum of supervision. It is useful to check how the dog has been living, so that you know whether she will need a little house training. The same applies to dogs that have come via rescue organisations.

Rescue Dogs

If lurchers are as special as I say they are, why are so many of them in the rescue homes? Is there something that I have not told you? Read on!

Proportionately there are not huge numbers of lurchers in the dog rescues compared with collies, Labradors, German shepherds, and crosses between these. However, they tend to arrive in the dog homes by a different route and are therefore often in poor condition; they are a shape that not everybody finds attractive, some folks preferring their dogs 'cuddly' rather than aerodynamically designed, and there are some lingering misconceptions about them, such as that they cannot be trained, will kill cats and smaller dogs, always have to be muzzled and kept on leads, and are delicate and need to have coats on all the time. This means that the ones that are in the homes tend to be in there for longer, especially the larger specimens, as people seem to think that the larger the dog the more exercise it needs, and there are plenty who want a dog but cannot be bothered to walk it on a regular basis. In fact all dogs, regardless of size, appreciate exercise, and some of the smallest are often the most difficult to tire out. Such is the perceived difficulty of re-homing lurchers that some rescues don't call their hounds lurchers at all, but refer to 'whippet cross' 'greyhound cross' or even 'lurcher cross'! Of course, these are all lurchers. There are some rescue kennels, unfortunately including some large organisations that should know better, who maintain that an ex-working lurcher is so undesirable and un-re-homeable that the dogs never get a chance, never mind the legal minimum of seven days, and are executed straight away, this system often being extended to working terriers. Where I live, it is very obvious that most rescue kennels have their share of lurchers and terriers, but one or two never seem to have any, which speaks for itself. So why are the lurchers in there in the first place?

The first group consists of youngsters, 'saplings' as they are known, aged roughly from six to eighteen months. Many of them are there because they are going through adolescence, with all the challenges that this implies. The cute puppy has been replaced with a lanky, bouncy hound that can seemingly get anywhere and reach anything, digs craters in the lawn and runs away. All breeds of dog go through this, but young lurchers going through the 'Kevin' stage are a bit taller, a bit faster and a bit brighter. Rather than train their dog, people have just let it grow, and now, rather than get help with training, have a fence put up and learn to put things out of reach, they put the youngster into kennels. Such is our throwaway society. Some very pleasant young dogs can be acquired this way which, with a very little application, go on to become lovely pets.

The next group are the 'found wanderings'. These dogs are in their youth to middle age, have often been living feral, and can be in terrible condition. Some dog rescues blame this on 'working homes' but nothing is further from the truth: the vast majority of people who work their lurchers keep them in tip-top condition, wanting for nothing. Sadly, there is a criminal underclass that uses the lurcher for poaching and gambling matches; instead of carefully raising and training their own dogs, they find it easier to steal them. When the dog is injured, or the match lost, they simply drive off and leave it. Those are the lucky ones: some die vile deaths, or are left tied up in abandoned buildings or in woods, or are thrown out of cars – surely no other type of dog has suffered so needlessly and so repeatedly as the lurcher in the hands of this particular group. Unfortunately, a dog's position in law is such that little or nothing gets done, and if your dog is stolen, you are very much on your own in trying to get it back, more of which shortly. The 'found wanderings' have often experienced the most terrible treatment, being injected with drugs, used to stub cigarettes out, or otherwise tortured, yet, amazingly, they can in the majority of cases be rehabilitated and still make loving companions, though they may for ever react in terror to certain kinds of men and, more rarely,

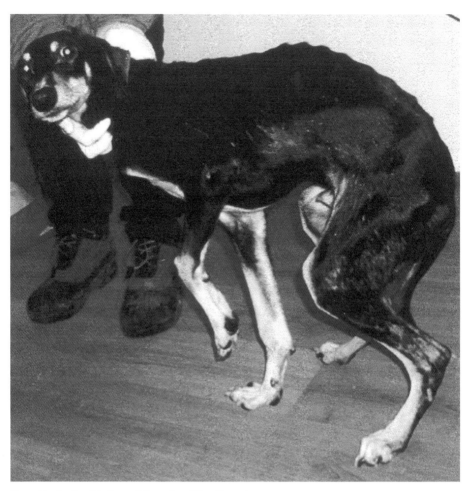

Rescued lurcher found in Surrey (Happy Breed Dog Rescue)

women. These dogs are physically and mentally scarred, but once you look past the wrapping, you find that they still have so much to give. They may have been run until their hearts and lungs are damaged – this condition is called 'blown' – or their feet are disfigured; no use then to the people who over-worked them, but ideal as pets for they will be so appreciative of the home you offer, and have neither the inclination nor ability to pose a problem on the recall. Sometimes quite young pups are 'found wandering' perhaps because they have seen their chance and escaped from a place that did not suit them, or because they have been 'tried' on quarry while far too young and have run off and just kept going. It is not uncommon for a dog being worked too young to refuse to work altogether, and that is another reason to find such a dog in the rescue kennels. Any of these will make delightful pets.

Finally you find the old ones. Old dogs of any breed end up in the dog rescue for reasons that don't say a lot about their erstwhile owners. They are there because they are making room for a new puppy, or because they have become infirm, or are starting to need medical attention. But a dog can also be there because the owner has suffered illness or accident, or had to move into accommodation that does not permit dogs, or only a certain number of dogs. Older dogs are gems, having left behind the follies of youth and reached a time of life where comfort and love are far more important to them than any lures of the outdoors. Divorce and its spin-offs can put dogs of any age into kennels, dogs that are well-behaved and usually well-trained. What you will very seldom find is a lurcher that is in a rescue home through any character defect of her own, though often through character defects of mankind. They are not dogs who adjust well to the noise and flurry of rescue kennels, and do not show themselves at their best, which is another reason why they do not get chosen as often as the more extrovert dogs that run barking to the kennel door whenever a voice is heard. Skulking, cringing and shivering in the furthest corner may be the dog that is destined to be the greatest friend that you have ever had, if you would only pause and look.

Old dogs have earned their comfort

There are quite a few things to be aware of when you take a dog from a place like this – and where indeed would these poor dogs be without them? First of all, it is useful to check whether the dog's name came in with her, or has been bestowed upon her arrival at the kennels. Next, be aware that her given age may be guesswork, as might the story behind her arrival. You have much to discover about each other, so take your time and keep your attitudes relaxed. Soon you will wonder how you ever managed without her in your life.

Theft

Having taken your lurcher home and started your life with her, you should treat her like any of the other precious things in your life, and make sure that she is not stolen. This means never leaving her in the car alone, nor in the back garden unsupervised, nor tied up outside a shop – not even for a minute. Whenever you leave her to go out, make sure that good locks separate her from criminal intent, and CCTV is by no means an extravagant addition to your security. If you are approached by strangers who ask about her, do not prolong the conversation, especially if they try to buy her. Often children are

Don't leave your lurchers outside a shop

sent first, to soften you up, though these children are sharp and streetwise, anything but childish. Do not tell them where you live, or anything good about your dog. She is old, she is lame, she is spayed, no use to anyone but yourself. She is not yours but belongs to your brother, who certainly will not sell her. Once when I was stuck in a traffic jam, two men in a pickup stopped and tried to wrench open the doors of my car to take my lurchers, and it was only the fact that I had central locking and that the line of traffic suddenly started to move, that saved us. It is not only lurchers that are stolen, but lurchers tend to get the worst of it when they are taken, because they are stolen for different purposes and go to a different type of owner from the pedigree dogs. The people who commit this sort of crime have all the time in the world to watch your comings and goings, as their days are not compromised by the need to earn a living. There is a significant amount of dog theft in this country, though for some reason, it does not command a high priority either in media reporting or police time, despite it certainly being on a par with having a child kidnapped in terms of grief for the owner. Sometimes the owner receives a ransom note, or is contacted after offering a reward – much easier and more lucrative than working for income, isn't it? And after all, a lot of people just pay up. In the case of lurchers, more often, the dog simply vanishes. Should dog theft ever happen to you or to anyone you know, the procedures for dealing with it are not what you would imagine.

A stolen dog may escape its captors quite quickly, or it may be several hundred miles away in a matter of hours. It can change hands a number of times in a matter of days. It may become a 'found wandering' in a dog rescue home which does not execute healthy dogs, or it may be picked up by the local authority in which case it has seven days to live and you have no time to waste.

Identification

What sort of identification does your dog have? Collar and tag is the legal minimum, but the collar may be removed. Tattooing and microchipping offer a more permanent form of identification, though each has its drawbacks. Tattooing is a painful, albeit quick procedure, and I would suggest that it is not you who holds your dog during it, as lurchers tend to remember things like this. Tattoos are usually done in one or both ears, though sometimes on the inside of the hindleg. If the latter, it is possible that no-one will think to check that area, especially on a large, distressed dog. Tattoos are easily altered, and the process is not any pleasanter than the type of person who does it: dogs have been found with their ears cut off, tattoos have been obliterated using primitive 'surgery' and dubious substances, and of the pack of beagles* stolen by animal rights activists in 2000, only one was ever recovered, the tattooed ear having been crudely mutilated by the self-styled 'animal lovers' in an attempt to deny identification. With microchipping, there are several types of chip and scanner, and not every chip will respond to every scanner. The chip can migrate in a significant minority of cases, or cease to transmit, or be found and cut out. With either method, the dog is at the mercy of the staff of the animal rescue, who may choose not to search for identification, or make only a cursory check. It takes twenty minutes to check a dog for a microchip according to the instructions of the manufacturers of these devices, and furthermore this check should be done in an area quiet enough to hear the electronic bleep. A quick sweep of the scanner across the neck, in front of a kennels full of barking dogs, is not the way to find a chip. It is quite common for dogs not to be subjected to any kind of search when they come in, and cases exist of missing dogs still wearing their collars and tags being in rescue kennels when their owners telephone in their details, and the connection still not being made. My own dogs are microchipped, and if you have taken in yours from a rescue centre, she probably will be as well, but there is no foolproof scheme that cannot be made to fail by a big enough fool; I think it is wise to have extra identification on your dog by chip or tattoo, but it should not lead you into a false sense of security.

I recommend that you take some good photographs of your dog that show any unusual markings, and keep a detailed record of how she looks. You need to have her height at the shoulder, colour, type of coat (rough, smooth or broken) any distinctive markings or scars, whether or not she is spayed (or castrated, for a dog) whether or not she has her dew-claws, any missing bits e.g. toes, tailtip, eartip, broken tooth, colour of nose or eyes if either is unusual, and note the colours of her nails – anything that will help you to identify her exactly. Don't rely on her identifying you, for she may be too traumatised to do so. Dogs do just as strange things as people after a bad experience: I was once at the centre of a nasty situation where a man's dog had been taken in to be re-homed, unknown to him, by his mother, who had claimed that she was the rightful owner. During the fracas that followed, the dog was brought out of kennels to be identified, but instead of running to his owner, the poor animal ran to me, whom he had never seen until that moment. The greeting he offered me was so intense that, had I claimed to have been the rightful owner, nobody could have argued with me.

---

*The Wye College Beagles, stolen and never recovered apart from one which had been mutilated. The others are presumed dead.

To recap: should your dog go missing, have a description to offer the police and the local dog rescues, and have some good photographs. Inform the police first, stipulate that the dog has been stolen (do not allow them to downgrade your problem to 'strayed') and get a crime number. This is very important: you MUST get a crime number. According to the law, your dog is 'a chattel' and not a great deal of police time will be allocated to solving the crime unless you have a sympathetic dog-friendly policeman at the right level to help you, or if the persons suspected of committing the crime – and the police might well have a good idea who they are – are suspected to be involved in crimes of a more 'serious' nature (their idea of serious, not mine or yours). This cannot be helped, no matter how irritating; in spite of your misery and anger, it does not do to lose sight of the fact that the police themselves find their restrictions exasperating too. Do not expect the central police communications office to circulate the dog's description to your local bobby, if you are lucky enough still to have one, or even to pass the details on to the next shift. Do not expect the police to necessarily know what a lurcher is, or the meaning of a colour such as 'brindle' or 'merle'. If you call into the station in person, take a copy of the photograph of your dog, along with a brief written description on the lines set out above, e.g. 'STOLEN two year old lurcher bitch, 22 inches high, broken coated black with white chest, toes and tailtip, scar inside right hindleg. REWARD for information leading to her safe recovery' (don't state the amount). Some dog insurances offer help with the reward but stipulate that the owner has to wait one or two days: believe me, you simply do not have time.

You must start your search at once, in case your pet has been taken in by one of those deplorable agencies that kills them after seven days, and in some cases does not even wait that long. Next, you need to circulate this description by telephone or in person to all the local dog rescues, large and small. There is no central list of these bodies, so you will rely heavily on the Yellow Pages, and also be sure to ask each sanctuary if they know of any others that you might tell, for the smaller ones are often unlisted. Some organisations are almost impossible to reach by telephone; fax and email can help, but there is no way of knowing unless you speak to someone whether this information will be circulated or just binned. Some animal rescues are very efficient and others have no interest in re-uniting dog and owner; some seem unable to understand the widespread theft of dogs that exists and blame the owners for carelessness! My own experience is that as a rule, the National Canine Defence League is head and shoulders above the rest for courtesy, co-operation and helpfulness; at the other end of the scale, you will meet with a degree of inefficiency, ignorance and apathy that would be funny if it was not so serious. Some of the smaller rescues can be very good, one of the largest ones is a nightmare, but you must deal with them all. It pays to visit in person, and to contact them every day, because sometimes details get passed on and sometimes they do not. You need all your friends and relations, and forty hours to each day to get it all done. Exasperatingly, organisations with several or many branches do not circulate information nationwide (or even between different staff members in one place) so if your dog has been found many counties away, there is no way of your finding out. Even more worrying is that if your local branch is full, or just on a whim, your dog may be transported far away to a different branch of the same organisation, but there will seem to be no record locally of her ever having arrived, never mind to where she has been sent. There is a large and famous dog rescue that claims never to put down dogs in its care and which has been caught doing exactly that; it (and many others like it) also moves dogs on to small private animal sanctuaries and boarding kennels, from where, again, no previous records of the animal exist and nor are details kept of her re-homing. I have been involved with a number of these organisations, which are so well intentioned, and are, after all, the only safety net that these poor dogs have, but the safety net is ragged and inadequate. The principle seems to be re-home at all costs, be economical with the record keeping, and don't give a moment's thought to the possibility of the so-called stray actually having a loving home already, and a distraught owner who is tearing the country apart trying to find his or her pet. I have no idea why this attitude should prevail amongst people who are otherwise caring. There are so few good homes available for dogs that it is common sense to save these for the genuinely homeless and make every effort to find the owners of lost dogs; the income for the kennels is the same, for everyone who takes a dog makes an appropriate payment, but maybe it is just less work? Yet in these days of computers, circulating information is hardly difficult or time-consuming. Whatever the reasons, those searching for lost dogs have a daunting task ahead of them.

Lurchersearch UK

There are agencies that can help, foremost of which is called 'Lurchersearch UK'*. This organisation, which relies on donations for income, keeps records of stolen lurchers and has an outstanding track record for finding and returning them to their owners. Lurchersearch has many ears and eyes, from people frequenting the showing and working worlds who notice a new dog, to the few helpful authority figures and kennel workers who, sometimes in the face of their employers' systems,

---

*Lurchersearch UK 01422 240168; 01598 753563; www.lurcher.org/lsuk

HAS YOUR DOG BEEN STOLEN OR LOST?

ENLIST THE HELP OF

LURCHER *Search* U.K.

We may be able to help you. By reporting to us the loss of your dog or any suspicious vehicle or incidents immediately, we can set in motion our telephone network of people nationwide including Ireland. Within hours these people will be looking out for your dog or making other people aware. We are in contact with dog wardens, rescue centres and police.

JANE : 01598 753563

KEZ : 01522 821074

KAYE : 01422 240168

BY JOINING OUR NETWORK YOU CAN HELP US TO STAMP OUT DOG THEFT!

Fax: 01598 753876

www.lurcher.org/lsuk

Lurchersearch leaflet

discreetly advise of new arrivals. I believe the record length of time is of one dog that was lost in the Midlands and found four years later in Wales. Lurchersearch's band of volunteer helpers covers the country, and circulates information on any lurcher that is found – as long as someone can tell them first. Despite providing email, stamped addressed envelopes, description forms that merely require a tick down a column, answerphone service, computer link, and free microchip scanners to kennels that do not have them, Lurchersearch still does not get the co-operation from some dog rescue agencies that it should have, but others are most diligent and deserve the highest praise. Other attempts have been made to centralise a lost-dog information system, and Lurchersearch liaises with all of these, so that only one telephone call is required on behalf of the bereft owner. Most of these other organisations have a short life, mainly due to the enormity of the task and lack of funding, though Battersea Dogs' Home has now initiated a system which, it is to be hoped, will continue to run. Once you have lodged your dog's details with Lurchersearch, do not relax your own search, but check on all your local dog homes, boarding kennels and animal sanctuaries every day. If you can get a mention on local radio (which is often very helpful) in the local papers (also very helpful) and perhaps even local television (not much chance but always worth trying in case they have a quiet day). Country magazines such as *Countryman's Weekly** will carry advertisements pertaining to lost lurchers, and your weekly free-ad paper is another useful one in which to put details.

Check that the posters of your dogs that you have put up in dog-walking areas, post offices and similar places are still there, for there exists a strange type of person that takes them down. List everywhere that you have put a poster, for when your dog is found, it is incumbent upon you to take all the posters down yourself, just as you should notify all the agencies that you have been pestering daily. You will be so deliriously happy that the task will be easy: I know, I've done it. Strangely, after your lost lurcher has come home, you may, as I did, get telephone calls for quite some time from people who think that they might have seen her, and would like the reward.

Now at last you have your lurcher, from whatever source, and you are looking at each other from either end of the lead, or else you have a tiny and rather worried puppy, her brow literally furrowed with concern – and maybe yours is as well. As soon as she is home, and has had a sniff about and emptied herself, you will introduce her to her accommodation and feed her. How you feed your lurcher is more important than you may think, which is why we look at it in such detail in the next chapter.

**The Countryman's Weekly*, Yelverton, Devon, PL20 7PE

3 FEEDING

You might be surprised to find a whole chapter on feeding before we discuss training, but with lurchers in particular, well fed is half trained. Many of the difficulties experienced with dogs in general, and certainly with lurchers, can be reduced to almost nothing simply by feeding them correctly. They are a very ancient type of dog, and so get the maximum nourishment out of their food. Feeding them food with artificial colouring or flavouring, or lots of chemicals in it, and most of all, feeding them on food that is too high in protein, means that you will reap the whirlwind with health and behavioural problems. By contrast, feeding them as closely to nature as you can will create a relaxed and co-operative hound, still brimming with joy and grace, but without that hard, fanatical edge that you may have seen in the dog that you brought home from the dog rescue. Don't be too hard on the rescue kennels: they are strapped for cash and staff, and have to feed as cheap and easy a diet as they can get away with. This will not do much harm as long as the dog is not in there for too long, but you can do a lot better.

Nutritional advice is everywhere for the new dog owner, and most of it is worthless. Dog food manufacturers tout for your custom by telling you that their various sacks and tins of processed food are carefully balanced to provide every nutritional need, and that feeding your dog one crumb of anything else will destroy this delicate balance – you must feed your dog exactly the same food for every day of her life. They will supply puppy food, adult food, senior food, maybe even diet food or elderly dog food, but heaven help you if you add anything to it. In an admirable entrepreneurial spirit, dog food manufacturers arrange visits and lectures for trainee veterinary students, and sadly, this is almost all the nutritional information that is presented to them. In due course, they will stock and promote this kind of dog food at their own surgeries, sometimes very aggressively, insisting that dog owners must feed it, and if they do not, all their dogs' subsequent ill-health will be down to inadequate feeding. Some of them even believe it. There is a huge mark-up on commercial dog food that is sold through veterinary outlets, and many practices depend on this income. Sadly, you cannot serve Dog and Mammon.

Your dog, not having been consulted, may feel differently about all this processed food. She may be very lacklustre about eating it, or eat it for a while and then refuse it. At the same time, she will eagerly devour carrion that she finds in the woods, horse, cow and sheep manure, grass, plants and fallen fruit. You are told not to spoil her by feeding her anything different from the recommended food. You are told that no dog has yet starved itself to death. Maybe not, but a fast-growing longdog can starve herself sufficiently to affect her adult strength and shape, and certainly anyone who has owned a deerhound or deerhound cross will confirm that they will starve themselves into anorexia before they will eat food that they do not like. If your dog does eat the food, and you have put her on one of the recommended high-protein diets, which range from around 26 to 33 per cent, you will learn the hard way that excess protein has the same effect on sighthounds as oats do on racehorses. Your dog will become hyperactive, ricocheting off the walls, tearing up anything she can get her teeth into, charging about on exercise until she is a panting, draggled heap. She will be unable to concentrate properly, and refuse to obey you. You will be uneasily reminded of a child on e-numbers. Well, that is just what she is.

By now you will be considering the discrepancy between what you have been advised, and sheer common sense. We are told to eat a varied diet of fresh food, and to avoid chemical additives, flavourings and colourings as much as possible. You are being told to feed your dog an unvarying diet of processed food, some of which is so unappetising that flavour enhancers, or even molasses, have been added. Dogs are prone to diabetes; molasses is neither desirable for their health nor their teeth. Processed food has, by necessity, to have preservatives in it; the colouring is added to appeal to the owner, not the dog. Read the bag or tin: it can be very depressing. Recently a criminal scam was uncovered where condemned food that was destined for the pet-food industry was redirected back into the human food industry. In and around all the brouhaha, a few pet owners registered the fact that this food was in a state of decomposition. So much for the 'prime cuts of best meat' in the advertisements! If pet food is labelled as (for instance) 'chicken' or 'beef' then that is what is in it, albeit the sort of chicken and beef that you may never have previously considered edible. If, however, the label states 'meat and meat derivatives' then the contents may be from a source that you would not care to feed to your dogs. A very large pet food manufacturer in Canada has decided that it will no longer use the corpses of euthanased pets in its products, one of the immediate spin-offs being that euthanasia now costs more there because vets no longer have a market for the dead bodies. These animals were processed complete with flea collars and any chemicals and drugs used on them prior to their demise, not to mention still in their plastic bags. Now, dogs are designed to eat whole carcases, carrion and even each other, but you might not like to pay premium prices to feed them like that. What they are not designed to eat is large quantities of (or any) cereals, pulses, and chemical additives. Not surprisingly, most commercial dog food contains wastage from the human food industry, and some of the more enlightened vets think that this may be one of the reasons why dogs are suffering from increasingly 'human' diseases, such as skin disease, immune system deficiencies, cancers, kidney and heart diseases, or diabetes, long before they get old. Maybe your new dog, staring woefully at her plate of kibble, knows better than we think.

That's all very well, I hear you say, but what do I feed her? You feed her what she was designed to eat; it is a little more trouble than scooping a bowl of pellets out of a sack, or opening a tin, it is considerably cheaper, and you will save the time it costs you in preparing it, which is maybe another hour a week, by not having to go to the vet except for her annual check-up. You feed her raw meat, raw meaty bones, and pureed fruit and vegetables. Let's start with the last first.

Fruit and Vegetables

Wild dogs eat a lot of vegetation, both in grass, herbs and fruit that they find for themselves, and in the stomach contents of the animals that they prey upon. They rarely eat cereal, and when they do, it is either in the form of stomach contents or fresh and green still growing on the stem. Pulses are not eaten in the dried form either. The canine stomach is not designed to extract nourishment from cellulose in the way that the herbivore stomach is, and indeed, herbivores either need to digest their food twice, as in cattle, sheep, rabbits and the like, or have stomachs like fermentation vats, such as elephants have. We humans cook our vegetables in order to break down the cellulose so that we may get more nutritional value, but too much cooking can destroy vital nutrients. Therefore it is useful to break down the cellulose either by the very lightest of cooking, or by whizzing up the fruit and vegetables in a liquidiser. You must use a liquidiser, as a food processor does not break up the cellulose sufficiently. Any vegetables are suitable for dogs, with the exception of raw potato and onion. All fruit is suitable. It is possible to obtain fruit and vegetables quite cheaply from suppliers if you arrange to take it just as it is on the verge of being past its best; cut out any bits that you would not eat yourself, liquidise, and freeze in meal-sized portions. We will come to quantities in just a moment. You can also add wild herbs, or herbs from the

Picking her own blackberries

herb garden, goosegrass, and green wheat, but not barley, oats or bearded wheat because of the sharp spikes on the awns. Nettles are extremely nutritious, but are better cooked, as they can be somewhat difficult to liquidise without stinging yourself. Beans and peas straight off the vine, pods included, are excellent. Do not feed too much of brassicas (cabbage family) all at once because large quantities can depress the thyroid; however, that is large quantities, and brassicas are otherwise extremely good. Aim for a wide variety of fruit and vegetables, just as is recommended for your own diet.

Meat

Any kind of raw meat is suitable for your dog, as long as it is of a quality suitable for human consumption. Although your dog can perfectly successfully eat carrion, and indeed is designed to do so, you will not feel happy about presenting it, and there is no nutritional gain to be had that cannot be equally served by eating fresh meat. There are various scare stories that you may hear concerning diseases that can be caught by handling or eating raw meat, but as long as the meat is fit for human consumption and you wash your hands after you have prepared it, neither you nor your dog is in any danger whatsoever. After all, butchers and slaughtermen handle raw meat every day, and you don't hear of them dropping like flies from foul bacterial onslaughts. These scare stories invariably have their source in those organisations that profit from the sale of processed dog food. The one exception to raw feeding that I make is in the feeding of wild meat, especially rabbit, which I cook thoroughly and then take off the bone. This is because sometimes it is possible for your dog to get worms from eating wild rabbit, but it is perfectly safe once cooked. Freezing the meat below −20° C for four weeks will also destroy worms, and so some of the rabbits we get are paunched, beheaded and then fed into an industrial-grade mincer, which pulverises the lot, hide, bones and all, into a very nutritious package which is then frozen for at least a month before being fed to the dogs. In any case, you will be worming your dog as usual (see Chapter 10) and the raw vegetables are excellent for repelling worms, but even so, there is no point in taking on any unnecessary extras. Lurcher owners tend to get a lot of rabbit, and it is a good food not to be wasted. Some of us like it, too, and it is not that long ago that British wild rabbit was considered gourmet fare, so please do not discard rabbit as a food source just because I mention worms. As long as you discard the intestines, and any livers that might look different from the norm, and do not feed anything that you would not eat yourself, the remaining meat will be an excellent food for your dog. She will tell you so, too. Heart, lungs and trachea (known as 'lights'), liver and tripe will all be very much enjoyed by your hounds. Do not feed organ meats to excess, though, especially liver, which should be fed no more than once a week. Muscle meat can be fed every day if you wish. Dogs enjoy fish, but raw fish can be very wormy and cooked fish needs thorough boning. A tin of fish now and again will be a good nourishing change of diet, and tinned fish has soft bones that will not cause harm, as well as many other nutritional benefits. Do not remove fat from meat as fat contains vital nutrients, and the oils will make your dog's coat shine. If a dog is underweight, I find a slab of breast of lamb once or twice a week will soon put weight back on. Just give her the whole piece, bones and all, and watch it go! Meat feeding need not be expensive, and there are several petfood companies that supply raw pet mince and tripe at very reasonable prices. However, the butcher is your friend here, and should be able to sell you all sorts of bargains, especially when it comes to bones.

Bones

Here be dragons! You see, meat by itself, and even meat and vegetables, is deficient in certain important nutrients, which nature arranged to be provided by bones. Raw, meaty bones complete the natural diet for dogs, and should be fed three or more times a week. If you use the bones in food sold for human consumption, then they will come from young animals, and your dog will be able to crunch them right up. Personally, apart from when I have teething puppies, I avoid marrow bones because the dog can wear her teeth too much in chewing them, and greedy dogs might chew off and swallow too big a piece. The bones I do use are the neck and spine of lamb, lamb ribs, pork ribs, veal neck, spine and ribs, and raw chickens. Yes, read it again, I really did mention raw chickens. You, like me, were brought up with the idea that, if bones in general were bad for dogs, chicken bones were fatal, and should never be fed, lest your dog die hideously with perforated or blocked intestines. You may have wondered fleetingly why the fox in the hen run did not die similarly, but the propaganda is so pervasive that I suspect, like me, you were convinced that the feeding of even one chicken bone would be a one-way trip to the great kennel in the sky. We could not have been more wrong: raw

Eating bones side by side – not many breeds have temperaments this good. Don't allow this unless you are sure of your dogs' behaviour

chicken carcasses are a marvellous food for dogs. I admit that the first time I fed them, I was awake for most of the night, listening for the cries of dying dogs, but many years later I still feed my dogs quantities of boned-out chicken carcasses from the butcher, and they have never been better. If you want to feed your dog up a bit, buy whole carcasses when they are on special offer, and have them quartered. Dogs thrive on them. It may well be better not to explain to your butcher why you want the boned-out carcasses, as he might, out of misguided concern, refuse to let you have them, because he believes that you will kill your dog feeding her this! One lady I know had this happen, and her butcher now thinks that she makes a lot of soup. Mine is much more relaxed about it, and lets me have all sorts of bones. To reiterate: these bones must be meaty, not dry, not marrow bones, and must be raw. Cooked bones do kill, and should never be fed, as they splinter, and also cooking alters the construction of the bone, making it liable to compact in the gut. Those of us who own thieving lurchers may have already experienced by accident the fact that they seem to be able to survive eating cooked bones, but there is no need to go looking for trouble, so do not feed them, and keep your rubbish bins lurcher-proof.

The feeding of bones has several immediate advantages apart from the nutritional benefit. The teeth of bone-fed dogs are sparkling clean and free from tartar. Even a filthy mouth will clean-up within a few days of feeding bones. You will never clean another tooth, never have to take a dog in to have an anaesthetic and her teeth de-scaled. No amount of biscuit or synthetic 'bones' will equal the cleaning effect of the real thing. At the other end, the stools will be much firmer, maybe even crumbly, and you might at first think that your dog is constipated, but she is not. Her bowel muscles will be strengthened, and her anal glands emptied quite naturally when she passes these firmer motions. Two more reasons not to go to the vet. – no wonder some of them do not promote the natural diet!

Balanced Feeding

Unless your vet is knowledgeable about canine nutrition, and few are, you can expect a lot of flak if he or she discovers that you are feeding raw food. You will be told of all sorts of diabolical dangers that will result, and have your arm twisted to feed the expensive complete food that is sold at the surgery. Obviously, this is disquieting, so at the end of this chapter, I quote some books and websites that you might like to read, so that you can make up your own mind in your own time. Is feeding natural food dangerous, or risk free? The answer is that it is not dangerous, and the risks are very tiny, but life is a risk, and your dog is more likely to choke on kibble than it is to choke on a bone. If the bone thing really worries you, either pulverise the bones in a blender, or substitute a mineral-enriched biscuit, though of course if you choose these options, you lose the tooth-cleaning benefits and the recreational aspects of feeding bones. Dogs love bones above all things, and get plenty of exercise and occupation from eating them. Unless you know that your dogs will not quarrel, separate or supervise them when you give them bones, for bones are a most desirable resource, and otherwise easy-going dogs may become possessive over them Still have reservations about feeding bones? You may consider that most kibble is a lot harder than a soft, pliant chicken wing, but the final choice is yours. Nobody can dictate to you how you feed your dog. I know a certain veterinary practice where natural feeding is thoroughly pooh-poohed, with much in the way of horror stories of e.coli, campylobacter and blocked or torn intestines, unverifiable of course. A client of mine took her shining, healthy puppy to one of these vets, and was unforgiveably harangued about feeding natural food; she took the pup home and continued to feed her how common sense told her. Six months later, when pup went for her 'free' check-up (which is actually used by this practice to put owners under pressure to have their dogs neutered) she was told that the dog was a picture of health, and you could see at once that she was now being fed a properly balanced diet!

The issue of balance is much misunderstood. Processed food is indeed nutritionally balanced according to laboratory experiments on captive dogs. However, any stockman will tell you that there is no such thing as a balanced metabolism. The same food intake will have some animals fat, some thin, some poor, some looking well and just right. Each individual body uses its nutrients in a slightly different manner. You will all know somebody who eats and eats and is always lean, and somebody else who eats only moderately and yet is quite overweight. The appearance of your dog will dictate how much you feed: if she looks fat, you feed less, if she looks thin, you feed more, if she looks fine, you have got it right. She will be fatter or thinner according to how much exercise she is having, the time of year, and if she is entire, the time of her season. Spayed and castrated dogs will put on weight more easily than their whole equivalents, but this does not provide an excuse for fat dogs. Feed less, exercise more, no secrets or rocket science. How much weight should she carry? Lurchers are lean dogs; you should be able to see the last rib clearly, and feel all of them under the skin. In saluki types, the hip bones often protrude, which is normal. You do not want a roly-poly lurcher that looks like a Labrador on four toothpicks. Now, how can you tell that she is getting all the

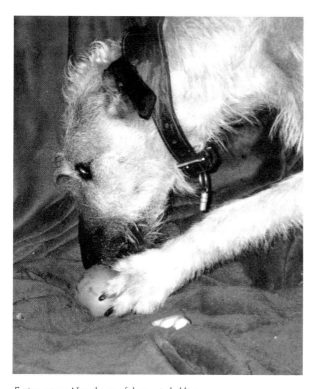

Eating a pear. Note the use of the toes in holding.

nutrients that she needs? She will tell you by looking well, with a shining coat, clear eyes, clean skin and bags of energy without hyper-activity. The secret is not that every meal should contain precisely the same nutrients – your food does not, after all – but that through the week, she gets sufficient of all that she requires. She does not need dairy produce, cereals, pulses or sweets. There is no harm in giving her cheese or biscuits as titbits if she likes them, but she does not need them. Milk, pulses and sugary things are positively bad for her, though the odd dog chocolate while you are training will not rock the nutritional boat. As long as she is getting plenty of fruit, vegetables, meaty bones (or fortified biscuits) and meat, she will not be going short of anything.

Great controversy waxes over the feeding of eggs; dogs like eggs and a few will do no harm, though when I used to work with free-range poultry, my dog was once introduced to a bucketful of eggs that had been dropped. She eagerly devoured the lot, unknown to me until it was too late, and suffered such horrendous sulphurous wind as a result that I telephoned the farmer and said that if she did it again, I would leave the dog in her bedroom for the night! No other harm was done at all, and a raw egg over food now and again can be a gourmet treat for your dog.

Some people like to add olive or human-quality flax-seed oil to the dog diet, which might loosen the bowels a little, others have dogs that like raw nuts (do not feed salted nuts), pumpkin seeds and the like. None of these will do any harm, but they are not essential. Vitamin and mineral supplements are not necessary with a proper diet, unless your dog is elderly or otherwise has a defective metabolism which might need a boost, in which case I would say find a holistic vet who is educated in animal nutrition. After you have investigated the natural diet to your satisfaction, and decided to adopt it, be aware that it is not vital to follow it to the letter, that there will be days when the food has not defrosted or you are in a tearing hurry and your overcrowded schedule means that commercial dog food has to be fed today. You have to live your life, and the odd junk food experience will not kill either of you. Take care to buy a food that has as little as possible in the way of additives, and the sky will not fall in if you feed her that on occasion, or the end of your toast crust, or a little something left over from the dinner party (as long as it is alcohol-free). There is nothing wrong with table scraps for dogs: if it is good enough for me, I reckon it is good enough for my dogs, though we do eat plain food here. As long as the bulk of your dog's intake is natural, the occasional digression will not matter at all. In my experience of several generations of working dogs raised naturally, the diet offers everything that the dogs need, and they look wonderful on it. More to the point, they perform well, heal quickly and cleanly when injured, and are glowing with health. It is a very little more trouble, but what marvellous results you get.

Introducing the Diet

Any new diet needs careful introduction. Some dogs take to the rawfood diet straight away – mine did – but others are very suspicious of any change. Remember that hunger is a great condiment, and start with a hungry dog. Give half of her normal rations, and add a tablespoonful of vegetable and meat that has been well mixed up with it. Gradually over the week supply less of her old food at each meal, and more of the new: you have been feeding half rations so she should be rather hungry by the end of the week. On one of the days, give her raw meaty bones for her meal and nothing else. Most dogs will be fully converted to the new diet by the end of the week. Then it is a simple matter to increase the quantity until she is satisfied by each meal, and does not look underweight. A raw egg cracked into the dish and mixed in will sometimes tempt a finicky feeder, but do not do this every day. Do not feed anything else at the changeover time, and she will soon come to really enjoy her new food.

The Shy Feeder

Lurchers are sensitive dogs, and many a shy feeder is acting that way not because she does not like her food, but because the restaurant that you are serving it in has no 'ambience'. Just as you would lose your appetite in a filthy, crowded, noisy greasy-spoon café, so your lurcher can be cowed by being fed among a crowd of other dogs, or in the hustle and bustle of a busy kitchen. If she is a reluctant eater, feed her on her own, away from noise, other dogs and human comings and goings. Some lurchers like your company when they eat and others prefer to be quite alone. I prefer to be in the same room but at a 'safe' distance if I have a nervous feeder: safe for the dog, that is, as many rescued dogs are afraid to eat if humans are too close. Sometimes, food and punishment have been disastrously related, or maybe they have had too much of shouting and barking and clattering dishes, and just want some peace and quiet.

Ignore the gung-ho dog training 'experts' that tell you to take the dog dish up if the dog has not eaten all its food in ten minutes: such rules might work with confident gundogs but not traumatised lurchers. Give her half an hour with her food, while you read a magazine and relax with your thoughts. She will eventually start to nibble at the food, maybe eat half of it and then retreat, or just sift up a few mouthfuls at a time. Even if she goes and lies down away from the food, do not stand up and pick up the bowl just yet, as she may be mustering the courage to return. She may come and 'chat' to you, boring into you with her huge, anxious eyes, or even touching you with paw or nose. Feel free to chat back, or offer a non-threatening touch such as a tickle of her chest. If after the half-hour some or all of the food remains uneaten, just pick up the bowl gently and quietly, and take it away. If she has eaten only half of it, that is the amount you offer next time. Do not feed except in the food bowl and in the quiet place, for even the most introverted lurcher will pretty soon learn to manipulate a soft dog owner into either offering better food (what you are eating is much more desirable than my food) or feeding by hand. Incidentally, a lot of rescued lurchers do not like the shine and clatter of metal food bowls or the smell of plastic ones – these can give off strong fumes when new – and you might find that simply changing to a solid, heavy bowl in earthenware or strengthened glass will be enough. Always supervise feeding, especially if the bowl is breakable.

When to Feed

The old-fashioned way of dog-keeping insisted on dogs being fasted one day a week, but being fed at precisely the same time on the other six. Lurchers and their relatives do not need fasting as they have relatively small stomachs for their size, and indeed, when you work them, it is quite difficult to keep the weight on them. The theory behind the fasting was that a wild dog would not eat every day. I would certainly contest this, as even a lousy hunter would find plenty to scavenge on a daily basis, and I suspect the truth behind this idea is that it is very cheap and convenient for the kennel owner who, after all, is saving fifty-two meals per dog per year! I am equally amused by the necessity of feeding dogs at precise times – that is the wild-dog theory out of the window, unless it can kill at exactly the same time on every day that is not a fasting day. This kind of arrangement is for the convenience of the kennel staff not the good of the dogs, and in fact is detrimental to the dogs, as they will become restless and demanding as the feeding time approaches. If you do not keep staff, or if you work your dogs, you will find it quite impossible to feed your dog at the same time every day and still have a life of your own. I have had a lifetime of feeding people and animals the best food at random times, and they do not suffer for it at all. However, it should be noted that when you feed your dog is just as important as what you feed her.

If you are training, you need a hungry dog, so feed her upon your return from training. If she is going to take part in strenuous activity, fast her for eight hours beforehand. If she has just had a hard day's work or competing, feed her a small meal, just four mouthfuls, upon her return, and the rest of her meal an hour or so later: a full meal bolted by a hungry dog can sometimes come straight back up again. If she has been running around and is still panting, do not feed her until she has recovered completely from her exertions, which will be upwards of about half an hour after she comes home. Likewise, never ever feed a dog and then exercise her. A dog should always take exercise on an empty stomach. Elderly dogs and pregnant bitches need to be fed more often than healthy dogs in their prime, and consequently will need to empty themselves more often as well. Puppies up to six months old should be fed four times daily if you can, and thereafter twice daily until a year old. Lactating bitches should be fed to appetite, and will commonly consume in excess of four times their normal ration; my method is just to keep feeding them! Again, they must be taken out to empty themselves often, especially as some will be reluctant to leave their puppies and so accumulate toxins by holding on to their waste matter. If you need to take a little weight off your dog, or have just taken one in that is overweight, feed a lot of fruit and vegetables and meaty bones, but relatively little meat. More and fattier meat is needed to feed up a scrawny dog, but do not feed any less of the fruit and vegetables; on the contrary, feed more, so that the extra protein does not stress the kidneys. Easy, isn't it?

Water

Good quality drinking water is every bit as important as good quality food. Every book that you ever read about dog care stresses the need for clean, fresh water to be available at all times. Tap water around the country varies very much in palatability, some being very pleasant to drink and others not all that many miles away being foul-tasting because of the added chemicals. An unfortunate offshoot of this is that your dog may not drink enough because the water tastes bad. We all know that a dog will drink eagerly from puddles, stagnant ponds and the like, in preference to the water in her dish, and this is because the water is soft and tastes better to the dog. In fact, such water might be contaminated with the run-off from farm chemicals, or sewage, or just the general detritus of pond life; it might give your dog diarrhoea, vomiting, or a few days of non-specific below-par health. In extreme cases, your dog could catch leptospirosis from infected rats, or die from the effects of anti-freeze in puddles, the latter being sweet to the taste and capable of killing in a very short time. Or your dog could live a long and happy life drinking from every available source without mishap. Personally, I don't let my dogs drink out of puddles or ponds, but am happy for them to drink from moving water. You cannot keep them in cotton wool, after all, or afford mineral water for them to drink (although I have noticed that mine really enjoy that). If your tap water is as nasty as it is where I live, there are several ways of improving the contents of your dog's water dish. You can filter the water – don't throw your hands up in horror at this blatant spoiling, but offer your dog the choice between filtered and unfiltered water; try a glass of each yourself and see what I mean. Or you can boil the water and leave it to cool. Or, the method I use, you can put a crystal in the dog bowl. Crystals are not expensive and last for ever, and are easily obtained from new-age sort of shops, or at craft fairs. I use clear quartz, but rose quartz and amethyst, while being more expensive, are very good as well. You do not need a very big crystal, though if you have a greedy dog (rare in a lurcher, but you may have other dogs) you need one sufficiently large that it will not be swallowed. Mine have never shown the slightest desire to eat any of their crystals, though on one occasion when I was away and my beloved had not noticed that the dog bowl needed replenishing, the oldest lurcher picked out the crystal and spat it into his lap!

I prefer a pottery or ovenproof glass bowl for water, rather than a metal one, though metal bowls are easier for foodstuffs. I keep away from plastic, as it is flimsy and often smells unpleasant.

Your dog might not drink very much at all on a day-to-day basis. There has been a fashion in human health to claim that we are all dehydrated and must drink large quantities of water every day. This is a nonsense, but sells a lot of water. Your dog will drink as much as she needs. If water consumption suddenly increases for no reason that you can see, and that increase is

Water from a cattle trough...

running water is better

maintained for more than a day or two, suspect illness and have her checked over (see Chapter 10).

Other Drinks

After severe exertion, electrolyte drinks can be beneficial, though it is unlikely that a non-working lurcher will ever push herself to the extent of needing them. However, if you race your dog, and she is good enough to go through several heats in a competition, you might consider giving them to her. Electrolytes, commonly used now in the horse world and that of human athletics, replace the sugars and salts lost during extreme exertion, thus helping to avoid muscle cramps and stress on heart and kidneys. Electrolyte drinks are offered at the end of a competition, though if there is a long wait between heats, a few laps may be allowed then. Most animals will take electrolytes when they require them, but if your dog will not and you know that she needs them, you can syringe them into her mouth. As an alternative, and a drink that dogs find very palatable, weak tea sweetened with honey or sugar and with a pinch of salt in it, will usually be taken readily. Dogs are better for potassium chloride, marketed as 'Lo-Salt', than ordinary table salt which is sodium chloride, but if ordinary salt is all you have, a little will do no harm. Adult dogs should never be given cows' milk as they lack the stomach enzyme necessary for its digestion, and it can cause scour (severe diarrhoea). Personally, I do not give puppies cows' milk either: in my opinion, it is wonderful for calves and not suitable for anything else. Dogs should not be given processed drinks such as colas, or coffee, or chocolate, which latter could prove fatal. Chocolate contains a substance called theobromine, which kills dogs. If you have a dog that really loves chocolate – I have – give her occasional treats of dog chocolate, from which the theobromine has been extracted. Never give a dog alcohol, though there are two exceptions to this: a small amount of beer very occasionally on her food can be a useful pick-me-up, and by small, I mean no more than a tablespoonful, and equally, a teaspoonful of brandy, well diluted, can be of use. Do not give either of these to lactating bitches.

Health

You will only get out in terms of health what you put in, in terms of food and drink. Money saved by feeding poor quality food is the worst of false economies. The dog that feels well will perform well, and even if you want nothing more from her than to be the delightful companion that she is, it is important to understand that the better she feels, the more co-operative she will be. The most difficult dog that I have ever owned changed beyond belief once I had the courage to fly in the face of received wisdom and feed her in the way that logic told me was the best. She went in a matter of about a fortnight from being a poisonous little sod to a charming and most devoted animal, and has remained that way ever since. One is tempted to ponder on how much human misfits might reform if only they were fed a better diet.

Self-service

Recommended Reading

Give Your Dog A Bone Dr Ian Billinghurst P.O.Box WO64, Bathurst NSW, Australia 2795

Grow Your Pups With Bones as above

Raw Meaty Bones Tom Lonsdale

All available from
Canine Natural Cures 020 8668 8011
www.caninenaturalcures.co.uk

Natural/holistic Veterinary Sites
www.holisticvet.co.uk
www.altvet.co.uk

We all eat junk food sometimes

Watching television

4 HOUSE MANNERS

You may want to start with a new puppy, or else be taking on an older dog, adolescent or fully grown. There are good reasons for each choice, or you have possibly had your lurcher thrust upon you by circumstances, and are having to make the best of the situation. Let's start, as so many people do, with a puppy.

Puppies

All puppies have a high cute factor, and personally, I think that it would be better for dogs as a whole if they did not, for then only people who really wanted them would get them. Although you have chosen a puppy, what you are getting is a baby dog: she will grow up into a dog, and the puppy days, puppy cuteness and puppy problems will not last long. She should come from her breeder with information on what she has been fed, when she has been

Puppies are cute (B. Hurley)

wormed, and whether she has been vaccinated. She may already be insured, as some companies will insure a litter right from the beginning, hoping that the new owner will continue with the same company. She will need a 'puppy starter kit' of her own bed, bedding, bowls and toys, collar, lead and identity disc, brush, nail clippers and flea comb, possibly an indoor crate. She will then show you quite unmistakably that she is not a blank sheet on which life will write experiences, but a mass of instincts, personality and quite possibly race memory, which you will need to mould into your way of life. Each puppy brings new challenges. You will think 'I won't make that mistake with the next puppy' and you will not: instead you will make completely different mistakes. But they are only mistakes and they can be put right. Your puppy will not be perfect, though sadly some owners expect them to be. You are not perfect either, but you can be an excellent dog owner with a wonderful dog. It is easy to forget how demanding and time-consuming a puppy can be, never mind how much they eat and how much clearing-up has to be done after them. The important thing to remember is that puppies must chew, dig, teethe, get into mischief and generally be puppies. Please do not take on a puppy if other big events are expected in the family. If there is a baby due, or an imminent house move, an operation, a family member moving back home, a promotion to a more demanding job – do not get the puppy until the dust has settled. In order to end up with that wonderful dog, a lot of time must be spent ungrudgingly with the puppy. The swan sailing serenely across the lake is paddling like blazes below the waterline, and the beautifully behaved dog has had two years of work put into her. Puppies are lovely, but please pause before you take one on, and consider honestly whether you can give her the commitment she needs.

The Adult Dog

The adult dog should have had most of the work done, and even if not, will have grown out of the most testing puppy behaviours. Make sure that you know of any 'ifs' and feel confident about managing them before you take the dog on, and also be aware that when a dog changes homes, there is often a 'honeymoon' period where she behaves like an angel. This can be followed by total hooliganism while she tests her boundaries, and afterwards you both settle into more or less the sort of relationship that you had hoped for. There are, of course, adult dogs that never change from being angels, and which came up for re-homing due to circumstances rather than fault, just as there are adult dogs which display a single aggravating, besetting sin which they exercise at every opportunity. Most of these sins can be exorcised with the

The older dog – plenty of life yet

right kind of approach, although there are some where a combination of compromise and vigilance has to be reached. Many people prefer to take on an adult dog and sidestep the traumas of puppy owning. There is also the physical aspect: if you no longer are as spry or supple as you were, and upon bending down you check if there are any more tasks you might achieve before struggling upright again, an adult-sized dog which is reliable in her house training and no longer needs to shred and scatter the contents of the waste bin will be much more your style than the infant that is hell-bent on mischief and is through every door that should not have been left open before you can cross the room.

The Teenager

Are you out of your mind? Well, I've taken on teenagers as well. Past the puppy chaos, young enough to grow into your way of thinking and not having paid the price of long-term neglect or abuse, the adolescent dog is a good choice, provided you can give her stability in her everyday life, and absolute consistency in her training. Most lurchers undergo a stormy adolescence, but

Two teenagers together

if you have help at hand or are otherwise confident in your ability to cope, they are very rewarding. You have the advantage of accurate knowledge of how she will look as an adult, and her behaviour can only improve. A lurcher that changes hands as an adolescent will often become a strongly bonded dog once she is past her insecurities, though initially you might feel as if you are living with the SAS.

Assuming that you will be keeping your lurcher in the house rather than in a kennel, you have two areas of training to tackle, one being house manners and the other being correct behaviour when you are out and about. First of all, take a look at the environment that you are offering her, being mindful that she may have been born in or living in kennels for some time before she arrived in your care. Do you have other dogs and cats? Do you have small children, or visiting grandchildren? Do you have rowdy teenagers? Are there rabbits and guinea pigs in hutches in the garden, or a hamster in a cage in someone's bedroom? Do you like the television or radio on all the time that you are at home? Is there a lot of domestic machinery going most of the time? All of these things, which are perfectly normal to you, can completely freak out a dog that is used to the quiet environment of her own kennel. Equally, the atmosphere of noise and bustle in a rescue kennels can traumatise a sensitive longdog, and she might take quite some time to come out of her shell once you have her at home. This period of transition can lead to a lot of misunderstanding.

The Sleeping Area

Above all, your new dog needs a place that she can call her own. This means a bed to which she can retire where she is out of the way of the rest of the household comings and goings, one that is away from the clattering of the washing machine and tumble drier, and which is not being constantly invaded by the vacuum cleaner. This means that whenever her new world overwhelms her, she can creep into sanctuary until she feels more comfortable, and she can come out and join in with the family, secure in the knowledge that once it all becomes too much, she can retreat again. Humans must respect this area: she should not have to endure heads and hands being poked into her space, or cats and other dogs making free with it. It is hers, and very necessary in the early days. She may wet on it, to make it smell more of herself, in which case just ignore what has happened and leave the smell there. Equally, no matter how houseproud you are, leave the mud and dog hairs on her bed for now. You might have a happy dog that moves seamlessly into her new home, but you are much more likely to have a frightened little creature with a traumatic history behind her. So give her something to call her own, just a bed and a little space, not too much to ask. Old-fashioned dog behaviourists who are still applying dominance rules will tell you that you should get onto the dog's bed from time to time and push her off it, to demonstrate your superiority. Please do not: it will be the last straw to a nervous dog, and achieves absolutely nothing. Once she is more secure, she will 'invite' you into her space herself, which is a real compliment.

You might like to house her in an indoor kennel: if so, put a blanket over the top to make it more like a den. Don't shut her inside it while you are with her, but let her come and go as she wishes. Leave a few small food treats in there for her to find when she goes in. If there is a problem with wetting/soiling or destructiveness while you are out, you can get her used to being shut in the indoor kennel for a few minutes at a time, building up to a maximum of two hours, but the root cause of the problem should be tackled as soon as possible, methods of which will be covered shortly. Situate her bed off the ground (a blanket on the cold concrete utility room floor is not adequate) out of the main line of household traffic, and as quiet as you can make it. It should also be somewhere with an easy-clean floor, and free from precious

Everything a bed should be (B. Hurley)

Part of the family but with his own space (B. Hurley)

items that might get damaged. Plan for the worst and it might very well not happen, but leaving her surrounded by (for instance) boots and shoes is asking for trouble. She should not be isolated from the rest of the family, and a kitchen is an ideal place to start a dog off, as there is usually somebody in it. As long as she can retreat out of the way when she needs to, or when the cook could do without a dog underfoot, she should come out of herself quite quickly. Another useful feature of the kitchen is that it usually has a door leading to the outside, so that she can go out to relieve herself when she needs to do so. In this atmosphere, the dog will learn quite naturally commands such as 'Go to your bed' which can be accompanied by a titbit thrown onto the bed, and 'Outside' when she goes to the door or otherwise indicates that she needs to empty herself. If you have a radio or television on in here, try to have the volume low; dogs are especially susceptible to laughter, and the roar of a studio audience can terrify them. If your teenagers crash in and out shouting, and like their music as loud as it will go, discuss before you ever get a dog whether they are willing to compromise during the settling-in period, and if not, delay your acquisition of a dog until they are either more considerate or have left home. Don't allow children to pull the dog about: very small children are largely powerless in their everyday lives and so really relish the power they can display over a dog, and the excellent attention-getting potential of hurting her. One of the phrases that I really detest is something like 'Oh he's so good with the children, they pull him about and he never retaliates'. No dog, no animal, should be made to endure this, and if he ever does retaliate, what happens? A child terrified, possibly badly injured, and a dog 'put down' – killed – for no good reason. Children should be taught to respect animals not torture them; a good way is to tell them never to approach the (or any) dog because when she wants to see them, she will approach them. Above all, never let the child into the dog's bed area, or interfere with her when she is eating. Older children can have an important training influence, and children and dogs can be joyous companions, but first of all, the child should be encouraged to take an active part in the responsibilities of owning a dog. Respect comes before love, and in many ways is far more important. The child that grooms, feeds and walks the dog will be much more dog-aware than the child that treats her as a toy.

Meanwhile, your new dog will settle better if she has a choice of whether to stay with noise or escape from it. When you wish to vacuum, tell her to go outside; if she dislikes the vacuum cleaner, she will quickly learn to present herself at the door as soon as she sees it. If visitors want to admire her, which is only right and natural with such a special dog, sit them with their cup of tea well away from the dog's bed and let her come to them. Do not let them feed her titbits unless you want a dog that is on the scrounge as soon as the biscuit tin is opened, nor should the visitor approach or make eye contact with the dog: the dog should be allowed to take her time going up to the visitor, and if the dog then offers herself for a caress, the strange hand should stroke a 'neutral' area such as the chest or sides of the dog. It is most impolite to touch a dog's head unless you are an intimate friend of that dog; just imagine if I walked up to you and touched your head! Heads are very personal and a vulnerable area; they should never ever be patted, and only caressed by invitation. A dog that ducks or flinches from the hand is not yet ready for it. Equally, do not allow people to loom over the top of the dog, which is very intimidating. If visitors result in your dog producing a puddle either out of fear or submission, do not punish the dog or even acknowledge the puddle beyond wiping it up; instead see that greetings take place outside until your dog is less fearful. Be patient: you have all the time in the world.

House Access

A frequent mistake people make when the dog first comes home is to allow her access to the whole house all the time. This is asking for grief, especially if the house is large and she cannot work out which doors lead to outside in time to prevent an accident on the carpet. Start off with the whole of the upstairs barred from access (a babygate is good for this, but make sure it has the bars blocked off so that long narrow heads and paws cannot be caught between them) and only have her in any room apart form 'her' room when you are there to supervise. When she is in another room, have a bed or a blanket on the floor beside you so that she knows where to be. If you don't mind her on the furniture, fair enough, but she must learn to get off on command because if she is in someone else's house visiting with you, they might not like to have her on their furniture; equally it can be annoying for human guests when there is nowhere to sit except the floor because the furniture is taken up with dog(s), or because they have just covered their good clothes with mud and dog hair. It is perfectly possible to allocate one chair or sofa for dog use and train her to keep off the rest, although you should not expect her to display a high level of self-discipline in your absence – so shut her out of that room if you want some furniture kept for humans only. She might like to be on your lap, which is very cosy, but she has to realise that this is a privilege not a right, and only come up on invitation. Otherwise there may well be upset when children or grandchildren want to be on the lap instead. Even if she is immaculately behaved in the house, it is good training to shut the door of her room so that

House rules – no dogs on the furniture?

she cannot be with you for a few minutes, gradually extending the time so that she is used to being on her own. For dogs with full-blown separation anxiety, this has to be very carefully managed, and will be dealt with in Chapter 6.

Resident Dogs

Other dogs in the household can be a blessing or a nightmare, each case being individual. Introduce the new dog in the garden, so that she has plenty of room to move out of range if one of the resident dogs becomes aggressive. Jealousy is a natural and very strong emotion: humans cannot cope with it and yet they expect dogs to do so. If you have several dogs, let them out one at a time, the top dog first, then put each dog away in turn until she has met them all as individuals. Then she can meet them – still in the garden – as a group. If all goes well, her bed can be near theirs, but be very careful of the situation for the first few weeks – yes, weeks, because once your new dog has settled in, she will be testing the pack status and her place within it. Your own attitude should be that there is only one person allowed to fight in this household, and that is the pack leader – you. Within those parameters, you will have to let the pack reorganise itself naturally, and your job is to reinforce the alpha dog's status, not demean her when she puts an upstart in its place, which is a human

Getting along with other dogs

reaction because we like things to be 'fair'. Dogs don't do 'fair' they do 'status', and if the human undermines the alpha dog by telling her off when she disciplines a social-climbing new dog, anarchy can be the result. Sometimes, the new dog slips in without a ripple, especially if your others are lurchers as well, but if you have a very dominant member of another breed, such as a terrier or GSD, watch out and be one step ahead at all times. Meals must be supervised, as they are a ready flashpoint, as are beds, and don't forget that one of the best dog training aids ever invented is the door – close it, and feed dogs or let them sleep in separate rooms if need be.

Cats

There is a prevalent idea that lurchers cannot be homed with cats. This is emphatically not so: lurchers can be trained to accept their own cats quite readily, and also not to chase outside cats (covered in Chapter 5) but you have to put a bit of work into the situation, and it is the cat side of things that defines the outcome, rather than the attitude of the dog. Introducing a kitten to a lurcher is very straightforward, and is usually quite simple, though it is wise never to leave them alone together in case the kitten's squeaks trigger a predator response. Some lurchers can become very protective of their cat, especially if it is a kitten, but each case must be taken as it comes, and you cannot predict how dog and kitten will interact, so play safe all the time. Adult cats that are used to dogs will treat the new one much the same as the others; expect very little problem there, but again don't leave them alone together. Many lurchers are trained not to chase cats before they ever get into the dog rescue, but equally some may not have been, and need to be acquainted with the word 'no'. Cats often do not help themselves in this matter; if you have a cat that taunts the dogs and then leaps just out of reach, don't get a lurcher, for she will be quicker than the cat; like teasing children, it is just not reasonable to expect any dog to endure it. Equally, if you have the sort of cat that makes friendly overtures and then claws at the dog, this is not a suitable situation for a lurcher, being likely to result in a dead cat and a dog that has been transformed from an amiable animal with cat-friendly potential to a cat-hating fiend. Don't assume, either, that your other dogs ignoring the cat will be sufficient to train the lurcher by example; the pack instinct might cut in at any time, and the other dogs join in a cat-hunt which can only have one ending. Jealous cats can start to use the dog bed as a latrine, which again cannot be tolerated; sadly this does mean that either the cat or the dog has to be re-homed, or else you (which is easy) and your family (which is not) will have to

Safe with cats

learn to shut doors and keep the cat permanently away from the dog bed, as cats do not seem to be able to get over this behaviour. Some will even start to soil the rest of the house, especially people beds, which again means great application in shutting doors. If your cat simply ignores the dogs, or uses them for warmth, then you have a more promising arrangement, as lurchers like warmth too, and my own working lurchers are very happy to share a bed with a cat, even though we do not have cats ourselves. It is merely a matter of introducing cat and dog in a supervised area, the dog being told 'no' if she pulls towards the cat in a predatory manner, but otherwise being allowed to gently sniff the cat, which may well, if it is an honest one, raise its tail, purr, and rub its face against the dog. It is at this point that I gently separate them, as some cats will then whirl and attack the dog, which is precisely what you do not want to happen. Dog and cat should spend plenty of supervised time with each other, but again be careful about food and feeding times. You will find lurchers very good at eating the cat's leftovers, not only in your own house but everyone else's, so unless the cat is fed somewhere that the lurcher cannot reach, which is quite difficult, the cat food should be taken up after each offering, and the cat may well learn not to be so fussy. Cats being great harbourers of fleas, there is a care and maintenance problem with cats and any breed of dog being kept together, and demands just that extra bit of application from the owner.

Small Pets

Rabbits, guinea pigs, hamsters and the like should be kept well away from all dogs, not just lurchers, as you can never tell when a predator response might occur, with tragic results. Many lurchers (and other dogs) will live in harmony with their 'own' rabbits, but it is never a good idea to leave them alone together. Secure pens and hutches, and constant vigilance is the answer.

Poultry and large livestock will be considered in Chapter 5.

The Kennel

You might prefer to have your lurcher in a kennel, or kennel and run, either all the time, just at night, or when you cannot be with her. If this is your choice, again make sure that the location of the kennel is quiet, is near the house where you can keep an eye on her and she is safe from opportunist thieves, and away from any area where children can hang over the fence and tease her. Lurchers generally take very well to kennel life as long as they have plenty of exercise and human contact during the day. They are not dogs which take well to being shut away for the greater part of the day and night, but after they have had a good run, maybe some training and a cuddle, they will settle quite cheerfully for a nap and a chew of the latest bone. Personally, I think you get a better relationship with a lurcher if she is in the house with you as much as possible, but it is useful if she is accustomed to being in a safe kennel and run at least part of the time. If she needs to convalesce, if you decide to breed from her, if she is on heat and you are going out for a few hours, or if the children from Hell are visiting, a comfortable alternative to the house is preferable to a perplexed dog suddenly being shut away in one room.

Kennels should be warm and weatherproof, beds should be raised and with generous bedding, for the angular proportions of a lurcher easily lead to sores, bald patches ('kennel rash') and callouses if the resting area is not sufficiently padded. Choice of bedding is up to you: we use discarded blankets and cotton sheets or duvet covers which are easy to launder; others prefer hay, straw, shavings or paper bedding. These last I avoid because hay and straw, although very warm, tends to harbour fleas and other unwelcome guests, and shavings are not very warm. Paper is warm and clean, but not so easy to dispose of, unless you live somewhere where you can have a bonfire. Some shredded bedding is of stronger material and can get caught around a leg or even a throat with tragic results: if it does not break easily, don't use it. VetBed is expensive but washes easily and lasts a long time unless you have a bed shredder, but by itself is not thick enough for a lurcher bed, so use it to top up other bedding; bean bags and duvets can make a lovely mess and a lot of entertainment for a bored dog, too, not to mention being difficult to clean. If a kennel is more convenient to you, don't hesitate to house your lurcher in one, as she will be perfectly happy as long as she gets plenty of company when you are at home. Curiously, many dog rescue organisations do not home dogs to places where they will be kennelled. As they keep the dogs in kennels themselves, this seems rather a strange decision. If a lurcher is offered a kind home where she will be trained, loved, exercised, properly fed and cared for, but spends some of her time in a kennel, I can find no fault with that. If you do choose a kennel arrangement, be sure that your dog has plenty of opportunity to go outside and relieve herself; do not put her in the position of 'hanging on' in great discomfort or else soiling her living area. Which brings me quite nicely to house training.

House Training

Probably more dogs of all breeds end up in rescue homes due to difficulties with house training than with any other problem, and yet helping a dog to be clean in the house is very easy. Tiny puppies come ready-programmed to be clean in their quarters, and will shuffle off their VetBed onto the newspaper to empty themselves even before their eyes have opened. If you get your pup from a breeder who has encouraged this natural instinct and allowed the puppies access to outside as soon as they are able to toddle, you will probably never have to house train your pup: I have never had to house train a puppy of my own breeding. If, however, the pups have been shut in with their own mess, and become used to being surrounded by it, you will have a little more of a problem. Rather sadly, a lot of dog rescue kennels (and quite a few boarding kennels) seem to actively encourage the dogs to soil in their living quarters: many of them shut the dogs into their kennels mid-afternoon and do not release them again until the staff come in the following morning. A major dog charity for which I have enormous respect otherwise, furnishes the dogs' living quarters with sofas and armchairs rather than conventional dog beds, the idea of which is said to be to simulate a domestic environment. Unfortunately, what it actually does is teach the dogs that climbing on the furniture is acceptable, and soiling in the domestic area is unavoidable. So if you have your dog, of any age, from a rescue kennels, or from the sort of breeder who has left the pups in their own mess, you will have a little work to do in order to house train. It really is only a little work, but for the duration of the house training, you will have to be utterly consistent and constantly vigilant.

It is important not to use litter boxes, soiling pads, newspaper, or any other device that allows the dog to relieve herself indoors, for this is a habit that is very hard to break once it is set. Instead, take the dog outside every time she wakes up, or has eaten, or has not emptied herself for three hours. For a pup, cut this time to one hour if she is very tiny, until you have established how long you can comfortably (that is, her comfort not yours) leave her. Tiny puppies simply do not have the bodily control to 'hang on' so don't expect her to; any indoor 'accidents' are your fault for not reading the signs. She is not doing this deliberately to annoy you; she is a tiny baby and when she needs to empty herself, the time is now, not in a minute. Think how long it takes a human child to house train! Your dog will be clean and dry in a matter of weeks, and the more you put into helping her, the quicker it will all happen. When she starts to sniff and circle, or look uncomfortable, seek out a dark place or begin to squeak, take her outside at once. Note that I say 'take' the dog out, not 'put' her out. This is a frequent mistake that people make, being so busy wanting to get back to the television or computer. If you put a dog outside in the cold and dark, all on her own, she will be confused, bewildered and quite possible frightened. She does not 'know' what you want, but she does know what she wants, which is to be back in the warmth and light and company of indoors. So she will wait on the doorstep until you let her back in, whereupon she will probably empty herself because that is now the priority, whereas when she was outside, she was worried and nervous and going inside again was her main concern. So take the dog out and be prepared to wait while she potters and sniffs and chases the odd butterfly. Don't huff and puff and stamp with impatience, because she will pick up your disapproval, not knowing why you are so cross, and may not do what you want her to because she is upset. Dogs pick up our moods so easily. So relax, admire the sky and try not to notice that the hedge needs cutting. When she performs, reward her with a titbit and lots of praise.

I find it useful to train dogs to empty on command, which is easily achieved by using that particular word or phrase just as she gets to the end of what she is doing – if you say it at the beginning, you will distract her, and may be in for another long wait. Do use a word or phrase that is repeatable in polite company – I'm afraid the one I use is not, so learn from my mistake –and also not anything that can come up readily in conversation. The Woodhousian 'quickly' and 'hurry up' are far too risky! After she has done what you want, play with her for a few minutes and then take her back indoors, otherwise she will delay emptying because the minute she has finished, so has her adventure outside. She will soon learn that play comes after emptying, not before, which will speed things up once she gets the idea. If the weather is good and your garden is safe, leave her on her own outside to do her own playing after she has had ten minutes or so with you, though you will likely find that she prefers to be with you all the time. Don't fret about that, for it is a valuable training aid. For night-time, go out with the puppy as late as you can, set your alarm for four hours later (if you come down to an 'accident' then try three hours) and then take puppy out as soon as you get up in the morning. I really do mean immediately: don't expect her to wait while you put the kettle on or find your dressing gown. The other option with a very young puppy is the cardboard box method. Line the biggest cardboard box you can find with newspaper and a blanket, put it beside your bed and put the puppy in it. When she wakes up and needs to empty, she will shuffle about and perhaps cry because she does not want to soil her bed. Carry her outside (don't expect her to walk as she has more urgent matters on her mind) and after she has obliged, take her back to her box. It will only be for a short time that you have to do this, as puppies soon become strong enough to last through the night, and time spent now will save you many an unpleasant surprise in the morning. If you prefer to clean up rather than get up – tough! Anything that you do to encourage the pup emptying herself indoors will

A dog crate – invaluable in so many situations

prolong the whole business, and if you are not consistent, you may well end up with a permanently unreliable dog. Do not worry about the few days beside your bed bringing on a dominance problem, or leading the pup to thinking that she will always sleep in your room – although it can be a pleasant arrangement if it suits you – once she is regularly lasting through the night, you can move her into her permanent quarters, still with her box, but lying on its side now so she can get in and out, and if she has grown out of it by now, her proper bed or dog crate. If you are able to leave a back door open so that she can take herself out when she needs to, all the better. Some people install a dog-flap, but these are a gift for burglars, which should be borne in mind. House training a pup is easily accomplished with just this couple of weeks of application.

The adult dog is trained similarly, though there may be a few more difficulties if she has come from a bad home via the dog rescue. Often, dogs have been punished for emptying indoors, but never shown that they should empty outside, the result being that they think it is the act of emptying, not the place of it, that is bringing such wrath upon them. This leads to a dog that will not empty when anyone is looking, the sort that can be walked for hours

– nothing – then taken home, left for five minutes and there is the result all over the floor. The reaction from the unthinking human is more wrath, probably punishment, and a really confused dog that hangs on as long as she can until she is on her own in a room. The way round this requires lots of time and patience: feed her a small meal to help things along and then walk her and walk her until she cannot help but empty herself. She will likely then cringe and grovel, expecting punishment, but instead, there is praise and fuss. Good heavens, this dreadful action seems to please this new family! There may then be a brief awkwardness while she checks whether it pleases you at all times, and may well empty herself indoors again. If so, don't make a fuss, just take her out so she will learn that outside is the place. Again, indoor accidents are your fault, so if they happen, just clean up and say nothing. Use either bleach or biological detergent when you clean up, as most disinfectants contain ammonia which smells to a dog as if this is a good place to empty. Take your dog outside frequently, and last thing at night, yes, even if it is raining, walk her until she obliges, then don't stop the walk as soon as you get what you want, but go on for another half-mile or so. Otherwise, the dog will delay emptying in order to prolong the walk, and you achieve the opposite of what you wanted. Instead of getting annoyed because you want to be at home, treat these outings as a bonding exercise; they can be a very companionable time.

Very occasionally, you will get a lurcher that finds it necessary to territory-mark inside the house; the odd bitch will do this as well as male dogs, the biggest offenders being entire males that have been used at stud. Initially, as a damage-limitation exercise, confine the animal in one room that is easily cleaned, unless you are there to supervise, and make sure he gets plenty of exercise and outside time. This is one occasion when your disapproval may be voiced if you catch the culprit in the act, but don't go on about it. A brief, gruff comment and putting the dog outside on his own should suffice. Most will get over it as they settle down: a few will always be unreliable, as it is usually a sign of deep insecurity. If you have other dogs, this sort of behaviour can be taken up by the whole lot, but then the new dog might well not feel insecure in a place on his own. If the behaviour persists beyond a few months, consider keeping the offender in a kennel and run outside, but do not use an indoor kennel constantly as it is inhumane to confine a dog so tightly for long periods. Castration of males rarely helps, as there is a tendency for this to go from a nervous behaviour to a learned one; however castration will reduce the smell, as entire male dogs add hormones to the urine which really does increase the smell even to human noses. Even when you have cured this behaviour in your own home, it can resurface in times of agitation, so this is not a dog to take visiting your friends unless you keep him on a lead close beside you while you drink your tea. Lurchers as a rule are sensitive dogs but very rarely oversexed, or even averagely sexed, one of the reasons why entire dogs of this type are so easy to keep, so the behaviour is almost always curable as its root is stress rather than sexual.

There are also physical causes for dogs wetting in the house. Old dogs of either sex can have continence problems, as do many people; if you catch yourself becoming impatient, just remember it might be your turn one day. Spaying is a major cause of incontinence in bitches, and when I used to spend time at an animal sanctuary, almost all the bitches we had in were there because of spaying-induced incontinence. I have a bitch who was spayed in her third year, a lean, fit working bitch, who was incontinent ever after, so do not believe the current hype that it is only overweight bitches that become incontinent, though the odds certainly increase if the bitch is too fat or spayed too young, as is the practice with certain animal charities. The condition can be treated a variety of ways, some more successful than others. Homoeopathy helped mine until the condition became so bad that she was leaking constantly, after which a drug that tightens the smooth muscles had to be used. Acupuncture can produce quite spectacular results as well. Hormone treatments are generally not so successful, and can cause unacceptable personality changes; further surgery or other drug treatments are available, but the situation is far from satisfactory, and it would be helpful if consideration would be given to improving surgical techniques, which research by Dr Peter Holt at Bristol University has shown to be at the root of the problem in the majority of cases.

Stealing Food

It seems curious that most lurchers have only a passing interest in food, sometimes to the extent that you wonder if they will ever keep body and soul together, and yet have a passion for stealing that rivals Fagin. Lurchers can reach a long way up, can learn to open refrigerator and cupboard doors with their long, agile paws, and some exponents of the art can even manage ovens and biscuit tins. Don't forget that stealing and poaching are part of a lurcher's skills. Dogs view unaccompanied food with a different set of morals from people: if it is there on its own, you obviously have eaten your fill and so a lurcher with an empty corner in her stomach is not committing a social crime. A dog that steals food needs an owner that does not leave food out to be stolen; if for some reason food needs to be left out, then doors should be shut. Even such an experienced lurcher owner as myself has sometimes come

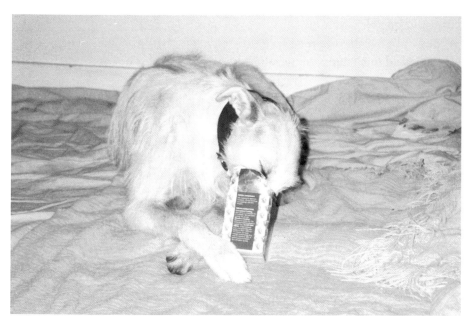

The bin raider

unstuck, most recently with a certain dog who looks as if butter wouldn't melt in his mouth proving that it did by eating half a pound of it on my bed, luckily very tidily. Others have fared far worse: a young couple had two of my puppies, though I did warn them that two pups together is more than twice the trouble of one on its own. They were a very good home, and sure that they could cope, and indeed they did. However, they did come home one day to discover that a bag of shopping had been left within puppy reach, and consequently the tally was half a pound of butter, six eggs, six bread rolls, six yoghurts, a packet of biscuits and – oh joy – a bag of flour that was opened and scattered to the four winds. What fun that must have been! The moral here is that you won't stop lurchers from stealing: it is one of the things that they do, so learn to put food away and close doors.

The Garden

If your garden is unfenced, you are not offering a safe home for your lurcher: she can get out, and other dogs can get in. If you cannot afford to fence the whole garden, fence part of it, or build a pen for her. Fences should be six feet high at least, and preferably with the top turned over, as some lurchers are very athletic leapers. The fence should also be dug in at the bottom, to discourage burrowing out. If you take the pen option, the pen needs to be roofed. Your lurcher is a hunting dog with strong instincts, and she will not stay put in an unfenced garden. She needs to be either fenced in soundly or under close control; it is no good expecting her to 'know' that she should not stray. Good fences make good neighbours; they also make safe dogs.

Do not even think about the option of the electric fence that is buried underground, the dog wearing a special collar and receiving a shock when she approaches the boundary. Lurchers live on adrenaline, and she will easily override the shock one way if the incentive is sufficient; she will then be unable to return home. If other stray dogs invade her 'patch' and attack her, she will be in terrible trouble,

Well enough fenced in? Just after this picture was taken she jumped over it

for she will be receiving the shocks and they will not. What you need is a good visible fence. Likewise if you take your dog with you while you get on with chores in the unfenced areas of your property, you will find that she can slip away as silently as water seeping into the ground. You will be absorbed with some task, look up, and your lurcher will be gone. While she is away she is in danger of being stolen, run over, attacked by other dogs, shot or snared; she could be worrying sheep, chasing other livestock, killing deer, harassing better kept dogs or getting in pup. If you really care for your dog, you will not take these risks. Two dogs make a pack: if she is meeting another stray, or if you have more than one dog, the drug of working as a pack will overwhelm any incentive that you can give her to stay at home, so do not put yourself in that position. This does not apply only to lurchers: most dogs will do this. The difference is that your lurcher can travel further faster and do more damage while she is away.

Digging

Lurchers are very good diggers, and if not checked will excavate much of the garden (I know one called Jaycee as in JCB). They need to dig, as do all dogs, so assuming you want to keep at least part of your garden free from that surface-of-the-moon look, you must provide a safe digging area for them. When you have chosen a suitable spot, put some fine soil or sand down loosely on the top, take your dog there and scrape at the soil with your hand, giving a command such as 'dig' in an excited voice. If she starts to paw the soil, praise her and encourage her to carry on. You can bury the odd biscuit there to give her incentive. Thereafter, if she starts to dig in another area, take her back to the 'diggery' and start her off digging there instead. Most dogs cotton

All dogs need to dig

on pretty quickly; a few die-hards will resist and dig where they prefer, in which case it is either fence her away from precious areas or resign yourself to a garden resembling the Somme. Likewise, you cannot expect a dog to 'know' that she should not walk on flower beds, so take her round the garden on a lead and show her where she can go, saying 'no' if she tries to take the short cut through the herbaceous border. Personally, I go for dog areas and non-dog areas, with a fence between the two, which is a good idea especially if your garden is important to you. Occasionally I come across people who are distressed because their dog's urine is causing brown patches in the lawn, and they want to know if they can give the dog something in her food to make the urine less acidic. Swallowing the observation that if grass is so important, they shouldn't get a dog, I can only say that the dog and the lawn should be kept separate, and the dog should be exercised as much as possible to give her the chance to urinate away from the garden. There is no justification for feeding a dog any substance to alter her physical processes merely for the look of a patch of grass, but the problem is brought to me sufficiently often that I have to address it here.

The Domestic Lurcher

Most lurchers fit easily into their new homes, and as long as she is treated with understanding and a consistent manner, you should have very little in the way of problems. Common sense and a light touch are what is needed, and you will soon wonder how you ever managed without her. She will lie at your feet and be a quiet, gentle companion when you wish to be quiet, she will tidy up leftovers for you, help you in the office by shredding paper, and add a general air of quality and nobility to your home. Once she has been exercised and fed, she will rest quietly until it is time to rouse and go out again. She will sleep on her back with her legs akimbo, or curled up so tightly that you will wonder how such a large dog can fold up to such a small circle. Lurchers, treated properly and given adequate training, are some of the most trouble-free dogs you could wish to own.

---

5 Outside Manners

A very long time ago, a well-known lurcher breeder told me a profound truth. She said, 'They are lovely puppies. They are wonderful adults. But they are horrible adolescents.' And this is largely why so many teenage lurchers end up in rescue homes. You may have just brought one of these home, and are wondering where to start. You may have reared one of those sweet puppies only to find her transformed overnight into a complete hooligan. Patience. You are closer to nirvana than you might realise. And please remember as you sob into your tea because she has taken all the washing off the line and danced on it, that all dogs, not just lurchers, are horrible adolescents, people are too, and dogs grow out of it faster.

Lurchers need to run (E. Dearden)

If you buy a puppy, it is tempting to think of her as a clean slate, and to have the idea that if you only present the right situations and avoid the wrong ones, she will become a perfect angel. It is true that a pup is easier to train than an adult dog, but not that much easier, and far from being a blank sheet upon which you may write, she is the product of her ancestors, with all their centuries of selective breeding, as well as – surprisingly – a result of whatever experiences she has had already in her very brief life. Gazehounds are the most ancient of breeds, the best of Crufts winners being but a recent upstart in comparison – unless that winner is herself a gazehound. As your puppy grows, her needs and drives will manifest in and rule her, and you should work with these not against them. By contrast, you may have brought home what the lurcher people call a 'sapling' – that is, a lurcher between six and eighteen months old. Or you may have taken on a mature adult in her prime at four or five years, or an old lady of eight or more. Just like any other breed of dog, these will have brought certain 'baggage' with them in the form of previous training or lack of it, good or ill-treatment, and the results of the moulding that comes from circumstance and environment. The most important thing for us all to remember is that you cannot train a dog of this type in the same way that you would train a more pedestrian breed. You can certainly train them, and you must train them if you are to enjoy your time together. It is not difficult at all, but there will be times when you need some support from those who understand this type of dog, which is why, after many requests, I have written this book.

Name

The name is extremely important. It should be easy to say, and not sound like any command or the name of any other dog that you happen to own. For instance, Poppy and Floppy will spend their lives not knowing to which one of them you are speaking, as will Daisy and Dizzy. Spitz won't know if you said 'sit', and Beau can't tell if you have said 'no'. Your dog may already have a name, and you may not like that name; if so, change it. If your dog has come via the dog rescue, the chances are that the name is new to her anyway; the staff have to call the dogs something, and tend to use the same names over and over. You change the name by using the old and new names together and then dropping the old name, for example 'Susie-Fly, dinner' can be changed to 'Fly, dinner' within a very few days. Decide on the name before you start, and then stick to it; don't call her Tina one day and Bess the next. You cannot really name the dog before you meet her, and it might take a day or two to decide, so until that time, don't call her anything. Once her name is established, you will observe that curious phenomenon known to most animal owners which is that you give an animal a perfectly good name and then she mysteriously acquires a nickname. What is even more amazing is that the animal, once she is settled in and secure with you, will understand that the nickname is her name, too. It is rather like a child knowing that the parent saying 'Nic' is in a better mood than the one saying 'Nichola', but not in as good a mood as when she is called 'Einstein'. I regret that all my dogs have nicknames, some bearing no resemblance to their proper name, and they all cope really well. But when you dog is new, this is far too much to expect her to deal with, so settle on that name and stick with it.

Early Days

Now that she has her name, use it when you speak to her, and precede any command with it, e.g. Sadie – dinner, Sadie – walkies, Sadie –NO! Do not, however, just say 'Sadie Sadie Sadie' when you want her to do something, because she already knows her name is Sadie and you have not told her what you want her to do. I see examples of this almost every day. The dog is running riot, and the owner wants it back, or the dog is barking incessantly and the owner wants it quiet, but do they say 'C'mon' or 'Hush'? Do they heck. They just shout the dog's name over and over, and expect it to know what they want, and to obey the order they have not given. You must tell the dog what you want from her. Please remember that your dog does not speak English or any other language; she merely associates certain sounds with certain results, so you can use any words you like to train her, but you must be consistent. We have words which can be used in several different contexts, but she cannot cope with that, so we, who are supposed to be the more intelligent, must make the system foolproof. A common problem, for instance, is misuse of the word 'down'. There is the dog on the sofa, and you don't want her on the sofa. You say something like 'Get down from that sofa, Tess, you naughty dog'. She hears an angry babble of sound, she can distinguish her name, and she has been taught to lie down upon the command 'down'. She is already lying down. You really go into one, thinking that she is defying you, 'I said get down, you know you aren't allowed up there, look at all those muddy pawmarks.' She knows you are angry, she would like you not to be angry, but you have said 'down' and she is down. She might wag her tail nervously or wet herself in fear, but she won't leave the sofa because you haven't told her to. If you then scream and shout and grab her and drag her off the sofa, you have frightened her, disturbed the bond between you and of course unsteadied her on the 'down' command because you said it, she obeyed it, and then you attacked her. So, when you want her to lie down, say 'down' and when you want her off the sofa, say 'off'. Not difficult, is it? And yet you will be amazed at how hard it is to get this simple fact into the skulls of other people you meet. Make a list of commands and pin it up somewhere conspicuous so that the rest of the family can comply. You will find training the dog much easier than training the family.

Useful Commands

No	Don't do that.
Sit	Sit. Do not, however, say 'sit down' because the dog does not know whether to sit or lie down.
Down	Lie down.
Off	Get off (the sofa, the chair, the vicar).
Out	Get out of (the flowerbeds, the shed).
In	Get in (the car, the house).
Stay	Do not move. I will come back to you.
Wait	Do not move. I will give you another command.
C'mon	Come here. Modern trainers teach 'Come' but most people find that hard to say. 'Here' does not carry over a distance. 'Come on' or 'C'mon' seems to trip naturally off the tongue.
Leave it	Don't you touch that (cat, pheasant, cake).

And – so very important – you need a release command, to indicate that the dog is now free of the last instruction that you gave her. Some people use 'okay' or 'free' or 'go play'; I say 'go on'. Find something that trips off your tongue with ease and use it. If you let the dog release herself, you are setting the scene for unsteadiness. I know so many people who thunder out 'sit' or 'stay' with great authority and then forget to release the dog from the command. Presently, the dog gets fed up and breaks the sit or stay, which teaches her that she can. If, however, you tell the dog when she is free of the command, you have reinforced its effectiveness. Timing is all with training, and if you see her just about to break her command, for instance get up from her 'down', give her the release command before she does so. That is the way to retain control. Because I work my dogs, I use touch as well, for those occasions when I need to be quiet: 'stay' is a touch between the shoulders, and the release is a touch on the chest. That will do for now. Don't be overwhelmed; it will all come quite easily, and if you have a second-hand dog, she may know most of it already. Like any long-term project, training is best addressed one step at a time. You need to give your dog ten minutes a day. If you are very tired or out of temper, scrap that day's training; this does not mean you give her twenty minutes the next day but that you forget the bad day and revert to ten minutes again on the following day. It doesn't have to be ten minutes all at once, five minutes twice a day often being just as productive. It isn't much, is it, for all the love and devotion that your dog gives you so freely, to bestow on her ten minutes out of the day just for as long as it takes to have her trained. Yet you would be amazed at how many people just cannot be bothered, which may be why your dog was in rescue in the first place.

Motivation

This is the chief stumbling block when new lurcher owners try to train by the methods which are currently fashionable. There are only three ways of training anything: reward and the absence of reward, punishment and the absence of punishment, and the conditioned reflex. Old-fashioned training was purely punishment, the dog being too afraid of the wrath of the handler to disobey. Modern training is solely reward-based, the idea being that the dog obeys because the reward of obedience is better than the reward of disobedience. The conditioned reflex – remember Pavlov's dogs, who were fed when a bell rang and then would salivate as soon as they heard the bell? – is rarely used now, but very effective. If you ever doubt the power of the conditioned reflex, ring a bell in the presence of a fireman, and watch him spill his beer. The best dog trainers use a combination of these methods; though one or other will work with many breeds of dog, the sighthound needs more subtle handling. They will quit cold if treated roughly, and are very difficult to reward. How difficult depends on how they are bred: collie and GSD crosses quite like toys, terrier and Labrador crosses usually respond to food. The more sighthound there is in your dog, the more of a challenge you have before you. You waggle a toy. She looks politely away. You offer a titbit. She couldn't possibly. You try to make a fuss of her. She gazes into the distance, putting up with it. If you have ever been involved with clicker training, the mantra is 'click and treat'. What if she doesn't want the treat? What if the reward of disobeying you is far, far better than anything you could offer her? Stop looking for the number of Samaritans. This is all perfectly manageable, but needs a specialist approach.

All dogs have their needs and drives. Labradors need to hold things in their mouths and get into water, so you teach them to retrieve, keep all your old towels and invest in an easy-clean floor. Terriers need to go down holes, and bustle through undergrowth, so you keep them well away from holes and take them to the sort of places where they can smell rats and rabbits. Spaniels need to crash into bushes and rush around after smells, so you take them for long smelly walks and invest in a good brush. Lurchers need to run.

In order to run, they need to go a long way away from you so that they can run back. If, on the way back, something jumps up that can give them an excuse for another run, they will chase that because after all, they know where you are and can run back to you after they have chased their new quarry. This can be a piece of paper blown on the wind, a jogger or mountain biker, or any one of an assortment of wildlife. Obviously there are incipient problems with this, but they cannot be solved by not allowing your lurcher to run. Running is in the warp and weft of her, she has to do it, and you would have to break her spirit to stop her. It is that laughing, glowing spirit that attracted you to her in the first place. If you do not allow her to run, you are keeping the lid on a boiling pot, and you are setting yourself up for big trouble at home, with a dog that may turn destructive because she is so unhappy. Uncontrolled running is a recipe for disaster. What you need to aim for is controlled running. Which means you would like her to come back when you call her.

Recall Training
The Puppy

Many pet dog owners never master the recall, but it does not affect them because they own small fluffy dogs. You, however have chosen to own a large elegant dog, which is a little more noticeable when it runs away, and although she is undoubtedly sweeter of nature than any number of small fluffy dogs, nobody except you is ever going to think of her as cute. Here comes that ten minutes a day again, and we will start with the puppy.

Puppies that measure their age in weeks rather than months will trot at your heels quite naturally. They are too young for long walks, but it is a good idea to take them to places such as parks and woods in the car and then let them toddle after you for a short distance. Do keep it short, or you will damage them because their joints and limbs are growing very quickly at this time. Every few yards, stop, and when your puppy comes up to you, give her a little fuss or a titbit, but sometimes give her nothing. Think about it: many people become addicted to gambling, but no-one has ever become addicted to a vending machine. If there is always a tickle or a titbit, coming in to hand loses its mystery, but if there is always a chance of something, your puppy will come in to hand just in case this is one of those occasions. In order to keep your puppy safe, choose times and places that are not overrun with other dogs or people, as you need her to concentrate on you. What of puppy parties and puppy socialisation classes? The best of these are very good indeed, and the worst will do damage. Go to several on your own, preferably before you get your puppy ('No time lost that is spent in reconnaissance') and pick a class where the puppies are divided for age and size – a six-month puppy jumping on a twelve-week puppy will frighten and might injure her – and where the puppy play is closely supervised rather than degenerating into a brawl where dominant puppies bully quiet ones. Puppies should be called away from play and then allowed to start again, so that they learn that playing with other dogs is under the control of you not them.

Don't expect your puppy to be perfect, and don't be downcast if she progresses two steps forward and one back, or does not progress at all for a few weeks. She is a baby, and will develop in her own time, not anybody else's. If she wants to sit under your chair or on your lap until she gains confidence, let her; do not be bullied by trainers of more extrovert dogs into forcing her to do anything before she is ready. Personally I am not in favour of classes where the puppies are passed around by person to person, as pups generally don't like being picked up and held, and young sighthounds have long legs that have to be folded up quite carefully if they are not to be injured. I also do not like my dogs to approach strangers, but that is my choice and if you feel differently, then go with your heart. If ever a dog trainer wants you to do something with or to your dog with which you do not feel comfortable, say NO and don't do it. Relatively few professional dog trainers have any experience with sighthound types at all, and nobody understands your dog or the way you want to live with her as well as you do. If you do not have access to good classes, don't fret, as you can accomplish a lot on your own by taking her out for those little trips. Sit by the side of the road with her, and let her see traffic, go to the level crossing and let her see the trains, sit on a bench at the shopping precinct and let her watch the crowds, take her to the primary school at playtime and let her listen to the children letting off steam. A word of warning – never tell children your puppy's real name, for they will then shriek it over and over, hoping to get a response from the dog, which will do your training programme no good at all.

As puppy gets older, take her for proper walks in safe places where there is not too much in the way of rabbits or squirrels, and let her run off the lead. She will meet other dogs, some of which will be amiable, and some not: this is part of her education. An adult dog telling a pup off can be very loud, but is usually no more than noise. Some adult dogs are not socialised the way that you are taking trouble to socialise your puppy, and can get nasty; if this is so, avoid them until your pup is older and can cope better. Don't forget that a dog on a lead is much more vulnerable than a dog off a lead, and if a bullying dog is off the lead approaching yours, let her off the lead also, unless it is in an unsafe area such as near a road. What has all this to do with recall? It is bringing new experiences to your pup with you in control. If she is used to coming back to you for reassurance when she is small and the world is new, you have laid a foundation that will last you for life.

Being a friendly dog, she will approach other dogs, sometimes running to meet them over quite a distance. But she has already learned her other-dog manners, and so, having said hello, she will perhaps try to play with her new friend, or else run back to you if the other dog tells her off. Seeing a rabbit or a fluttering piece of paper, she will give chase, because that is what she needs to do, just as Labradors have to run through puddles. This is a hairy time for you because you don't know whether the other dogs, or more likely, the other owners, are friendly, but it is a phase that soon passes. What you don't do is stand in the middle of the park like a lighthouse, bawling your dog's name, while she runs happily about ignoring you. She knows her name, she knows where you are, you don't seem to be in a good mood, and she is having fun. This is why you don't call your dog and then put her on the lead, because why should she come back until she has completely finished what she is doing, if you are going to spoil her games? Never set yourself up for disobedience, because it teaches your dog that she can disobey you. If your dog has launched off to go and chase that rabbit or see that dog, calling her will do no good at all. What you should do is hide. Dogs see movement well, lurchers see movement far better than other dogs, but if you stand up against a tree and stay very still, she will likely not be able to see you. If there is no tree, run away, or if, like me, you are built for comfort not speed, walk very fast in a different direction. Having made her introductions or lost her rabbit, she will look about for you – and you have gone! How unreliable you are. Now she will come barrelling back to find you, and when she does, greet her with joy in your voice, and carry on with her walk. As she runs back, crouch down and turn your head slightly away from her. Do not make eye contact – dogs find the unwavering human stare very intimidating.

She may want to lick at or nuzzle your face when she returns, which is 'proper' behaviour in the dog world. Some humans will allow this, some will not, but if you come into the 'not' category, don't spurn her greeting completely, but give her a hand to lick instead, or turn your head so that she gets your neck or ear. Some dogs can be very accurate when licking your face, and it is an action that really does please them. If yours manages to break through your defences and place a deadly tongue on or even in your mouth, don't panic, you won't die of it, and be more careful next time. It is true that such a greeting is unhygienic, but no more so than a human kiss, and just think of the dreadful things you can catch off children – two things your pup will never give you are threadworms and head lice. If, when she runs off, she knows you will be there to come back to, she will not worry, but if you disappear as soon as she turns her back, she will take a lot more notice of you, which is what you want. Don't even think about training discs, because you will need the reflexes of an Olympic athlete to use them in time with a dog that can do 0 to 40 in two strides. Relax. At the age she is now, the rabbit will go down a hole, the other dog will either play with her or shout at her, and if the other dog owner can't accept a puppy's antics then that is their problem. Some folks expect people to have more control over a little puppy than they have over their own children! Having said that, most dog-walkers are very understanding. We like to socialise and dogs do as well, and I have made quite a few dog-walking friends where the puppy has made the introductions.

Let's pause and take stock. The pup looks back at you often when she is off the lead, in case you disappear. She comes up in the hope of a titbit when you call her, knowing that she will not be put on the lead for the rest of the walk. Periodically, you put her on the lead for a few yards and then let her go again, using your release command. Or you call her in and keep her at heel for a short distance and then send her away. All of this will subtly reinforce your control over her. If you have other dogs, exercise the pup on her own at least once a day, otherwise she will bond with them and not with you; sometimes a steady old dog will teach the pup to come back when you call and do the job for you, but it is not unusual for the opposite to happen, and the steady old dog not only to become wild, but also teach the pup sins that she would perhaps never have considered on her own. I exercise my pups on their own until they are completely steady, which takes a year or more, much to the ill-disguised scorn of most of the local dog walkers ('What – isn't she trained yet?') although afterwards what I hear is 'Aren't you lucky your dogs are so good'! It isn't luck, it is work and application, albeit a very pleasant process. Work put in now means you can metaphorically put your feet up for the rest of your dog's life. Where does the adult dog fit into all this?

The Adult

Assuming that you have a second-hand, or more, lurcher, you may be faced with considerable difficulties in establishing a reliable recall. To start with, the name you are using might not be her original one, and she needs time to get used to it. If she has been through several homes, she may be wary of bonding with you in case you are not worth her trust. If she has been allowed to run in

Excellent recall – back as fast as she went out (E. Dearden)

an uncontrolled manner, or has been worked without preliminary obedience training, then she has had a considerable taste of honey far sweeter than anything that you can offer. If she has always been kept on the lead, she will make damned sure that once it has been taken off, it is not going to go on again. This is not her fault; it is circumstance. She is not going to be impossible to train, but both of you will need to come halfway to meet each other, and it will take time. If your lurcher is a delight in every way (as most are) but will not come back, you really only have one problem to tackle, so don't give up on her now. Take the issue one step at a time.

First of all, you have to be worth coming back to. You have to be pleasant, you have to be fun, you have to be unpredictable to maintain your dog's interest. And (this is the difficult bit) you have to offer greater value than all the distractions around you. Weigh the dice in your favour by taking the dog somewhere very dull, with no stimulus in the form of other dogs, people moving fast e.g. joggers, and small furry things which might need to be chased. Make sure that your dog is hungry by cutting her rations down to half of normal the previous evening, and feeding no breakfast. Breakfast is something for which you have to go home, which means you need to come back. Now put in a bag in your pocket some specially yummy treats instead of normal dog biscuits. Cheese is useful, and travels fairly well, bits of rabbit or chicken are messy but very appealing – this is not for ever, just while you are training – perhaps a few doggy chocolate drops, but not people chocolate, which is dangerous to dogs, sweet biscuits or savoury crackers, or some liver baked in the oven until it goes hard and then crumbled into treat-sized nibbles. How big is treat-sized? The very smallest you can achieve. In the other pocket, put a squeaky toy. This toy must never be seen by your dog: it is a squeak which lives in your pocket. Then you need to attach a long line to your dog's collar, rather like a horse's lunge-line, approximately thirty feet long if you can manage it. Do not use an extending lead because they are not man enough for the job; the lead may have a breaking strain equal to your dog's weight plus the power of her kick-off stride, but neither the plastic handle nor the nickel clips will withstand it, and possibly neither will you. A lurcher that really means to go can pull a human over quite easily.

Let your lurcher sniff your fingers that have just stroked the treats in your pocket and then send her away with your release command. When she gets to the end of the line, walk along with her, let her sniff and explore at that distance, empty herself if she needs to, and just about the moment when you see her looking about herself for something to do, break into a jog for a few steps, call her name enticingly, and as she turns to consider coming back to you, break your eye contact, turn away from her, and move so that she has to run to you. Still avoiding eye contact, tempt her right up to you by turning your head aside, crouching and opening your arms. Offer the titbit when she is as close as she can get: if she will not come close, throw her the first titbit, but only once, for she needs to know that she has to come right up to you for the others. Then send her away again, before she is ready to go, before she has satisfied herself that the titbits are there for her. Do not reel her in with the line, for longdogs are adept at snaking out of their collars, and also you want her to come of her own volition. The line is there for your security, and to show her at what distance she may go away from you.

Obedience is a habit, disobedience too, and so you are subtly instilling a good habit. It is easy for a lurcher to run three or four hundred yards away from you off the lead, and they are quite happy with this distance because they can get back to you at top speed any time they like, but of course there are few places where it is safe to let a dog go this far, and the further away that she is, the less control you have. Thirty yards is reasonable, and if you prefer her closer, you can shorten the distance over a week or so, bearing in mind that this lesson takes longer for some than others to learn. Sometimes call her in and ask her to walk to heel for a short spell, sometimes sit down with her for a few minutes and just relax, for this kind of training is very demanding for both of you, though not one iota as demanding as losing your dog or having her running off and causing mayhem and possibly landing you in court. Remember the vending machine principle, and do not offer food every time. Squeak the toy in your pocket sometimes, while wearing an air of innocence. Praise her with great warmth in your voice when she comes in, run a few paces sometimes with her running along beside you, making your voice excited and squeaky, or crouch down on the ground, turning away from her, to let her gallop up to you and lick your nose. Resign yourself to looking like the village idiot on these occasions: the time will soon pass, and you will look a bigger idiot bawling at the rapidly disappearing rear end of your dog if you don't teach her recall. Keep these lessons short, and intersperse them with brisk lead walking sessions so that she gets plenty of exercise.

While you are engaged in this period of her training, find either a riding school with an indoor arena or a round-pen, or some stock-fenced fields that a farmer will allow you to use (without the stock in). If neither of these is available, a fenced tennis court is a lot better than nothing A small crossing of palms with silver, a bunch of flowers or a bottle of something warming is considerate; many people will not take the money but it is always appreciated when something is offered. Let your dog run off the lead in these places, and really run for all she is worth: when she stops running, chase her and make her run again. When she is tired, she will come in to you, and when she does, make her welcome and sit down and rest together. Do not take her straight home as she will not then come in so readily in future. Instead, when she is rested, send her round again. These intensive play periods, that always end with a fuss and maybe but not always a titbit, will bond her to you. Warning: if she is a jumper, the stock-fenced fields are not a good idea until you know each other better – instead use somewhere from which she cannot escape. You will be much more relaxed as well, because you do not fear her running off, and if you are relaxed, she will be relaxed too. If this all sounds like a lot of bother, please think again: all dogs run off if not trained, and any dog can get its owner into trouble. The only reason most get away with it is that they don't run as far or as fast as your lurcher can. This little bit of effort now will help to form a lovely friendship with your dog which will last for her whole life. Regard it as a pleasure, not a chore; it really gives a wonderful sense of achievement when she begins to respond to you.

Off the Line

Presently, and much sooner than you anticipated, she will be ready to walk off the line with you in unfenced areas. This is a tense time, and you will not have one hundred per cent success. Damage limitation is the name of the game, so your on-line lessons can be changed to more interesting places, because you need the boring places for her first steps of freedom. She must be hungry, and she must be tired, so do this after one of your galloping stints in the horse arena or wherever else you go. Owners of more pedestrian breeds will often take toys, balls, frisbees, etc to throw for their dogs, but it is a rare lurcher that will respond to these. Their attitude tends to be that if you wanted it, you shouldn't have thrown it away in the first place. They may chase once or twice just to humour you, but lurchers have a very low boredom threshold compared to (say) a collie, which will chase the fiftieth ball with the same manic fervour that it ran after the first. Just so with food treats; a greedy terrier or Labrador will eat until it is sick, but the majority of sighthounds are only interested in titbits if they are ravenous. You will need to vary your titbits too, for one day cheese will appeal, and another day chicken is better. Different 'sweeties' on the same walk will also create more interest than a pocket full of the same thing, for maybe *this* time, there will be a chocolate drop. So take off the lead, let the dog sniff the titbit smell, and then send her away. She will gallop off probably further than you would like her to, but watch her all the time and keep her watching you. Don't be predictable: walk or run or curl up, lie down or hide, or squeak the toy, and don't put the lead on for the final time at the same place. Keep the first off-lead session short, and repeat daily, lengthening the time of freedom and gradually going to more interesting places. If she tanks off after another dog, keep moving, preferably in a different direction from the one she anticipates, and do not call her until she looks back at you. Then run away. When she runs up to you, welcome her, because the thing above all others that you want from her is that she comes back to you, whatever the circumstances of her leaving. She must be aware that you are always safe to come back to, that you do not shout or punish. If she ignores your first call, do not repeat it, just move away from her. Above all, do not be downcast if it does not all come together at once; believe me, you are both doing just fine, and perfection is not for mortals.

Chasing Wild Animals

Inevitably, she will find a squirrel or a rabbit to chase at times, even though you are somewhere where squirrels or rabbits have never been seen before. This is her instinct, in every drop of her blood. Do not panic. Squirrels run up trees, rabbits run down holes. Once she is poised, puzzled, looking up the tree or down the hole, she will be ready to come back to you. Other animals are more difficult: hares, foxes and deer run a long way, and may take your dog across roads or into other danger. It is possible for some lurchers to be trained by some people not to chase these, but remember that you have a hound, and her desire to do so is very strong. This means that aversion training has to be very harsh: there is no way that reward-based training will stop a hunting dog from hunting, because the reward of fulfilling her instincts is better than any alternative. It also means that dogs so trained must be allowed to fulfil their instincts in other ways, or else they will be spirit-broken and desperately unhappy. Working dogs are taught that they can chase these animals but not those, but if you insist that your dog is not to chase anything, you will have a troubled dog, and what is more, one that may turn destructive and disobedient in her frustration. Therefore, keep ahead of the game. 'The price of freedom is eternal vigilance', write it on a pad, etch it into your brain, embroider it in cross-stitch, but never forget it. Owners of less vital dogs will be able to mooch along deep in thought or conversation, but you must always have an eye out not just for your dog but all around her. It is sensible to call her in to heel before you go through a gateway or over a stile, or anywhere that you cannot see ahead of you. When you know that ahead is safe, you can send her on. Wear distance glasses if you need to, and always check along the line where woodland meets meadow, in case deer are grazing. If her head goes up and she starts air-scenting, then looks back at you to see if you are taking notice, call her in and put the lead on for fifty yards or so. If her tail goes up and her nose goes down – here be dragons – so do the same again. The lead is the most underrated piece of dog-training equipment: used correctly (not hard across her rump, tempting though it may be on occasion) it will de-fuse any incipient disaster, establish the fact that you are in control, and take the pressure off both of you. Dogs feel insecure if they have to make decisions (should I chase that or not?) so be sure that you are aware at all times of what is happening, and make the decision for her. She will respect you for it, and love you all the more. Keep away from areas that you know have wild animals, especially at dawn and dusk, which is when they are most active – or else keep the lead on. Don't exercise her in the dark off a lead, for her night vision is much better than yours, and she may well have been trained in night-hunting. She might have been trained to follow a beam of light, so be careful with torches and car headlights, lest she follows those instead. Remember that as far as she is concerned, she is being obedient, so don't scold her, just avoid the situation, and if it cannot be avoided, put her on that lead.

Running Off

Watch dogs – not just yours – when out off the lead. They will look at their

I might come back – when I'm ready (E. Dearden)

owners as if to check 'all right?' several times; if the owner returns the eye contact briefly (a good time to do it, unlike recall), murmurs an endearment, maybe strokes the dog, the dog is secure. If the owner does not complete the communication, the dog will frequently mutter the canine equivalent of 'okay, then, I'm off!' and slope away to do its own thing. This can be quite dramatic or go unnoticed, depending on the dog and the attitude of the owner. It makes my hair stand on end sometimes, when I see what some dog owners perceive as acceptable behaviour. Anyone can lose a dog on occasion, for they are sentient beings and their agenda is not always ours, but to repeatedly allow a dog of whatever breed to run out of sight and make no attempt to correct it is anti-social and irresponsible. Please do not exercise your dog with dogs that are allowed to behave like this until you are quite satisfied that she is trained, because two dogs make a pack, and she will go further and for longer with another dog for company, whereas it is the lurcher way to go afar and then come straight back. If she starts to show signs of joining in even after you have trained her, then take a few weeks away from your friends and exercise solo again until you are satisfied that she is back into the habit of obedience rather than testing its boundaries. If she does run off, wait where she left you, for that is where she will return. Make an enormous fuss of her when she returns, no matter how late she has made you; I cannot stress hard enough the fact that you must be the nicest person in the world to come back to every single time.

Your objective is to have a dog that comes back, and you must never lose sight of it. If you give her a hard time upon her return, she will not understand that it is her going away that made you angry, but think that it is the coming back, and so will be much less keen to come back next time. If she has had a previous owner who has punished her for coming back, she will return to within a few yards of you and then circle you, diving out of reach if you attempt to catch her. She terribly wants to return to you, but is afraid of a hiding, or worse. This is easy to cure. Welcome her with great warmth in your voice, trying to block out the fact that you are furious, because she will pick up your anger. Think of her as a frightened, bewildered animal, which is what she is, even though in your annoyance, you might see her as a cocky little minx. Then run away from her. She will follow, albeit at a distance. Drop to a brisk walk, then a slow walk, not looking back. Sit down with your back to her, and wait for her to approach, which might take a few minutes, depending on how much she has been punished in the past. Still not making eye contact, take a titbit and hold it out. If she does not dare to take it, drop it and continue to sit. Chat to her in a soft voice. When she eventually approaches you, do not take hold of her. Change your voice to disappointed, but keep it soft. 'Oh, Willow, how could you?' will elicit a much more positive response than, 'Willow you little B!'. You might well find her head thrust into your lap quite suddenly, in which case make a gentle fuss, but still do not catch hold of her. After this is over – or if she still does not dare to approach you – (poor little dog, what she must have gone through if she is still so frightened) get up as slowly as you can, still avoiding eye contact, and walk away. She will follow, and she will gradually come closer. Tap your leg and invite her to come to heel, talk sweetly, and she will soon be beside you. Now she can take a titbit from your hand, and you can slip the lead on while she is eating it, and then give her another.

This would be a good time to go home, if your nerves are in shreds. You have both been stressed and need to relax, so go home and have a cuddle with her in the safety of your home. When she is home and feeling mellow, every time you fuss her, take hold of her collar and release it immediately, as if you touched it by accident. Dogs that have been grabbed by the collar and hit in a previous home need to learn that having their collar handled is not a prelude to a beating. Similarly, if you, or a previous owner, has taken the trouble to teach the dog to 'down/stay' do not put her into a down/stay and then walk up to her and grab her. She will not allow that trick twice, and you will have unsteadied her again. However, it can be useful to put the dog into a fairly lengthy down/stay and then call her to you when she begins to look restive, crouching, opening your arms and avoiding eye contact as you do so. Make her welcome when she arrives, and then walk away as if everything is normal. Well, it is normal, isn't it? She is back, and you can relax, and there is that walk to finish. She has not made you angry; only you can make you angry, and it is not productive to be angry when things go wrong. Dogs do not set out to annoy you or spite you or get revenge upon you: those are human traits. She is simply being a dog and doing dog things, and has not the mental capacity to think into the future or imagine what you are suffering, or what dangers she might be in when she runs off. She has found something interesting to do, and she is doing it. When she has finished, she will come back if you are nice, and delay if you have proved to be unfriendly. Your job is to interfere quite subtly before she actually goes off, and in the beginning you will sometimes misread the signs, but you will improve with practice.

Commands

We have had a look at what commands to use, but it is worthwhile before we go any further to examine how best to issue those commands. You see, they are commands: not requests, not invitations, but orders, and you must give them in a manner that compels obedience. Modern methods of human interaction are too soft for dog training, tending to situations such as this:

Owner: If it isn't too much trouble, please would you come here?

Dog: Go away, I'm busy.

Owner: If you would come here, we could have a brainstorming session whereby I could explain to you the mutual advantages on offer.

Dog: Shove off.

Obedience is not a question, and 'no' is not a word that you like to hear.

Dogs feel comfortable and secure in a firm hierarchy, and interpret negotiation as weakness. Weakness does not sit well with animals; it makes them feel not protective but insecure, possibly even predatory. They like defined boundaries that are consistent. You need to speak to them with authority, which comes more naturally to some than to others. Practice on your own if you need to. Authority does not have to be loud; my mother, a very experienced dog trainer of the old school, could say 'sit' with a chilling firmness that was barely louder than a whisper, and would have every dog around her sinking to its haunches, even if it had never seen her before. To understand something done well, it is often useful to see it being done badly, for which I would recommend a trip to a large supermarket. Therein, you will see disobedience being rewarded, and commands given with a kind of helpless despair, as tiny children run rings around adults. You will hear requests for certain behaviour being ignored because the pattern is that the request is then repeated with a whining plea, as in 'please leave that alone', then the child makes a lot of noise while it disobeys and is rewarded with a titbit. The quiet, obedient child (admittedly in rather short supply) is not rewarded but ignored. Should you be unfortunate enough to have such parents as your friends, you will be told that they give in 'for the sake of peace' but of course the opposite effect is true, because, as Kipling said, once you start to pay danegeld, 'You never get rid of the Dane' and you certainly do not get peace: you get a scheming little monster with an eye to the main chance, ruthlessly pushing boundaries as far as they may go. If, however, boundaries are clear and consistent, bad behaviour is not rewarded and (most vitally important) good behaviour is rewarded, then good behaviour becomes the rule not the exception. Do not talk to your dog with that weary, futile, expecting-to-be-disobeyed voice that you hear from the parent in the supermarket, nor nag it with the loud ranting voice that you will also hear from the despairing parent. Both advertise the fact that the situation is out of control. Speak to your dog in a friendly, confident manner that leaves her in no doubt that you expect to be obeyed, and she has no option but to obey you. The situation is non-negotiable.

Stock Training

It is absolutely vital that your lurcher does not get the opportunity to chase domestic livestock. Most working dogs are actively trained with livestock so that they learn not to touch them, but few people outside the working dog world take the trouble. If you have a second-hand lurcher, this job may have already been done, or else she may have already chased livestock which is why she has been passed on. If you seldom or never exercise in areas where

Safe with sheep

sheep, cattle or horses are kept, then you can manage without doing this job, though if you then move house to an area where livestock is kept, you may wish that you had. Unless you are surrounded by livestock, you will probably cope by simply putting your dog on a lead where you see stock. If the footpath that you are on goes through a field of sheep, then this is all you need to do, but the situation with cattle and horses is different. Cattle will often attack dogs, and a dog on a lead is terribly vulnerable, as are you because they may attack you as well, though they would have ignored you if you had been without a dog. Horses, especially horses that have been hunting, are likely to gallop up and investigate you and your dog; they seldom attack unless they are stallions, or mares with foals, but can hurt you unintentionally. Keep out of fields with horses or cattle! If this means taking the long way back, or retracing your steps when you had hoped for a pleasant circular walk, it is merely annoying, and far safer than risking injury. Dogs and dog walkers have been killed by cattle before now. Likewise, if you exercise your dog on bridleways, put her on the lead if there is the slightest chance that she will chase a ridden horse. She could cause a terrible accident, frighten the horse so that it injures itself or is terrified of dogs for the future, or end up crippled or dead from a blow of the horse's hooves.

117

Safe with poultry

Do not forget that fowl are livestock as well, and if a footpath takes you through a farmyard or anywhere else where free-range fowl are pecking about, put your dog on a lead. If she chases poultry, she may well put them off lay or even frighten them to death, and if she catches one, she could very likely kill it.

If you wish to put in the time to train your dog to leave livestock alone, you will hear plenty of strange tales of how to do it, and someone will assure you that you should pen your dog with a ram and let the ram batter her, or else tie her in a passageway and drive a flock of sheep over her. Please do not. Both systems are cruel and quite possibly illegal, even supposing you could find a farmer who would let you do any such thing. The reality of stockbreaking is just like any other form of training: take it one step at a time.

Passing fields of stock, if your dog seems to be taking a lively interest, you should have her on the lead. Jerk the lead and tell her sharply 'No! Leave it!' Do not use a titbit on these occasions as she will consider it a reward, and therefore think that the behaviour that she has just offered is acceptable. If there is a path through a field of sheep, you can take it, keeping her on the lead, and scold her by voice if she pulls in the direction of the sheep. Some sheep hold their ground and others run away: a dog that ignores steady sheep might well be quite undone by the sight of them running. A dog that ignores adult sheep can take a most unhealthy interest in lambs. If your dog seems really keen on the sheep, you can use a noise distraction such as a rolled-up newspaper or short length of hosepipe whacked against your leg; a rape alarm is spectacularly loud, but if you do use one, make sure it is the sort that has an on/off switch, not one where you need two hands to replace a fiddly piece of plastic in order to stop the noise. A small tin of stones shaken suddenly can help, but the dog must not see you shake it. Once she has responded to the distraction, call her close to heel. This is one occasion where the rough voice only is used, because you must leave her in no doubt that interest in the sheep is wrong. If, however, she trots happily along beside you and does not show any interest in the sheep, you can praise her in your sweetest voice. Next, back on the long line in the field, and if you have the slightest doubt of her steadiness, attach the line to a harness that she cannot slip out of, rather than a collar. Do a few stay and recall exercises, walk her back and forth along the path. If you can get the farmer or shepherd's permission, so much the better, because you can then walk through the flock, but it is inconsiderate to do this otherwise, as the sheep may be in lamb. I have a very helpful farmer friend who lets me stock-train my dogs first with the bachelor males, then the ewes, and lastly with the ewes and lambs.

Once you consider your dog to be completely trustworthy – and a month too late is better than a day too soon – she can be let off the lead and kept to heel when passing through the flock. Never have your dog at any other position than close to heel. It is different with working dogs, because they have to be able to hunt through a flock of sheep if necessary, but for yours it is sufficient that she will walk past them. If in doubt, put that lead on her. If this is all more trouble than you are willing to take, then make sure that she is never loose within a mile of farm livestock, and never think 'Oh, it will be all right' just in case it is not. If farmers are displaying signs telling you to keep your dog on a lead, please respect that and do so, no matter how trustworthy you think your dog might be.

You cannot do this with horses or cattle, so please keep out of their fields, for their safety, yours, and your dog's. With ridden horses, take her on the bridlepaths on a busy day – a sunny weekend, perhaps – stand well to one side, and let her watch the horses go past. If she lunges at them, chastise her severely. If she watches calmly, praise her and offer a titbit. Horses have been described as 'dangerous at both ends and uncomfortable in the middle', well, they are certainly dangerous at both ends when frightened or angry, so keep

When she starts air-scenting – get that lead on

well away from the ends. Riders are sometimes pre-emptively aggressive, which is a pity when your dog has done no harm, but a direct result of less conscientious people allowing their dogs to attack horses. It has happened to me many times when riding, and is very frightening. So if you do run foul of what seems to be a bad-tempered rider, please find a little forgiveness, and explain, if you can, that you are being responsible, unlike the dog-walkers that he or she has encountered previously.

Dog Training Classes

Like the puppy socialisation classes, these can be of differing value, and are best checked out before you go near them with a dog. The running dog will not tolerate overt dominance or rough handling, and sadly, a lot of training classes still exist where this is the norm. My advice to you is to watch how the 'down' is taught: if the dogs are thrown or otherwise forced into position, this is not the training class for you. Also, you will need an instructor who is flexible enough to understand that sighthounds are different. The long backs make the 'sit' very uncomfortable for some, and if the instructor cannot cope with that and insists that all dogs 'sit' then he or she really does not have what it takes to help you with any other problems that you may be having or else trying to avoid. Equally, many lurchers do not have a strong retrieving instinct, nor are they playful in the way that collies (for instance) are, so they are very limited in what they can be taught using toys or play as a reward. It is no accident that serious dog trainers tend to use border collies or GSDs, occasionally retrievers, but I doubt that you will ever see one competing with a beagle or a saluki. This is fine if your trainer understands the differences in approach that are necessary with different breeds, but if they treat every breed as a potential collie, save your money or go elsewhere.

Class lessons can be fun, and you can make some new friends, but if you are already experienced with training dogs, you can give them a miss with a clear conscience, for there are rarely problems encountered in training lurchers except for the odd hiccup with recall. Certainly, that is what I get most letters about. Once the puppy socialisation is complete, and that part is very important, you can carry on in your usual way. If you encounter a specific problem not mentioned here, I would suggest that you have one-to-one sessions with a dog behaviourist who is accustomed to your type of dog, if you are not too confident of training on your own. You will need someone who is quiet in their approach and quick on canine body language to succeed with a lurcher, and knowledge of the sighthound mind is much more useful than any amount of qualifications or show-ring rosettes. Although the dog behaviourist

Under close control – both dogs are obedience champions

may seem expensive, it is money well spent, and an investment in the dog's future; it is also considerable moral support at a time when you may be in need of it. Don't be despondent; I can assure you that there are dogs far, far worse behaved than yours, for lurchers are rarely as bloody-minded as some other breeds. They are obliging by nature, and capable of loving their human very deeply, are rarely quarrelsome and seldom stoop to dominance. That is for upstarts and parvenus: the lurcher has shared history with kings, sheikhs and chieftains, and social climbing or canine politics is beneath them. If you are halfway worthy of it, they will become your boon companion and soulmate, but fawning deference and bullying dominance is, for most, completely outside their remit.

Safe with cats

6 Home Alone

One thing that the modern dog has to experience which was little known in days gone by is to be left alone in the house for long periods. There, she is on trust not to steal, wreck, escape or make unnecessary noise. This is a tall order, and many people who expect this of a dog could not guarantee it of their children. However, our lives are such that we make these arrangements, and expect our dogs to fall in with them: amazingly, some of us even think that such a situation can be achieved without training. Sometimes it can, but more often a little effort is involved. Just like any other training process, it is not difficult, but it does require sensitivity, consistency and understanding.

In the old days, dogs were often left chained up in yards, to bark and pace their lives away until their family came home from school or work. Less conscientious owners allowed their dogs to roam free, and some still do. Both of these options cause untold grief to neighbours and often to the dogs themselves; if this is the only way to keep a dog then a dog should not be kept. Much more humane to both dogs and neighbours is the kennel and run, which offers a dog every comfort while nothing can get in and the dog cannot get out, or keeping the dog in the house, or part of the house, with access to outside so that she can empty herself. Some people arrange to go home at lunchtime and take the dog out, or else have a friend, neighbour or professional to do the same kindness. While it is easy to pontificate about dogs not being left alone, the truth is that even people who do not work outside the home frequently have occasion to leave the dog, and busy mothers with small children might be physically in the home but are not available to offer company or attention to the dog, which is often shut away from the rest of the family for long spells. Therefore the dog should be gently introduced to short spells alone, which can be gradually extended to longer periods of time. Like us, dogs prefer company, and leaving them alone is not always an easy process.

Leaving a Puppy

I cannot over-emphasise that a puppy is a baby, and cannot be expected to

Home alone (E. Dearden)

develop any faster than her mind and body will allow. It is downright callous to leave a little puppy on its own for long spells when it has always had the company of its mother and siblings. Of course she will cry, forget her house training, and become destructive in her terror at suddenly being alone, so do not put her in that position. Instead, introduce her step by step to being in the same room with you but in her pen with the door closed so that she can see and hear you but not get to you. Then you can be elsewhere in the house for ten minutes or so, and she can be in her room rather than in her pen, separated from the rest of the house by a baby gate, but able to hear you vacuuming, singing, talking on the telephone and so on. Keep these spells of separation very short so that she learns that you are going away and then coming back. A radio or television playing softly – very softly please – in the background will give comfort. Some pups are bolder than others, some go through a clingy phase just like children do, so take matters at your puppy's pace and subordinate your own agenda until she can safely be left for the maximum time that you need to leave her. Put on your coat and shoes at random times, pick up your keys and go out, then come straight back in again. Start the car and drive around the block, and come back. In the evenings, she can be in the living room with the rest of the family, but during the day she should be confined to the kitchen, utility room or wherever she is going to be left when you go out. Some people call the pup to go into her room, and then wonder why she does not want to go in it. She has worked out that her family goes out and leaves her when she is put into this room, and she does not want that, so she tries not to go in. Never, ever call your dog for something unpleasant, because that will weaken your recall. Instead, put a little food down for her in her room, and let her follow you in. When you are leaving, do not play with her or do anything to excite her immediately beforehand, because you want her to be calm. A tired puppy is always more settled than a lively one, so before you leave, make sure that she has had a romp in good time, been outside to empty herself, and is in a frame of mind to sleep or chew her bone. When she is older, she can have her walk and a few minutes of training, and then something relaxing like a brush, before you attend to this and that around the house, and then quietly and without formal goodbyes, leave.

Some people like to make a ritual out of leaving, which creates quite a stressful situation for the pup, as she begins to anticipate your going. I do know people who leave with a command, such as 'stay', which is appalling, because the dog is being told to remain exactly where she is until the owner returns! Just leave your little one in her place, with safe toys and/or food. I used to leave cardboard boxes when a pup was at the destructive stage, so that she could have a lovely time tearing up things that didn't matter, rather than cruising around looking for something to do. Damage limitation is the name of the game: pups need to chew, so give them something to chew that will not harm them or grieve you, because if you don't, they will find their own occupation. There are dog toys that you can stuff with treats which the dog can then roll around the floor to extract the goodies, and which are very good, although I have to say that a lot of lurchers will not even consider them. A box or several paper bags with a single biscuit inside is usually well received, and although I don't normally hold with giving dogs junk food, an unopened bag of crisps can offer quite a challenge. Nothing quite beats a bone, but make sure it is a safe one that can be eaten right up, like a chicken carcase, or else, for teething pups, a huge uncut raw marrow bone. I do not recommend marrow bones for dogs with their second teeth, as they can wear them prematurely, but each dog is an individual, and if you can get good marrow bones and your dog copes well under supervision, then you could let her have them. The reason for not giving her a cut marrow bone is because she might wedge part of her narrow jaw in the hole as she tries to get at the marrow. Never ever feed cooked bones (see Chapter 3). Do not leave bones with more than one dog if they are kept together, as, without your presence, they could fight over them and do each other harm. These lovely animals that we share our homes and lives with are still wolves under the skin, and their priorities can be a lot different from ours. Pups that are left alone on a system of gradually increasing their time apart from you, that are given plenty of occupation, and are tired when you leave them, are seldom any problem. As they outgrow the teething and destructiveness of adolescence, you will be able to relax house rules and give them the run of the house if you wish to do so. Just don't expect them to keep off the most comfortable chairs, or to ignore food that they can reach! Likewise if you have small hutched or caged pets – no matter how well-behaved your dog is while you are there – do not risk the lives of these little creatures, for they are prey and any dog, not just your lurcher, is a predator. Finally, do not leave your dog alone in the garden, for many lurchers are stolen that way.

Welcome Home

Lurchers are not the most effusive of dogs, but they will offer a handsome welcome upon your return from being away, even if you were only out for a few minutes. Some modern dog training manuals say that you should not allow this greeting, and instead, you should ignore them and only greet them when they have settled. These dog trainers know nothing about lurchers: follow their instructions at your peril. If you are so ill-mannered as to snub a greeting straight from the heart of a lurcher, she will lose respect for you, and rapidly stop greeting you altogether. Lurchers are perfectly capable of withdrawing from all social interaction if they do not consider you worthy of them, and they can sulk for England. They are seldom either demanding or dominant, and they have natural good manners. These same dog books will tell you to refuse to fuss a dog that comes up seeking a fuss, and only to be demonstrative on your terms. Again, this is not the way to behave with lurchers. If they come up to you with waving tail and laughing eyes, put a long arm up to tap you, or push a snout where no snout has any business to be, then for heaven's sake greet them back!

If you have been working, and your lurcher arrives, stretches before you in greeting and then suggests in the politest possible manner that it is desirable for you to have a little time off and preferably to spend it with a lurcher, then why not? If you really cannot stop working, at least acknowledge her presence

Welcome back

with a caress and a kind word. Lurchers may not bark a lot, but they have a huge vocabulary of noises known to lurcher folk as 'lurcher talk'. They can squeal and chunter, moan and mumble, and make disconcertingly human-like yowls. If your lurcher comes and talks to you, talk back to her. Lurchers are not in-your-face dogs always with an eye to the main chance like terriers, or seeking to find weakness in the way of (for instance) a GSD. But they are terrific communicators, and don't take kindly to clumsy attempts at belittling and rank-reducing when they have simply been 'talking'. For those who are receptive, lurchers are very telepathic, definitely on a par with Thoroughbred racehorses. Remember the old saying: 'Dogs looks up to you, cats looks down on you, but pigs is equals'? Well, lurchers treat you as equals as well. They do things with you not for you, and are the most loyal of companions, as long as you deserve them. There is nothing wrong with showing an animal respect; after all, you would respect something bigger and fiercer, would you not? Lurchers like their own space, and have practically knighted you by allowing you inside. This does not mean that your lurcher should be anything other than obedient, but you will never achieve that obedience by bullying or by displaying bad manners by turning aside her love or her greeting to you. I had an interesting example of this not long ago, when a friend took on a saluki cross of just under a year old. This dog, from an unknown background, was very protective of her space, and had snapped at several people who had invaded it. Ordinarily, a lurcher would never display this sort of behaviour, but who knows the stresses this young dog had been under? I walked a little too near to her space that she had made for herself under the table, and she produced the tiniest, softest of growls. I was mildly annoyed at her, but almost immediately realised that she had no other way of asking me to back off, and as growls go, that was probably the politest that I would ever hear. I moved just out of her space, not so far that she could think she had intimidated me, but sufficient to comply with her request. And let us be clear, this was a request, not a demand. The result was that shortly afterwards, she came out from her safe space and laid her head in my hand, drowning me with her eyes. That was her thanks that I had acknowledged her need, and respected her. To put your head in a stranger's hand is the ultimate submission, and she made it not because I had followed the dominant dog-trainer route of bullying a dog that dared to ask me for something, but because I had displayed understanding and tact. Ever after, this very proud and feisty hound has made a point of greeting me with the softest of licks and her head laid briefly in my hand, and I am able to go into her space as much as I want, by her invitation and not my dominance.

When I first became involved with dog training, everything seemed to be about pack leadership and dominance, but this is as old-fashioned now as the old system of 'first break a dog, then train it'. Instead, the lurchers in my life have taught me the good manners and grace that should accompany our dealings together. It is difficult to describe the lightness of hand that you need with a lurcher; they should be in no doubt that you are the one who calls the shots, but at the same time, there is no need to be egocentric about it. With a lurcher, you get obedience without subservience. The nearest I can get to describing the relationship is that they are like the bravest and most loyal of troops who follow a loved and trusted senior officer into battle no matter what the dangers, where they would be likely to shoot a bombastic and blustering one in the back.

Leaving the Adult Dog

A dog that has been accustomed from puppyhood to being left alone using the system described will be quite tranquil about being left as an adult, and indeed may barely be properly awake in time to welcome you back. You will get up

Tire your dog out with a good run before you leave (E. Dearden)

early to walk her while the morning is still fresh, and I don't mean twenty minutes on a lead but the best part of an hour of free running. Leave her breakfast with her, then off you go to work, leaving the radio on low if that is what she is used to. Quiet households like my own, where radio or television seldom feature, do not need this, but if your dog is accustomed to background noise, then the hush of an empty house will be alien to her. A pleasantly tired dog with a full tummy will want to sleep, and as dogs, like all predators, are designed to sleep for around eighteen hours out of twenty-four, she will probably be quite settled until your return. If, however, you have taken on a second-hand dog, you may find that you are the unhappy owner of a dog with separation anxiety, and this can be a daunting problem to overcome, simply because you are not there when it happens.

Separation Anxiety

This should not be confused with its smaller relation, which has been referred to by that excellent dog behaviourist Dr Ian Dunbar as 'Separation Fun'. Separation fun occurs when you are not at home to issue the No and the Don't, and you have not sufficiently damage-proofed your dog's quarters. In the absence of your nagging, the dog can have a whale of a time tearing and chewing, digging, jumping up onto surfaces that dogs should not jump up onto, and eating anything remotely edible. I once came home to find a dismembered bean-bag, and little white polystyrene beads spread the length and breadth of the dog room; in fact I even found them inside the freezer. What fun that must have been! Nothing for me to do but clear up as best I could, and remember not to give that particular dog that particular opportunity again. If your dog is prone to having just this sort of entertainment while you are away, then your best bet is to confine her in a kennel and run, or a place free from objects that you do not want remodelled, and full of safe toys and/or bones. The latter are very important it is no good expecting a dog to settle if she has nothing to do. Exercise her properly beforehand, and keep her off high-energy foods with artificial colourings and flavourings, which can make dogs and particularly lurchers hyperactive. Vegetables can make good chew toys, and will do nothing but good if eaten. Swede, turnip, carrot, apples, a whole cabbage or cauliflower, all offer lots of chewing potential, but do not leave potatoes, onions or maize on the cob.

Proper separation anxiety is another matter entirely. It can vary from slight to severe, but describes a dog that is deeply distressed at being left on her own. She might bark, howl or scream, salivate, mess and wet herself, self-mutilate, destroy her surroundings, or display all of these behaviours. She might be quite all right most of the time, but experience a trigger-factor on some occasions that sets her off. Common causes are strangers coming to the door, the answerphone activating, particularly if the recording is of the owner's voice, or one member of the family leaves a message for another, which means the dog hears the longed-for voice again but no-one shows up, dustmen, car or burglar alarms going off, or rows next door. Or she might be totally out of her mind with panic on every occasion that she is left.

Much can be done to help the dog with separation anxiety. First of all, do not take one of these dogs on if you have to leave her straight away, because the remedial therapy can take months in severe cases. Conventional veterinary treatment offers tranquillising drugs to get over the initial periods of separation, and these are fairly successful in less dramatic cases. Adrenaline is, however, an amazing hormone, and fear can override these drugs; long-term drug use is also undesirable for health reasons. Holistic vets have a plethora of treatments at their disposal, and it is possible to have your re-training period buttressed with homoeopathy, flower remedies or herbs which can be very successful at taking the sting out of separation anxiety. These treatments are safe and effective in the majority of cases, but the treatment has to be suited to the individual dog, which is why the best results are obtained from a vet who is qualified in these therapies. In dire emergency, Bach Rescue Remedy in the drinking water can hold the fort until a therapist is available to assess the animal. Reiki healing can give quite stunning results as well, and there is no bar to using all of these methods on the same dog as they are completely safe.

Along with these treatments, take the same route as I have recommended with the new puppy: leave the dog for a few minutes at a time, accustom her to being in one part of the house while you are in another (dogs with severe separation anxiety try to follow you from room to room) and tire her out with exercise. You cannot cure this problem in a few days or a few weeks, but you can certainly cure it. Remember that the dog is not being spiteful or deliberately awkward: she is frightened, miserable and insecure, you are her only comfort, and she is devastated when you go away from her. Remember that solitary confinement is still used to punish prisoners. Remember that she is only a dog, and cannot reason or see into the future the way that you can, nor can she occupy herself with crossword puzzles or daydreaming about what to do when she wins the Lottery. Above all, remember that this is temporary.

I know of someone who took on a lurcher with very severe separation anxiety, the cure being effected quite accidentally by the weather. That winter was one of the wettest on record, and rain hammered down day after day. The owner worked out of doors on her farm, and the dog followed her everywhere, but after a few weeks of being soaking wet from dawn until dusk (he was a wimpy lurcher, remember) he elected to stay indoors in the dry more and more. Obviously there were setbacks, and the one-step-forward two-steps-back that you get when treating a major behavioural problem – and this dog was the worst case of separation anxiety that I have ever come across – but progress was made because it was the dog's decision to stay indoors away from his beloved new owner; he had not been shut away by forces outside his control. At first, he would cry, pace and salivate if left even for a few minutes with another person, but gradually he built up a few special friends with whom he could be left in his own home, and the time that he could be left with them extended until it was all day. Additionally, he made some dog friends, including one of my lurcher bitches, and would settle in their company as well. Then came disaster: his owner had to go away unexpectedly, and there was no alternative but to put him in kennels. The kennels experience unhinged him, despite the provision of tranquillisers from the vet, and set his therapy back severely. Another such experience was unavoidable – life is like that sometimes – and the kennels refused to take him again. The owner was in a desperate quandary, for she had to go away to be with a dying relative, and there was no provision for the dog, and no-one that he knew and trusted who could care for him in his own home. I suggested that she tried a greyhound training kennels, as the owners would be much more accustomed to that type of dog. It was a roaring success: he was kennelled with a lady greyhound, in the sight of others, and looked after by people who understood longdogs. No medication was required, and there were no problems of any description. He now goes back regularly and happily, and his separation anxiety is very much in the past. It took nearly a year, but it was not a great problem for most of that year; he is three years old and could easily live for another ten. A pretty good investment, by any standards.

Dog Company

Is the cure for separation anxiety another dog? Sadly, it is seldom that easy. The other dog might become anxious as well, or join in the dirty or destructive behaviour. The troubled dog is unlikely to draw reassurance from the presence of an untroubled dog, any more than you take comfort in a crisis from someone who is not suffering telling you that you will be fine. The stresses might be so acute that the dogs might fight. However, look at the experiences of the dog mentioned above. The conventional kennels exacerbated his fears, and the kennels that was used to accommodating his type of dog never had a problem to start with. Sighthounds have a natural affinity for others of that ilk, and he was immediately more settled to be with his own kind. If you have a lurcher, you will know that she doesn't have much time for other breeds of dog, except special friends that she goes walking with, but is delighted to see another lurcher, whippet, greyhound or other longdog. Then there is the sex side of the matter. Dogs of all breeds are much happier as one of a pair with the opposite gender: if the greyhound kennels had put him with another dog, he would have been far less settled, especially as the dog rescue had castrated him. But he was very much at home in the company of a gentle bitch. He also had other bitches around him, that he could see and communicate with. A professional greyhound kennels is run on rather different lines from a professional boarding kennels; while each is good of its kind, the greyhound keepers can gear their routine specifically to suit this calibre of hound. If you take on a dog with separation anxiety, boarding kennels of any type should not come into his experience until his rehabilitation is complete. However, life does spring some unpleasant surprises, as it did to the farmer, and it is as well to give thought to what you would do if caught in a similar dilemma. If boarding kennels is the only option, as it was for her, then let the dog visit several times before you need to leave her overnight, or for several nights, so that at least she knows you are coming back. This is a good plan even for dogs that do not suffer separation anxiety as such, because being apart from their home and family is stressful for the most laid-back of dogs. Boarding kennels vary very much in their routines and systems, and you would be well advised to shop around and look at several, rather than simply picking the nearest one.

The Dog Sitter

Although at first sight a rather expensive option, having someone to stay in your house to look after your dog can be a useful alternative. This is the only option for people who choose not to have their dogs vaccinated annually, because all boarding kennels insist on this. This is not the kennels being difficult, but a requirement of their insurance, without which they cannot hold a licence. I used to farm- house- and dog-sit, and the animals are very happy with this arrangement. You can use a company that specialises in this, knowing that whoever is sent will have been thoroughly vetted and insured, or else a private individual, but if you take the latter choice, make sure that they carry adequate insurance, and it is wise if a form of indemnity is drawn up by a solicitor and signed by both parties. Particularly with dogs, the sitter and the animals must be introduced beforehand; you cannot expect dogs to obey a stranger. Equally, if there is any doubt about your dog's behaviour, for instance on recall, with livestock, or in the company of other dogs, the sitter must be warned so that they can take appropriate precautions. Any 'ifs' or 'buts' must be made quite plain: for instance, I once had two dogs to look after for six weeks, which I had to keep on leads or kennelled for the entire stay, because one was likely to run off. This meant extra time to exercise them properly, but the stay was uneventful. However, a previous dog-sitter for the same person had ignored this request, and a dog had run off and been killed while trying to cross six lanes of traffic. Another time, I looked after a full kennel of dogs for a professional trainer, and we had to set up a situation to ensure that the attack-trained guard dog allowed me in and out of the house! He was marvellous, being so well trained, and during the stay protected me from a rather intimidating unwanted visitor.

The more dogs that you have, the better the cost of the sitter compares to the cost of kennelling, but the best are not cheap. What you are paying for as well as the care of your animals, is having somebody on the property, and for that person's honesty (I do know of some people who found me too expensive, and had a family friend to stay instead, who emptied the drinks cabinet). You are also paying for the fact that the sitter is not earning anything else while you are away. Each agency or individual has their own arrangements: I used to supply my own food and pay for my own telephone calls, stock the larder if required for the householders' return, water house and greenhouse plants, and leave the house and garden as I found it. Some people will cut lawns and do the garden for you, but this should not be taken for granted. Just as the sitter should not abuse your telephone or wine cellar, so the householder should not leave the sitter with a series of difficult situations: I have been left with a fortnight's building work to endure, sick animals requiring experienced nursing, dying animals that should have been put down before the owners went on holiday, people telephoning to buy puppies after an advertisement had been placed to come out in the owner's absence, relatives descending on the place and leaving it insecure when I was responsible for security, and many, many times houses and gardens that simply had no safe areas to leave animals if I wanted to go out even to buy a newspaper. Unruly and plain vicious animals were mine to care for on frequent occasions. By contrast, I have stayed in some lovely places with delightful animals, where every care had been taken to make our time together a positive experience. Lurchers do not give their loyalty easily, and take time to make friends with other people, but if you are away a lot, then the sitter can be a better solution than putting your dog in kennels. Some people will even look after your dog in their own homes, and I have done this too. Be careful, though, because strictly speaking, they should have a licence from the council to do this. However, in the case of separation anxiety that takes time to resolve, it could be a lot cheaper than making good the damage to house and garden.

Dog Appeasement Pheromone

This is a new method of helping the dog that is under stress, and may be of use in certain cases of separation anxiety. The DAP device emits a pheromone identical to that produced by a bitch when she has very young puppies, and is supposed to exert a calming effect on the dog that smells it. Most testers report that dogs respond favourably to it, but the degree of success obviously depends on the individual dog. Obtainable only from veterinary surgeries at the moment, the DAP is well worth a try, not only for a dog with established separation anxiety, but to stop the behaviour developing in the first place.

Noise

There is a lot that can be done in practical terms to limit the damage that a dog going through a destructive phase can do, but noise can be very frustrating to deal with. Lurchers are not given to unnecessary barking and some never bark at all, but they can howl, and some do. In fact, my youngest dog is nicknamed 'Pavarotti' for his addresses to the full moon. Howling *per se* seldom goes on for any length of time, and to my mind is really rather tuneful: it is a normal dog communication, and hound breeds tend to use it more than non-hounds, which by contrast bark and yap. It is not a sound of distress: it asks if anyone is there, or it can just be singing. Again, if I come home and my dogs are in the right frame of mind, we can sing together, which is good for bonding and leaves everybody fulfilled. However, most of us have to be mindful of neighbours, some of whom would like to sleep: as an ex-shift-worker, I can relate to that! One of the big exasperations of dog ownership is that the dog's normal behaviour is seldom treated with tolerance, and people who make your days a misery with screaming children or endless strimming, and wreck your nights with letting out cats to yowl and fight under your bedroom window, can bring the full power of the local council down upon you if your dog makes a noise. You can even have your dog taken from you, and the farmer's lurcher with the separation anxiety which I mentioned earlier had been removed from his previous owner under a Noise Abatement Order. Not long ago, an old man's terrier was taken from him because its constant yapping resulted in complaints by one neighbour; originally the dog was under a death sentence, but it managed to avoid that, being re-homed instead. The poor old man was left without his pet; what a shame nobody thought to enlist the help of a dog behaviourist! There is plenty of help available for someone who is home all day with the dog, but what if yours howls while you are out?

See if you can find a 'day nursery' for your dog – some kennels will board dogs on a reduced rate for a regular customer, and you will probably find that after a month or so, you can have your dog back at home for one day a week, then more, working quite quickly up to all of the week. It is a matter of breaking an established habit. During this time, backup treatment with homoeopathy and/or Flower Remedies will be of use. You might be able to find a private individual who is willing to dog-sit either at your house or his/her own, or who has a dog with which yours is friendly, so that they can

A strong bond

spend the days together. This is one behaviour that often responds favourably to the presence of another dog, though there are occasions where two dogs sing a duet instead of your singleton performing solo. You will not know until you try, and it is better to try this way with a temporary dog than to acquire a second one on a permanent basis only to find that you now have twice the trouble. Two dogs, like two children, sometimes get on so well that they bond with each other rather than you and therefore give you a training problem, or else there is jealousy and discord where you had hoped to create companionship. A dog that is on good terms with yours and that goes home at the end of each working day is unlikely to cause either of these problems. Make sure that the two dogs really are friendly, and don't expect it to be automatic. Opposite sexes usually work better than same-sex combinations, but unless one or both is neutered, there will be times when they cannot be together, and it is politic to make alternative arrangements well in advance. Have them together under supervision before you ever try leaving them both, and when you do, be careful to remove any bones, food or toys over which there could be strife. You can, as an alternative, have the dogs in adjacent rooms or runs where they can see each other but not reach each other, in which case they can each have whatever you like to leave them with in terms of food or playthings – unless of course this causes one to bark at the other! The radio playing in the kennel area can often stop neighbours complaining, as they think you are at home. Outside dogs can be victims of goading by children or cats, which causes them to make a noise, in which case you have little alternative but to have them safely indoors. It is important to feed your dog a diet as free from additives as you can, and to exercise her properly before you leave. Leave a radio or television on, with talking rather than music, as the latter does tend to stimulate singing in susceptible dogs. You can buy collars that fire a spray of citronella – a smell dogs hate – when the dog makes a noise, but this is not tackling the underlying issue. Much better to get back to basics and remove the incentive for your dog to make a noise. Is she somewhere where sound echoes? Does she feel threatened by external noise? Do some homework and sit quietly close by the house, so that you know how long after you leave that she starts making a noise, and for how long. Of course, this also identifies whether it is in fact your dog that is making the noise, as it is not uncommon for the wrong dog to be accused.

Compared to other dogs, lurchers are very rarely noisy. You can keep them for years and never have any sort of problems with noise at all. If, however, noise does become an issue, then as you see, there are many ways to resolve the matter. One of the many joys of this type of dog is how very easy and pleasant she is to have around, so if there is a matter on which she and you cannot agree, please do not give up on her when there are so many ways that you can both be helped.

Greyhound/Whippet lurcher, out for the day

7 SHOPPING

To your lurcher, the world is one vast pick-your-own site. Her breeding and instincts make her a hound: a hunting dog. This does not have to be a problem between you, but it must be acknowledged if you are to live in harmony with each other. Every breed of dog was originally a worker: even ladies' lapdogs were required to catch the rats and mice that plagued houses in days gone by, and they were also used for rabbiting in the enclosed warrens in which rabbits were reared. Your lurcher is a gazehound, sighthound, and running dog: she is designed to find quarry and chase it until she either catches or loses it. Although she can use her nose, she prefers to use her eyes, scanning the far horizons for movement. How much easier this is than owning a dog that hunts by scent, and which will put its nose down and run for miles, for your lurcher will return to you once she has lost sight of whatever she was chasing. You might feel that there are advantages in owning a dog that is capable of catching her own supper and yours as well, for that was her original purpose, and that is the life of most of today's lurchers. If you are happy with her talents, and perhaps would like to polish them and learn a little more about the ancient arts to which she was born, then there are plenty of books, magazines, websites and a couple of good videos which will help you, as well as clubs that you can join to meet like-minded people. If, however, this is a side of her nature that you would prefer not to develop, then you have to take a little extra care. As with anything, prevention is better than cure.

Nature

All dogs hunt, every single one. Often their owners are blissfully unaware that Snookums is hunting when she puts her nose down and snuffles about, but the fattest, most pampered lapdog is a wolf under the skin. The only difference between Snookums and your lurcher is that your dog is capable of catching what she pursues. She is also clever, and tractable enough to learn that she must not chase certain animals, such as horses, cattle and sheep. Does this mean that I am going to tell you simply to train her not to chase any animal at

A lurcher's purpose – catching dinner

all? Not quite, for that would be a dreadful cruelty to your dog. Guard dogs need to guard, herding dogs need to herd, gundogs need to flush game, and these behaviours can be modified so that the dogs are able to fulfil their needs without causing worry to their owners. If, however, a natural behaviour is totally suppressed, the result is a suffering dog and one that will develop bizarre behaviour to compensate for her frustration. Snookums can puff along in the wake of a rabbit that went down a hole twenty minutes ago, her needs utterly met and her owner likely in ignorance, but you will have to be more aware of your lovely running dog and her requirements.

You can handle this in one of two ways: either there are some things that you will allow her to chase, such as rats and rabbits, but make it clear to her that anything else is not allowed, or you never put her in a situation where she will have the opportunity to chase another animal. If you choose the former, you will have a happy dog but will have to cope with the occasional catch; lurchers are not stupid, and will quickly kill a rat, but you might find bunny is brought back to you quite unharmed, which is the correct way for a working dog. If so, take the rabbit, praise your dog fulsomely, and either restrain and distract her while you let bunny go, or else if you are capable of recycling this free-range organic food into a meal for yourself and your dog, then despatch it humanely, empty its bladder by running your thumbs down the belly from middle to between the hindlegs, and pocket it to deal with later. Never ever scold a lurcher for retrieving her quarry to you, because not only will you cause untold distress because she is doing something right and being told off for it, she might take the next one off and eat it. Then you really are in trouble, and have completely lost control of what is, after all, a very straightforward situation.

If you do not like the idea of touching the rabbit, either put on a glove or keep a plastic bag in your pocket (you probably carry them anyway, for clearing up after your dog) and put your hand in the plastic bag before you take the rabbit. You cannot catch anything from the rabbit, so do not worry about touching it; it is only an animal covered in fur just like your dog. If it is alive, it will wriggle, so catch hold of it across the back so that it cannot accidentally scratch you. Rabbits have nice loose skin which is very convenient for this. It may also squeal; remember that it is a wild animal, and stroking will not comfort it. Either kill or release it as soon as possible, and praise your dog again, whichever you do, because she will be rather shocked if you are so clumsy as to let her rabbit go, and may try to catch it again. That is why I recommend distracting her attention first. Let bunny go in some undergrowth if you can, rather than in the open; he will have learned a lesson and not be overwhelmed by the day's events because rabbits have constant near-misses with death until finally one of their numerous enemies catches up with them. Rabbits never die of old age! If the rabbit has eyes which are pink-rimmed or swollen shut, and is not moving freely, then it has myxomatosis. You and your dog cannot catch myxomatosis as it only affects rabbits. It is, however, a slow and miserable way to die, so be brave and put the poor creature out of its misery. The easiest way to do this is to catch hold of the back legs in one hand and place the other over the head so that your hand is in front of the ears and behind the eyes. A quick pull with the head hand is quite sufficient to dislocate the neck. If you are very squeamish and cannot do this, then the little fellow will have to be left. If you are happy to despatch a rabbit but have no experience of doing so, or of how to prepare one for the table, I have a list of books to help you at the end of the chapter. Of course, you will not be eating myxomatosed rabbits, though you would come to no harm if you did. They do not look very pleasant and seldom carry much flesh, so leave them for the crows and foxes.

If you allow your lurcher to catch food for you, she will be so pleased, and

A working lurcher is trained to ignore sheep and other livestock

it will bond you closer, for nothing is as close as the relationship between a working dog and the person for whom she works. If, however, this is something with which you simply cannot cope, then it is incumbent upon you never to put her in such a position. This is a small price to pay for the company of what is otherwise a very easy dog; have you ever wondered why so few beagles and bassets are allowed off the lead, or felt relieved that the retriever covered in slimy essence of pond is not yours to take home and wash off? All you have to do with your lurcher if you do not want her to hunt is take a few simple precautions.

Avoidance Tactics

Let me give it to you straight: you will never be able to call off a lurcher in full flight. Fully trained working lurchers can be trained so, but it is a long hard road that only the most dedicated trainers travel, and the only reason that they have such a high level of control is because their dogs are allowed to hunt, encouraged to do so, and therefore the dog knows that she will have plenty of other opportunities to fulfil her needs. A dog that is not allowed to give rein to her instincts and suddenly gets the opportunity to do so will not pass up the chance. Neither would you! No matter how persuasive professional dog trainers are about the virtues of clicker or disc training, these methods will not work on any dog – not just a lurcher – that has its heart set on pursuing quarry. So your only way is to ensure that your dog never sees any. This means never exercising at dawn, dusk or in the dark with your dog off the lead, keeping clear of woodland and other places where you know there are wild animals, always going through gateways and over stiles first, and having a good look around before you call your dog forward, and getting to know the country signs that denote the presence of wildlife. Wear your glasses if your distance vision is iffy, and keep a constant scan on the landscape, particularly watching those areas where forestry joins meadow and watching out for the bright smudge of russet or sudden movement that denotes a deer, fox or hare. Rabbit droppings and crops nibbled in a characteristic half-circle mean that your dog must be on a lead before a rabbit is found, and sharp little deer hooves will leave slot-marks in soft earth.

If you walk footpaths across farmland, do not let your dog off the path; apart from politeness to the farmer, there may be animals lying-up in the crop, particularly during the breeding season. Animals move around more at certain times of the year, such as when young males are driven out by older males, or when harvest is dispossessing a variety of creatures that have lived happily in the crop all summer. Local flooding or drought will have an effect on wild

Warning – she's seen something. Is that fence high enough?

animals' movements either into or out of your area, and sunny days will bring all manner of creatures out of the seclusion of the woods into the open. In winter, organised shooting will move animals out of the estates where they normally live, though usually only on a temporary basis; if you exercise near a shooting estate, keep away on shoot days. The estate will be happy to supply you with details of when the coverts are being shot, especially as an unknowing owner disturbing the woodlands by letting a dog run through them will create a lot of problems for the hard-working keeper. Nobody needs bad feeling, and it is just as easy to be considerate. In any case, keepered ground tends to have far more wildlife than other places, and I would suggest always keeping your dog on a lead as you go through or past. You will have a lot of pleasure in wildlife-spotting, for although you are doing it out of duty rather than recreation, you will see far more than dog owners who are not tuned-in to the natural world. I have watched a roe doe suckling twins a few hundred yards off a popular footpath in constant view of dog walkers, none of whom noticed her. Also watch your dog, for she will tell you at once if she sees or scents something that might need chasing. If she air-scents and looks sideways at you, put her lead on at once, and if she freezes on point and stares at a bramble bush, ditch or tussock of grass, she knows that something is in there. She will be very unlikely to be distracted by a toy or a titbit at such a time, so put the lead on first and then offer one or the other.

You need to be alert all the time, and your dog walks will not be spent deep in thought or enjoying the wild flowers, for you must be diligent in your watchfulness. There will always be some places where you can relax and let your dog free, such as beaches or public parks, and there are some areas which are much frequented by dog walkers and therefore have little in the way of wild animals. At 'moving' times of year, though, you can find animals where they have no business to be: foxes are common in built-up areas, and I have seen deer in suburban back gardens on a surprising number of occasions. Should the worst happen, and your dog finds and pursues something that you had no idea was there, it does not have to be the end of the world. Rabbits and foxes go down holes, squirrels run up trees, and if one of these was the object of desire, then your dog will be back fairly quickly, unless of course something else jumps up to beguile her when she is on her way back. Hares are so fast and agile that a dog will quickly run out of steam running after one,

Ears right forward means that he has found something hiding in the ditch

A risky place – rabbit warrens and no secure fencing

for hare-catching dogs need to be very fit. Deer are another matter, for they are relatively slow, and even a Labrador can catch a roe deer. You really do not want your dog to chase deer, and indeed the majority of working dogs are not allowed to chase them either. Do not delude yourself that your dog 'only wants to play', she is not playing, she is deadly serious. Do not think that if your dog is small, she 'can't do any harm'; I knew of a pair of border terriers that were allowed to run in an uncontrolled manner, and took to killing deer.

You can work around most situations, but on this you must be utterly implacable: your dog must not be allowed to chase deer. Deer can go a long way, across roads or into other hazards, so keep a wary eye out for them at all times, and if in doubt, put that lead on your dog. There are six species of deer in UK, plus the Sika/Red hybrid, and most rural areas have a high population of the smaller ones, so always be on the alert. Many dogs chase deer, not just lurchers; don't get yours involved just because other people are less caring, and don't exercise your dog with another person or people who let their dogs chase. The controlled use of hunting dogs by knowledgeable handlers is one thing, but uncontrolled dogs running wild are quite another. If your dog does

'Marking' unseen game – she is tense and ready to chase

In full flight (E. Dearden)

run off, wait at the point where she left you, because it is to there that she will return. If you can get a better view of the area from a high point nearby, then leave a jacket or similar item of clothing where your dog was last with you, and if she returns unseen, you will probably find her lying on that when you return from your lookout spot. Lurchers can be very furtive, and pass by without anyone ever seeing or hearing them – in fact you may have noticed this trait in the house – and will often come back without you seeing. Make her welcome upon her return, no matter how frantic you have been at losing her, because if you are forceful, she will associate your reaction not with her disobedient departure, but with her willing return. Next time, she may elect to stay away for longer.

Muzzling

I have been asked about whether it is a good idea to muzzle a lurcher, so that if she does chase after something, she cannot hurt it. While a laudable idea, this one is fraught with dangers. To begin with, any muzzle needs to be wide enough to allow the dog to pant, which labels as unsuitable the soft cloth muzzles. If your dog attempts to run while wearing a muzzle that restricts her jaws, she will still run but be unable to cool herself by panting, and in extreme cases may not be able to breathe properly. If she has had a run and cannot pant, she may die. It is as stark as that. The soft cloth muzzles are therefore unsuitable for this particular purpose and this particular dog. The wide plastic muzzles, or the wire racing muzzles can trap a claw or a paw if the dog tries to scrape her muzzle off, and injure her. If she does not return to you for one reason or another, the muzzle will stop her from eating and drinking, and she will not survive for long, whereas a lurcher can take care of herself quite adequately if she has to live feral for a while. The muzzle will cause more, not less harm to wildlife, for she will be unable to effect a quick catch and kill (or catch, carry and return) but may batter at the quarry with her head, which will damage both her and whatever she is chasing. A squirrel or a rat could bite her through the muzzle, and she would be unable to defend herself. If the quarry is the sort that fights back, such as a fox, mink or deer, she may sustain some very bad injuries. Muzzled dogs are in danger of attack from unmuzzled dogs, which are quick to sense a disadvantaged animal and act upon it, and people can react most unfortunately to the sight of a muzzled dog, assuming her to be vicious. Likewise, racing greyhounds, the most gentle of beasts, are often considered vicious by those who know nothing about them simply because they wear muzzles for their work. Although it might at first seem to be a way that you could let your dog run free without worrying about her catching an animal, muzzling is far too risky.

The ex-Professional

If you have a rescue dog, it is possible that she was initially intended as a hunting dog or even used as one, before proving inadequate in some way. Or she could have been very good, but stolen or otherwise fallen into the wrong hands and thus into the rescue home. She may have had to live feral for a while, catching her own food. I heard of a pet whippet that was lost on the moors in the North of England, and though she had never hunted, she lived through a bitter winter, catching her own food and finding her own shelter. When her owner finally managed to catch her, the little dog having grown very wary, she found that her whippet had grown a thick coat, and was an accomplished rabbiter. Luckily, she had never attempted to touch the plentiful sheep in the area. Such dogs cannot be de-programmed, but you can live with them successfully and happily, as long as you understand that as far as they are concerned, what they are doing is right. In fact a properly trained working dog can be easier than one that is all instinct and longing but no experience, for the trained dog knows that she must come straight back to you after she has run, and she will probably be quite safe with livestock. Don't take chances though, on what you do not know, but put her on the lead if you do not want her free in a particular situation. Older dogs are generally quite happy to take life a little easier after a hard few years' work, though she will still find game and turn almost with a conspiratorial wink to see if you would like her to take the matter further.

Sighthounds

Of all the breeds of hound, the sighthounds are the only ones with which you can live easily. As a human, you use your eyes as the primary sense, as do the sighthounds, but your sense of smell is vestigial. Where the pet ownership of a beagle or basset is fraught, and a foxhound impossible, because you have no inkling of the scents that are beguiling your dog's nose, the sighthound owner simply has to keep a good lookout, and avoid those times of day and night when wild animals are on the move. You will soon get a feel for times and places which are best avoided. Your lurcher does not have a manic desire to herd, which can result in some rather awkward situations, nor does she want to fight, or get into smelly muddy water, or find something to guard that she will not let anyone near. She does not want to go down holes or bark at everything she sees and hears. She will not run for hours on scent. All in all, the hunting instinct is something of which you need to be aware, but it is pretty small beer compared to what owners of other breeds have to work around.

Further Reading

Understanding the Working Lurcher Jackie Drakeford, Crowood Press, Ramsbury, Marlborough, Wiltshire SN8 2HR. First published 2000.

Lurchers and Longdogs E. G. Walsh, The Boydell Press, P.O. Box 9, Woodbridge, Suffolk IP12 3DF. Reprinted 1988.

The Lurcher – Training and Hunting Frank Sheardown, Swan Hill Press, Wykey House, Wykey, Shrewsbury SY4 1JA. Published 1996.

The New Complete Lurcher Brian Plummer, Swan Hill Press, Wykey House, Wykey, Shrewsbury SY4 1JA. Published 1998.

A large selection of lurcher books from Coch-Y-Bonddu Books, Pentrehedyn Street, Machynlleth, Powys SY 20 8DJ and Tideline Books, P.O. Box 4, Rhyl, North Wales LL8 1AG.

8 SHOW TIME

Lurcher shows are very popular during the summer, and it is possible for the dedicated enthusiast to be out showing every Sunday from March until the beginning of October. Some clubs, such as Sussex Longdogs, hold an indoor show at Christmas-time as well. The shows are run by Hunts and lurcher clubs, and are sometimes part of a larger organisation, such as a Game Fair or a Country Show. They raise money for the organisers and usually for charity as well, are open to anyone with a lurcher, and are a fun way of meeting other lurcher owners, prospecting for a suitable mate if you want to breed from your lurcher, and stocking up with leads, dog coats and other lurcher paraphernalia. The easiest way to find out about lurcher shows in your area is to read *The Countryman's Weekly*, which carries a list of shows every week.

Not only are there showing classes at a lurcher show, but also other events such as speed jumping, high jump, lurcher obedience, which is very different from the highly stylised Kennel Club obedience competitions, and sometimes light-hearted events such as 'fastest recall' or 'fastest retrieve'. Lure coursing and racing events are sometimes held either before or after the showing classes – to hold them at the same time is to invite disaster, as the dogs in the show rings become very unsettled at the noise of the speed events. Prizes are generally small; maybe a trophy for the winners and champions, perhaps a sack of dog food from a sponsor, sweets for the children, and rosettes for all placings. Lurcher showing is strictly for fun.

Showing Classes

These are divided into Rough or Smooth, usually Dog or Bitch, and then by height, the cut-off being either 23 or 24 inches. There should be a measuring facility available for you to check your dog's height if you are unsure. Often there are classes for purebred sighthounds, and novelty classes such as 'best rescue' and 'veterans', not forgetting the ubiquitous 'child handler' which may be divided into two age groups. A typical schedule will read thus:

A typical showing class

1   Puppies, dogs or bitches, 6 to 12 months, rough coated
2   Puppies, dogs or bitches, 6 to 12 months, smooth coated
3   Champion puppy, winners of classes 1 and 2
4   Large rough dogs 24 inches and over
5   Large rough bitches 24 inches and over
6   Large smooth dogs 24 inches and over
7   Large smooth bitches 24 inches and over
8   Large lurcher championship – winners of classes 4, 5, 6 and 7
9   Small rough dogs under 24 inches
10   Small rough bitches under 24 inches
11   Small smooth dogs under 24 inches
12   Small smooth bitches under 24 inches
13   Small lurcher championship – winners of classes 9,10,11 and 12
14   Greyhounds, dogs and bitches. Class may be divided if sufficient
     entries
15   Whippets, dogs and bitches. Class may be divided if sufficient entries
16   Any other purebred Sighthound

17   Rabbiting dog or bitch 21 inches and under

18   Best Rescue

19   Veterans over 8 years

20   Child handler up to 8 years

21   Child handler 8 to 12 years

22   Supreme Champion – winners of classes 8, 13, 14, 15, 16 and 17

There are local variations, but normally puppies are ineligible for other classes, and whippets may enter the rabbiting class. If in doubt, ask the show organiser before you enter the class. The term 'rough coat' can be open to interpretation, so if your dog has a coat that seems neither rough nor smooth, check with the judge which class you should be in. 'Any Other Purebred Sighthound' means exactly that, and it is lovely to see wolfhounds, deerhounds, pharaoh hounds, borzois, salukis or sloughis in the ring. The judge will judge them not according to Kennel Club rules – he or she is seldom a Kennel Club judge – but as healthy, fit sighthounds ready to do the job for which they were originally bred. Other classes that you sometimes see

Not many shows hold a progeny class – sire (centre) and two yearling pups (B. Hurley)

can be 'pairs' – sometimes judged as a matched pair, sometimes as a hunting pair, best to check with the judge which applies on the day, and a 'hunting group' which is three dogs of mixed type, one of which must be a lurcher or sighthound, which would hunt well together, usually a combination of lurcher(s) and terrier(s) but sometimes a gundog completes the group. Watch out for judges with a sense of humour here: I have been known to ask the handler to remove the leads as a hunting group must be controllable. You may also get classes for collie types or Bedlington types, or classes for a particular colour of lurcher, such as merle, white or pied.

In The Ring

Normally, your entry fee is taken by a steward when you go into the ring. The judge will wait until all the entries are in the ring before beginning the judging, though no doubt taking a shrewd look at each from a distance. There is no set format for judging, but most judges follow a similar pattern. With puppies, my concern is that it is a pleasant experience for them, so I only ask them to parade once around the ring and then come in for an individual check; no puppy is penalised for being shy or wriggly, and the ones that lick me do not get extra marks! Sometimes people ask me if they can bring in a younger puppy just for the ring experience: I am happy for this to take place, and such puppies are not eligible for placing, but it is good for them to have a look round and leave when they have had enough. Dogs that are in adult classes are judged – with local variations – as follows:

First, handlers are asked to stand their dogs up. Dogs must face to the right, have their weight equally on all legs, and their head facing forwards. I do not like to see dogs' heads strung upwards in an unnatural line *à la* Kennel Club; this fashion is largely dying out in lurcher shows thank goodness, though a few old-fashioned judges still like to see it. If in doubt, ask your judge how he or she would like the head carriage; a good judge will tell you in any case. I always stress that I want a natural head carriage, and if someone then strings their dog up, they lose marks for it. The judge will look along the line of dogs from a distance, taking in their general symmetry and conformation, and then ask the competitors to 'take them on round, please'. The dogs are required to walk around the ring at a brisk pace so that the judge can see how they move; generally once round the ring is enough, though if the ring is small or there are a lot of entries, dogs may be asked to go around twice. During this time, let your dog show herself; do not let another competitor crowd you, and keep well back from the dog in front. Go right into the corners of the ring so that you have plenty of space to let your dog stride out, and don't let her drag

RING 4
LURCHERS
OVER 23"

Waiting his turn. The ears and shape show that this is probably a collie/greyhound/whippet

behind or leap up at you or other dogs.

After you have been round, you will stand in line and wait for the judge to call you forward in turn for a detailed examination. I have heard people claim that they know the winner as soon as it comes into the ring, but believe me, no judge knows what a dog is like until it comes under their close scrutiny. Eyes, ears and teeth are checked for health, nails must be the right length for a working dog, toes must be tight and free from injury, legs angled correctly and bodies the correct weight. The overall appearance should be of a dog that is fit and ready to go. Some judges place a lot of importance on tail length and carriage, though I do not; true enough a long tail is usually a sign of a fast dog simply because a long tail indicates a lot of greyhound blood, but there is a lot more to a lurcher than speed. Tail carriage varies with the breeding: a 'gay tail' carried high is almost inevitable in a terrier cross, while saluki crosses can produce curly tails. Neither affects the dog in its work, and regardless of whether the dogs in the ring are workers, pets or both, the judge should always use 'work' as the benchmark when judging this stamp of dog, not 'does it work' but 'could it work if given the chance?' The coat should be clean and

155

Judge at work

free from evidence of parasites; anyone can pick up a flea at a show but evidence of untreated infestation – those giveaway dark specks and red areas of skin – is not acceptable. As a working dog, it is permissible for a lurcher to be scarred, or to show evidence of recent injury, providing that injury has received appropriate treatment. Some judges will not place castrated dogs, which is a nonsense, for they should be judging working dogs not breeding stock. In any case, it is a judge with x-ray eyes that can tell if a bitch has been spayed! Bitches in season should not be shown, as it is most unfair on the other competitors, and can spark off a dog fight, especially if there are terriers being shown in the ring next door, terriers never needing much in the way of reason for a scrap.

It is hard for judges of pedigree dogs with a strict breed standard to understand how a lurcher judge can judge a type of dog the appearance of which varies according to how it is bred. It is, in fact, quite straightforward in that you judge each dog not against each other dog but against the way a perfect specimen of that type would appear if it was in front of you. That way, the long, strong feet of the saluki or deerhound cross are not unfavourably compared with the tight catlike feet of a border collie cross, or the well-knuckled feet of a whippet; instead what the judge should be looking for is perfect feet in each type. Similarly, the narrow, wasp-waisted saluki cannot be compared with the broad haunches of the bearded collie, for each is a very different stamp of dog, and therefore each is mentally compared to a flawless specimen of that particular cross. Coat colour is irrelevant in that a dog does not catch quarry with its colour; all colours occur in the lurcher world, and all are beautiful to somebody. Outside the show ring, I definitely have my preferences, but once I am judging, my preferences take a back seat, for what I am looking for is the lurcher which most nearly achieves perfection of its type.

After the detailed examination, the judge will ask the handler to walk a triangle, so that the dog can be viewed moving from the front, the rear and the side. The judge is looking for correct movement and a free, swinging gait indicative of a dog that can gallop. Though the dog cannot be seen galloping, a dog that can move correctly at walk and trot will be able to gallop. The running dog should move on one track, like a fox, not two tracks like a horse, so that the paws leave a track that is almost a straight line rather than a 'leg at each corner'. This can be compared to a human baby that at first staggers along moving its legs in parallel, but as its physique develops, so it steps under itself and walks with footmarks in a slightly offset line. The dog should equally move straight, not throwing a leg, not swinging elbows or hindlegs out from the body, and certainly not lame. The whole impression should be athletic and springy. To allow a dog to stride out, the head carriage should be left *au naturel*; stringing the dog's head up will cause it to mince rather than daisy-cut, as it is difficult for a dog to stride beyond its head. Lurchers naturally have a long, low head-carriage to balance the long limbs, and forcing them into an unnatural line does them no favours; nor does it fool a good judge, for I have seen that tactic used to disguise lameness on several occasions.

Once the 'triangle' is complete, the judge will thank you, you will join the end of the line, and the judge will proceed to the next dog. Some judges like the dogs to be stood-up all through the judging, so that they can look from one to another of similar type, but I prefer a dog to relax when it is not actually being shown, and accordingly will make it clear to competitors that the dog can sit or lie down if it wishes. With the large classes we get in the ring nowadays, it is unreasonable to expect a dog to be 'at attention' for half an hour or more, especially in the blazing heat or sluicing rain that often accompanies a lurcher show. Dogs quickly get sour about such discomfort, and they have no conception of winning, only knowing that their handler is either happy or disappointed. As a judge, I try to make the experience as pleasant as

Puppy champion, eleven months old

possible for them; however much we enjoy showing, the dogs only go along with it to please us.

After the dogs have all been checked, the judge will ask the competitors to stand them up, and then to walk round again. It may be necessary for two or more circuits of the ring to be completed, while the judge picks out the placements. Dogs placed will be called out, and stood up again, while the judge looks at them one last time; the other competitors will be thanked and this is their cue to leave the ring. Please do not be disappointed if your dog is one of the unplaced, because the standard is very high nowadays. If the contest is close, two dogs may be asked to run-up again, to compare the movement. Then rosettes will be presented, and the winner's name will be taken for the championship. If your dog has not been placed, or never seems to get placed, and you would like to know why, most judges are happy to be approached after the showing has finished and they have had a cup of tea, and they can tell you how to improve your chances. Often it is something simple such as the dog having dirty teeth, or nails too long, or being too fat. Sometimes it is a case of showmanship – this is a show, after all – some dogs do not show themselves to their best advantage, and some handlers let their dogs down. Please remember that the judge has had a long journey and probably bent over dogs in the boiling sun for the best part of five hours, usually without a drink or a break, and that judges donate their services free, often not even taking travel expenses. If you disagree with their opinion, that is your privilege; it is, after all, only one person's opinion of one dog on one day, but please don't start an argument. This is supposed to be fun, and to each of us, our dog is undeniably the best that ever looked through a collar. Often, I have left unplaced a dog that really took my eye and heart, a dog that I would love to own, but in purely showing terms, there were better dogs there on that particular day.

The novelty classes are similar but not so strict: for instance, nobody expects a rescue dog to be physically perfect, although some are, and the veterans are bound to have some lumps and bumps, and bits missing. For the child handler classes, the marks are for the child's handling of the dog, not for the appearance of the dog, so make sure that your child can follow instructions, and also that he or she knows a little about the dog. Conversations too often reveal that this is the first time that the child has encountered the dog, and does not even know its name, which makes heavy weather for the judge!

Obedience Tests

If the showing is – or should be – fun, some of the most deadly seriousness ever seen in the show ring occurs with the obedience tests. Lurcher obedience is geared to the requirements of the working dog, and so you will not need a dog that is glued to your leg and in danger of tripping you up, nor do you need a dog that sits every time you stop. What the obedience test is designed to produce is a dog that you would not be embarrassed to take onto someone else's land for the purposes of pest control, and before you run away and say that this is nothing to do with you and your dog, please do continue with reading this section, for lurcher obedience asks nothing that a well-behaved dog cannot produce. The obedience tests were originally created to prove to a doubting world that sighthounds are perfectly trainable and not automatically a liability as soon as they are let off the lead. They are also an essential preliminary for anyone wishing to compete in lurcher field trials, as it is not generally realised that a good hunting lurcher is more highly trained than a police dog. This last may not be for you, but your pet lurcher should be able to give a good account of herself in obedience tests, and if she is a rescue dog and has previously been worked, you will have every chance of taking her to the highest levels of competition, if you want to. Or else just enjoy yourself with the local shows.

Tests are divided into Novice – open to dogs that have never won a test – and Advanced, open to all dogs. It is perfectly permissible to run a novice dog in an Advanced test, but if you want to use the novice test to warm-up an advanced dog, it is at the judge's discretion, and cannot be scored. Judging obedience tests is very hard work, so do not be offended if the judge does not allow you to run a dog *hors concours*. At the very highest level, there are the qualifying tests for the field trials, but if you do not wish to get involved with the working dog side of lurcher ownership, these are not for you as a competitor, though you may enjoy watching them for their own sake. The field trials themselves are open only to competitors and judges, for the very nature of lurcher work means that spectators would ruin the dogs' chances, wild rabbits not being given to approving of large numbers of humans.

The Tests

Novice tests require you to demonstrate that your dog is under control on or off the lead, that she will stay until called, demonstrate a good recall, will stay out of sight of the owner, perform a simple retrieve, and jump a straightforward obstacle. Advanced tests build on this, and you may in addition have to call the dog off a moving dummy, perform split retrieves, jump retrieves, and prove that the dog will not break from the down-stay despite distractions. The very advanced tests will sometimes require a dog to simulate longnet or ferreting work, to retrieve cold game or a raw egg, to mark a hidden rabbit, and to leave or catch the dummy as instructed. A good rapport and quiet control is what the judge wants to see; the loud, repeated orders that are acceptable in non-lurcher competitive disciplines will lose marks. Tests vary according to the preferences of the judge and, it has to be said, the facilities provided by the show organisers. I have, more than once, had to eliminate the jump from my test, because the obstacle provided was not safe. Equally, as a competitor, I have had to refuse one exercise or another because it would have been detrimental to my dog's welfare or working requirements. Most obedience tests are excellent, but a few are not, and ask the wrong questions of a dog. If an obedience test is not to your liking, don't do it; your dog's steadiness is much more important than any circus tricks. Or do it and leave out the exercises that you don't wish to do; I have still had dogs placed under those circumstances because the rest of the test went well. Obedience judges often allow competitors to enter several times, and take the best score as the final one, which can be useful, although some people are tempted to over-run their dogs. Twice, in my opinion, is plenty for an obedience test; dogs sicken of this very quickly, and more than one good obedience dog has been stressed by an over-enthusiastic owner to the point where it ran out of the ring. If the judge refuses your entry on the basis that your dog has given her all and should not do any more, respect that decision and learn from it.

If you win an obedience test or two, allow yourself to feel good about it; you and your dog have done well. Finally, if obedience really isn't for you, please respect the fact that it is very important to others. Concentration and control taken to the level of competitive obedience are such that interruption can be disastrous, so don't let your children run through the ring while a test is taking place, don't, as happened to me when judging at the Midland Game Fair one year, sit on one of the test obstacles and start your picnic, don't let your dog run into the ring and attack or seduce the competing dog, or take the dummy from under its nose, and if you are part of a happy, noisy crowd of youngsters and dogs, please keep well away from the obedience ring to have your fun. If you are organising a show, please site the obedience ring well away from areas of noise or distraction such as the agility ring, the bouncy castle, the clay-shooting area, helicopter rides, and racing or jumping events. Lurchers are sensitive souls, and this sort of haroosh can freak them out completely, sometimes permanently.

Speed Jumping, High Jump and Long Jump

Speed jumping consists of a line of hurdles which your dog jumps while being timed with a stopwatch, and you usually get three tries per entry fee. Most lurchers enjoy this. Sometimes there is a variation where the lurcher picks up a dummy at the end of the line of hurdles and races back with it. High jump gets fiercely competitive; the UK record for dog high jump is held by a lurcher at something in the region of 12 feet. If you want your dog to compete in this discipline, be sure to check that the landing side of the jump is adequate; most organisers are careful about this and provide a thick layer of straw or a sandpit, but I have seen the sort of landing area that is likely to injure a dog. Remember that a dog lands on one front leg, usually the same one, and so the risk of injury is significant on bad ground. Also remember that if your dog can clear a considerable height and knows it, you might have to alter your fencing arrangements at home. Long jump takes place over a line of thin poles designed to be safe if the lurcher does not quite make the length. Long jump landings also have to be considered, as it is not always appreciated that, to clear length, a dog has to achieve height, and is still coming down onto that one front leg. The UK canine long jump record is also held by a lurcher and is, I believe, something in the region of 22 feet.

Muzzled for racing, and waiting eagerly

Lurcher Racing

This is another area of fierce competition, and if you have ever stood in a line-up of so-called racing lurchers with a real one, you might well wonder what on earth you are doing in the midst of what are near as dammit pure greyhounds, whippets or crosses between the two. You do get the odd rough-coated lurcher which can account for itself in lurcher racing, and I can think of a couple that were quite outstanding, but mostly they are dogs bred for the job, and though there is no betting and the prize is usually little more than a rosette, lurcher racing is taken very seriously by its fans. That does not mean they are unfriendly – quite the reverse – but once the dog is lined-up, they are deadly serious.

Dogs are required to wear racing muzzles, which are often available for hire at a nominal fee, and coloured knitted collars, again available for hire if you do not have your own. Colours are red, blue, green, yellow, pink and black -and -white If you are bitten by the racing bug and start to do a lot of it, you will want your own equipment; a lovely old lady knitted me my racing collars many years ago, and they are still going, though I don't race my dogs now. Sometimes dogs are started from traps, as with real greyhound racing, but more often they are 'hand-slipped' which means that the handlers stand in a row behind the 'start' line, dog held by the collar and just in front of the loins with the handler standing over it. The lure, often just a white plastic bag, is wriggled in front of them until they are squirming and shrieking in an ecstacy of desire, then the lure is dropped and flickers away from them as the starter signals GO!' At the other end, the lure disappears under a blanket, and, being sighthounds, the runners mostly pull up and run back to their owners, though you do get the odd canny hound that tries to extract the lure from its hiding place. Few sighthounds are aggressive, but the muzzles are most necessary as, at the end of a race and in the heat of the moment, one dog may snap at another. They have big mouths, and can do a lot of damage. A dog that consistently 'turns its head' ends up being disqualified, as less forceful dogs can still risk being injured even with all racers wearing muzzles, or else be frightened off following the lure. Many lurchers will not follow the lure at all, especially if they have been worked on live quarry, but others really love their racing. Some work and race equally well, but not that many.

Racing champion at a meeting that finished in the dark

Like showing, racing is divided into height limits, usually under 21 inches, under 23 inches and large lurchers. Sometimes there are veterans' races, for racing lurchers seem to go on for years. They are built and bred to run, kept very fit and fed on the best, and usually very much part of the family.

Lure Coursing

This is called 'lure chasing' by the purists, as it bears no relation to coursing, and is sometimes mistakenly used in arguments against fieldsports that claim it could substitute for coursing. It is quite different, and not suitable for every dog, but great fun for the ones that take to it. The lure, usually driven by a car battery, follows a zigzag course to the 'finish' line, and dogs are run in pairs. They are required to follow the exact route of the lure and pass through a series of 'gates' indicated by poles at each turn. Good lure-coursing tracks do not have too sharp changes of direction, though it has to be said that a rabbit or hare can turn more sharply than any course ever set up! Clever dogs will only follow the lure once, and thereafter will run from the 'start' to the 'finish' to intercept the lure as it arrives – this is a very typical bit of lurcher thinking, but does not win lure-coursing competitions. If yours is a smart lurcher and

Lure coursing

tries this, just appreciate her fine intellect and enjoy watching the other dogs run. There will be plenty of other activities she can shine in.

Bits and Bobs

Some lurchers, though not many, take to doing dog agility, though if this is your particular discipline, I would recommend using a different type of dog. Lurchers are often very sensitive to noise, and the shouting and ceaseless barking that accompanies agility sessions can be very distressing for them. On a physical level, their long backs and legs can make some exercises more difficult than they are for a lower-slung wider-set dog. Equally, although there are lurchers that can put up a creditable performance in Kennel Club-style obedience tests, most would find it far too stressful, or even pointless. Much as lurchers like to please you, they are not the sort of dog to persist in any activity that is without pleasure for them as well, and they are not the only type of dog to feel this way, which is why serious Kennel Club obedience competitors use border collies or GSDs. Tracking is rather out of a lurcher's remit as well, not because they cannot use their noses – they have excellent noses, which is one of the reasons they are such versatile working dogs – but because the rules of tracking competitions make no allowance for the use of air scent as opposed to ground scent. Lurchers are capable of putting up a very good show at gundog scurries, but are seldom allowed to compete, these competitions normally being restricted to Kennel Club registered gundog breeds. On the occasions when a more relaxed attitude allows non-registered dogs to compete, lurchers have been known to almost sweep the board.

Lurcher Displays

Lurcher display teams are becoming more and more popular at Game Fairs and Country Shows, and it is well worth watching these to see simulations of lurcher work, as well as the standards to which it is possible to train lurchers. Some teams are professionals, such as Dave Sleight's display, others are given by volunteers, but all are equally enjoyable. Between displays, members of the public will be encouraged to come and talk lurchers, and there is always something more to be learned in congenial company.

All in all, lurcher shows are a great way of relaxing and having fun with your dog during the summer, and of meeting lots of other beautiful lurchers. I have made some good friends at lurcher shows, and if people-watching is your sport, you will meet an extraordinarily diverse cross-section of humanity.

(Above) *Strong deerhound and saluki influence can be seen and she also has border collie/greyhound in her*
(Below) *Down and stay – the merle dog is a field trial champion*

9 LURCHERS IN AMERICA AND ELSEWHERE

Such a useful beast as a lurcher would invariably have accompanied settlers to new lands, and crossbred running dogs became established everywhere that the climate and topography lent itself to coursing. Once again, the lurcher's job was to put meat on the table. Just as it has in UK, so the lurcher type became tailored to the quarry it hunted and the terrain it hunted over. In some areas, such as India and the Middle East, running dog breeds of great antiquity already existed, perfectly adapted for their environment and work, and these were the obvious choice in preference to imported stock, especially as bloodlines were jealously guarded, and crossbreeding discouraged. Thus the lurcher did not flourish as a type, its appearance in these places being the result of only the occasional mismating or import. In other countries, such as America and Australia, there was no native-bred coursing hound, but excellent, if harsh, conditions in which to use them. In each case, the larger coursing hounds were crossbred to give the desired result, and evolved through trial and necessity into the kangaroo dogs of Australia and the staghounds of America.

It must be remembered that the gazehounds from which these types came were a world different from the show dogs of today. Wolfhounds, deerhounds and borzois were still field-tested and able to do their original job. Frank Sheardown writes of his time in Africa*, working lurchers that were bred from a wolfhound and an Alsatian (German Shepherd Dog), commenting that the wolfhound was quite small compared to the modern version. No doubt the GSD was far less of a cripple, too, than those that we see nowadays, with their bent backs and hindlegs. While anyone wanting a lurcher from these types of hound would have to choose their breeding stock very carefully today, there were many more specimens available then that were not oversized or exaggerated in build, could still run and leap, and had not lost

---

*Frank Sheardown: *The Working Longdog*, Dickson Price Publishers Ltd. Hawthorn House, Bowdell Lane, Brookland, Romney Marsh, Kent TN29 9RW, published 1989; *A Man of the Field*, Huddlesford Publications, address as above, published 1988

any of their prey drive. Hard work and hard living would weed out any lingering weakness, and because of the vast distances involved, limited breeding stock would result in different local 'types'. In each case, however, the result was a large, narrow hound capable of great speed, with a strong hunting instinct. In Australia, the kangaroo dogs were also used to protect person and property; while the sighthound character was retained towards its own people, a stronger guarding instinct was encouraged to develop than that with which the British lurcher owner was familiar. Similarly the Middle Eastern saluki is, even nowadays, required to protect the possessions of its owner, and it is a foolhardy person who answers the challenge offered by a guarding Afghan hound in its own land. The UK lurcher, by contrast, was and is naturally shy and suspicious with strangers, but not aggressive, as the poacher wanted a dog that would make itself scarce in the event of trouble. Such dogs were encouraged to hide their catch, and retrieve or lead the poacher to it when the coast was clear. It is an inbred behaviour, and many modern lurchers will do this without being taught. This natural diffidence is often mistaken for surliness or even cowardice when people who are used to more ebullient dogs first encounter a British lurcher. However, I am given to understand that kangaroo dogs are best treated with a respectful caution by strangers. The early Australian settlers needed meaningful guard dogs, and have evolved several breeds and types that are decidedly up for that job; though the Australian cattle dogs are a herding breed, they have a very strong guarding instinct, and there are many breeds I would rather be confronted by!

Modern Australia has little need for lurcher types, coursing being illegal or very restricted in most areas, and legal quarry such as feral pig needing a chunkier type of hunting dog, moreover one that makes a lot of noise when it has its quarry to bay, or 'bailing' as is the correct term there. Nevertheless, the kangaroo dog has not died out, and maybe still fulfils a useful role in Australia's more lonely places. Truly, such hounds are a valuable part of the continent's history.

New Zealand Lurchers

Again, the type is not commonly found, and most people have never heard of them. A few individuals work the British-type lurcher to a variety of quarry – there are fewer legal constraints in New Zealand than in Australia, and plenty of rabbits, foxes, hares and other non-indigenous nuisances, as well as possums to be caught. Again, there is a strong culture of feral pig hunting, and though, as in Australia, a different type of dog is preferred, greyhound blood does creep in here and there. Such animals do not often appear as pets, though immigrants from Britain sometimes bring their lurchers with them.

American Working Lurchers

America has a long and magnificent history of settlers and sighthounds, and the descendants of the coursing hounds brought over by the pioneers established a sporting history shared by such prominent men as General Custer, 'Teddy' Roosevelt and Ernest Thompson Seton, all of whom valued the practical as well as the aesthetic uses of good hounds. From the Midwest to California, from North and West Texas to New Mexico, the coursing hounds are still used to hunt jackrabbit, fox, coyote and sometimes wolf. The hounds used are primarily staghounds, which are a distinct type that has its origins in borzoi, deerhound, wolfhound and greyhound crosses, sometimes with a dash of a good scent-hunting hound. They are quite different from the English staghound, which is a larger type of foxhound, and hunts by scent. American hunters use what they term cold-blooded greyhounds, which are unpapered (unregistered) greyhounds with maybe a dash of something else a long way back, as well as greyhounds which are registered and bred originally for racing (often called hot-blooded greyhounds) and crossbreds of these, with additions of borzoi and deerhound blood. Saluki influence is gaining as well, both with purebred and crossbred hounds, their legendary toughness, stamina, and inbred ability to take heat, cold and rough terrain in their long loping stride, gaining them fans all the time. Dutch Salmon in his book *Gazehounds and Coursing** writes of using an Afghan hound as an experiment: she shed umpteen generations of show breeding to give an excellent example of what her ancestors had been used for, coursing with great courage and verve.

American quarry requires exceptional hounds, whether matching the extraordinary speed and endurance of the jackrabbit, which is a type of hare, or the cunning, speed and stamina of the coyote, with a bold dog needed at the end to bowl it over and hold or kill it. American terrain is hard as well, and it takes the cream of the crop to course this land, where mere humans need a horse or a vehicle to keep up. Thus the hounds are traditionally worked in twos and threes (the British would say in braces or leashes) of hounds with differing strengths: the greyhounds to burn off the initial speed of the quarry, the saluki types to then take over and work, seemingly tirelessly, when the sprinters have done their job, and then the crossbreds to effect the catch and,

---

*M. H. Dutch Salmon *Gazehounds and Coursing* published originally 1977 revised 1999 High-Lonesome Books, P.O. Box 878, Silver City, New Mexico 88062

where appropriate, the kill. The result is hounds of immense toughness, agility and power, thoroughly field-tested, sound and strong. There is a saying among British running dog owners that working a dog to see how good it is, is one thing, but the true test is working it until you find out how bad it is. This means testing a hound thoroughly until it reveals any flaws in its makeup. Certainly, the big coursing hounds in America are tested on hard ground and hard quarry, and are splendid examples of their ilk.

So where does this leave the pet owner? The position is interesting. Large coursing hounds that are bred for work tend to go to working homes, and there is not a great deal of this type of animal available to pet homes, nor, it has to be said, are there a great many pet owners who would countenance such a creature, which needs to be confined when not under direct supervision, trained with care, and exercised well. Some undoubtedly do come up in the dog rescue homes, but their initial purpose tends to put people off, and I have read instructions from several of these homes in the USA that coursing hounds should always be muzzled when being exercised, lest they suddenly decide to slaughter another dog. Because lurchers are not as extrovert and grovelling as some breeds of dog, their self-contained natures can be misread, but it is very unusual indeed for a lurcher to display antipathy to another dog, even if that other dog becomes overbearing. They will stick up for themselves if they have to, but very seldom, no matter what quarry they have worked, will they take the fight to another dog. Where instances have occurred, it is usually because owners have ignored warning signs that have been in evidence for some time. However, my contacts in America advise me that some strains of staghound are distinctly touchy, best kennelled alone, and well supervised when with other dogs.

Though working lurchers do not often come up for rehoming in the USA, retired racing greyhounds, by contrast, are available in quantity, as they are here. Most pet owners who want the larger type of gazehound go straight for the purebred saluki, borzoi, wolfhound and so on. Because there is no tradition of the running dog/working dog cross in America – there is no job there for this type of hound – the middle-sized hounds that make up the most part of British lurcher breeding simply do not exist. Of the smallest size, again, people tend to have whippets and Italian greyhounds, rather than the plethora of small rabbiting dogs that are available in UK. However, some breeders with an eye to a gap in the market have created an appealing little lurcher type known as 'silken windhounds'.

The origins of this type are very controversial. They are purportedly from a strain of long-haired whippet, the existence of which is vigorously denied by whippet breeders. Genetically, long, rough or broken coats are recessive. The creators of the so-called long-haired whippet argue that, until the nineteenth century, whippets appeared in long and short coated versions, and that all they had to do was assemble a breeding nucleus of whippets with this recessive gene, put them together and breed on from the long-coated pups. However, this is stretching genetics a little. It is true enough that, two hundred years ago, greyhounds and whippets could have broken (not long) or smooth coats, and breeding was rather more flexible than nowadays, but those broken coats came from outcrosses, just as they do in lurchers today. The original Rules of the Swaffham Coursing Club, the oldest in the country, specify that no rough-coated dog is to be allowed to course, so that distinction was well established even in the sixteenth century. Greyhounds and whippets in the UK are still bred for performance, and as the smooth-coated ones were faster than the broken-coated ones, the broken coats were bred out long ago. Neither whippet nor greyhound has thrown back to a properly broken coat in hundreds of years, though occasionally a greyhound with a slightly hairy tail will appear. This is so slight that it could not even be called feathering, and is hardly noticeable; nevertheless it exists. Long coats, however, are a quite different issue, and it is worth noting that the American long-haired whippets first appeared at a kennels that also bred borzois. Knowing how a bitch can hold service to more than one dog, and observing that 'nothing propines like propinquity', it could be that, although the breeder remains convinced that the whippets were purebred, at least one of the hounds knew differently.

Breeders of the silkens are quite open about having crossbred the whippet with borzois to produce what, in looks, is a miniature borzoi. Some say that other breeds have been used to enhance the coat, and certainly some of these little lurchers do have a look of the Shetland sheepdog about them. It is relatively easy to fix a type in any breed, and British lurcher breeders have been doing this all along, with many sub-types of lurcher being easily recognisable, such as the Hancock, the Norfolk or the Tumbler. The rule is: breed close and cull hard. As far as lurchers are concerned, I would like to add 'test hard' as well, for field-testing quickly shows up any undesirable traits of body or mind. With a small gene pool, even dogs as healthy as sighthounds will throw up a variety of physical and mental faults, and in the early stages of creating and fixing a type, many pups are born which do not conform to the desired type.

Dr Brian Plummer, who created the Plummer terrier, has documented the pitfalls in the creation of his own breed, which is waiting for acceptance by the UK Kennel Club, expected shortly, thus making the transition from type to breed. On the way to achieving this, he has had to breed out all manner of faults, some quite serious, such as cleft palate, hydrocephalus and Legge-Perthe's disease, and in temperament, a vicious, combative tendency that appeared in the 1980s.

The silkens appear to have good temperaments, but are still in the early days regarding appearance, with some very much more miniature-borzoi-like than others. Some physical faults have occurred, and are being rectified by the breeders, though as these little dogs are unlikely to be field tested except for the odd individual, it is doubtful that they will ever achieve the splendid soundness that the average ordinary lurcher owner expects of his or her hounds by right. Except for cottontails (rabbits) it is difficult to know what quarry these silkens could be used on, and it is evident that, although they were created, as one breeder has put it, to fill the gap that exists because there are no long-coated small sighthounds, the silken windhound has been bred for the pet market only. As with other lurchers, they come in all colours, and are a most attractive little hound. Few exist in Europe as yet, where the lurcher type is in any case not common. As with the Middle East and India, purebred indigenous sighthounds exist over much of the European mainland, and are used in preference to imported stock. Being of a useful middle size, and bred for the terrain and the climate, there has never been the need to create a lurcher where the native dog already exists. Equally, there is little tradition of pet dog keeping in such areas, the dog still being viewed very much as a worker. In some European countries where there is a stronger pet-keeping ethos, such as France and Germany, the true use of the sighthound is either limited or illegal. The UK is the cradle of the lurcher type, and we already have a wealth of small and medium variants, so whether the silken windhounds will catch on as pets is unknown, though I have no doubt whatsoever that if they do appear here, some of us will have them out after small game as soon as possible! In the interim, they have certainly filled a niche in America, and will probably become immensely popular.

There is a lot of interest in lure-coursing in the USA, with many competitions for purebred sighthounds which would surely extend their remit to the lurcher if the demand was there, though competitions of which I have been given details are very firmly for pedigreed dogs only at the moment. No doubt the silken windhounds will hold competitive meets, for where two sighthounds meet, there surely must be a race! The British type of lurcher that has a proportion of non-sighthound blood is rarely successful when raced with pure sighthounds and their composites, and the lurcher obedience competitions that are so popular in the UK are unknown elsewhere simply because their various disciplines such as ferreting and longnetting are not part of the American field culture. Although you can create a lurcher wherever the raw materials exist i.e. a running dog and a working dog, outside the plains where fast quarry are hunted, such animals are simply not required. Quarry such as groundhog and coon is more usually hunted with a combination of terrier and gun; larger quarry has a tradition of scenting, baying hounds being used. A few Americans import British lurchers, but the cost is high, and these hounds are imported for working purposes. A few people emigrate to the USA from UK and bring their beloved lurchers with them as part of the family, but apart from the big coursing hounds, the type barely exists otherwise and is certainly not deliberately created on anything like the same scale as it is in its cloudy homelands.

The older dog enjoys shorter walks with stopping places

10 HEALTH AND FIRST AID

L urchers are generally healthy beasts. Not only do they have no inherited diseases or unsoundnesses, the very fact that they are working dogs means that usually only the best are bred from, and the parents are roundly tested in the field. There are, of course, exceptions to this, but you can expect your lurcher to have been bred from good stock. They are easy to rear, the only precautions needed being not to give them too much exercise too young, and not to let them become overweight.

Exercise

Generally, the bigger the dog is likely to grow, the more this applies, so a lot of deerhound or greyhound blood means that you will not be going for long walks until your dog is well into her second year. Saluki and whippet lurchers mature much younger, and will be tearing about with no regard for their own safety at less than a year old. I take mine very steadily until they have reached their second birthdays, after which they get as much exercise as I can give them until they start to slow down at about nine years old; then they tell me how much they want. My old girl of sixteen still manages two one-hour walks most days, provided the going is more or less level, and not too muddy. On wet, cold or windy days, however, she opts to stay indoors except for the odd sortie out for hygienic purposes. Before you panic at the amount of exercise and say that the dog rescue told you (as they mostly do) that two 20-minute lead walks every day would be quite sufficient, don't forget that my dogs are workers and have been kept very fit all their lives. Your dogs will manage through the working week on the nearest you can do to two one-hour walks daily, and they must have free running. The old and the very young will need much less, however. At weekends, you can give your lurcher as much exercise as you like. Greyhounds and whippets are speed not stamina dogs, but the other breeds that are crossed into them to make up the lurcher give them stamina. Salukis have great stamina, and deerhounds are not far behind them, but that is stamina in relation to sighthounds, rather than the stamina of, for instance, herding dogs, which are bred to run up and down hills all day, or

Plenty of free running

foxhounds, which can easily cover 70 miles in a day's hunting. So on days when the weather is vile, and in the depths of winter when daylight is short, your lurcher will cope with less exercise, as long as you can give her more at the weekends. The better a lurcher is exercised, the better her behaviour will be for the rest of the day, and she will settle down quite happily until her next walk.

Sleep

Predators are designed to sleep for long spells, and this sleep is light, easily disturbed, and full of dreams. We have already covered the need for a dog's bed to be warm, draught-free, adequately padded, and in a quiet spot. Sleeping dogs really should be left to lie. Your normally silent dog may yip, bark or howl while she is dreaming, wag her tail, chew with her jaws, or paddle her limbs. All this is perfectly normal. If you do need to wake a sleeping dog – and this applies to all dogs – never do this by touch, for the transition from sleep, especially dreaming sleep, to wakefulness, activates the primitive brain before the rational brain, and the dog may snap before she is fully awake and can remember where she is and who you are.

176

Instead, speak softly and kindly to her, and she will awaken pleasantly and gently.

The Skin

Lurchers have quite delicate skins, and not always a great deal of hair. They do not suffer from skin disorders in the way that, for example, West Highland white terriers or shar-peis can, but they can be sensitive to chemicals, stress and parasites. Avoiding chemical allergies is simple: always rinse floors thoroughly after you have washed them, and make sure that kennel surfaces are quite dry before your dog goes back in there after you have washed them down. Avoid biological detergents if you can; if you really do need to use them, wash the item through a second cycle with no detergent at all, to make sure that it is rinsed absolutely clean. Try not to use synthetic material, which can make your dog miserable if an electric charge builds up. I have to do the same, being very susceptible to static, and the resultant shock is sufficiently nasty to make me sure that I wouldn't want my dog to experience it. I know about static: they don't, and the shock for them would be emotional as well as physical. Some synthetics, such as VetBed, don't seem to build static, and I have never had problems with this. Disinfectants should be animal-friendly, of

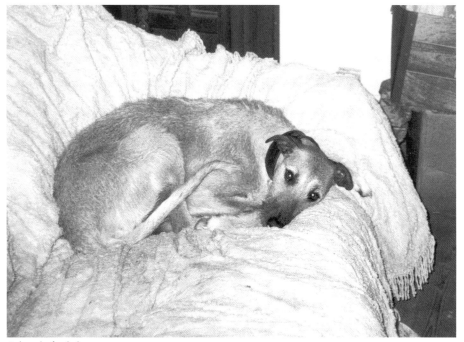

A draught-free bed

which several excellent ones are available. Remember your dog's sensitive nose, and give her quarters ample time to air before she is returned to them.

Mange

Stress brings on a type of mange which is commonly seen in newly-rescued dogs. This is called demodectic mange, and the mite responsible for it is cigar-shaped. This mite lives dormant under the skin of most animals, us included, and usually causes no trouble for a lifetime, but if a dog is severely stressed, the mite will activate, breed, and cause widespread loss of hair, though usually little or no irritation. The cure is to remove the source of stress and boost the animal's general health; unfortunately, most kennels treat this condition with strong chemical washes, which have exactly the opposite effect. The mite is passed from bitch to pups, and some bitches will develop demodectic mange with every litter that they whelp, the condition clearing up spontaneously when the bitch finishes suckling the pups. Just to really confuse the issue, hormone changes may also cause a suckling bitch to lose her hair. Demodectic mange cannot be passed from one dog to another except in the bitch/pups situation, where the transfer takes place in the first few days of separate life. Nor can it be passed from a dog to us, or any other animal. Fox mange, or sarcoptic mange, by contrast, is caused by an oval-shaped mite, and is readily passed from one animal to another, or to us, in which case it is called scabies. The mite will only cause problems in people whose immune systems are below par, and usually clears itself up, but it really does itch, and scratching the irritation can cause skin infections. A dab of neat lavender or tea tree oil directly on to irritated areas is usually sufficient to clear it up in humans, and is much safer than using corticosteroid creams.

A dog with sarcoptic mange is very itchy, and can lose a lot of hair, the skin beneath sometimes being so affected that it is grey and crusted. From that state, it is prone to further infection from lesions caused by scratching. There is a characteristic unpleasantly musty smell, the dog suffers severe irritation that is exacerbated by warmth or handling, and is acutely miserable. Left untreated, sarcoptic mange will kill; nor is it straightforward to treat. Foxes with advanced mange can be seen in some areas, especially where there is overcrowding, and they can lose all their hair, dying slowly of cold, starvation, and infection. Dogs that frequent areas where these foxes lie up can be at risk also. Customary veterinary treatment for sarcoptic mange involves bathing the animal in harsh insecticidal chemicals, for rather like the human head louse, the mange mites are tough and resistant. A few vets still prescribe organophosphate washes, which carry considerable risks both to the animal and the human treating her; after you have read the instructions on the bottle, you may prefer not to use these substances. Some vets will inject ivermectin, which is authorised for use on farm stock but not for dogs. The reason is that ivermectin has been known to kill certain types of dog and is particularly risky with collies and huskies. Your dog is unlikely to have any husky blood, but many lurchers have collie in them, even if a few generations back, and it would be a sad day if yours was one of the dogs that died as a result of using this.

Because the conventional mange treatments are so harsh, they damage the immune system and the major eliminatory organs; once the immune system is damaged, the mange will return. To illustrate the importance of the immune system in combating either type of mange, I offer my own experiences with working dogs that regularly catch foxes with mange. Because my dogs are fed a rawfood diet and kept very fit, they do not catch mange from the foxes. When they need medication, they are treated by a homoeopathic vet and so their systems are not damaged by over-use of drugs. This is not to say that I am opposed to the use of drugs, for there are times when they can do great good and are entirely appropriate. I am, however, opposed to the unnecessary use of drugs, and so avoid them whenever I can. If you acquire a dog with mange, or she develops it while in your care, the first stage of treatment is to establish which form of mange it is, which is achieved by the vet taking a skin scrape. If demodectic, then the dog's immune system needs to be boosted, and her general health improved. If sarcoptic, then as well as those two actions, the mange mite needs to be tackled. The best and safest way to do either is in my opinion by homoeopathy. A properly qualified homoeopathic vet (as opposed to a regular vet who has completed a weekend course) has an arsenal of treatments at his or her fingertips. Homoeopathy treats the whole animal, not just the symptoms, and each patient is seen as an individual, so the treatment for one may not be the treatment that is best for another. This is why the vet must see your dog and examine her. If your dog has had a close encounter with a mangy fox and has developed a few ominous patches around her mouth but not yet full-blown mange, then a dab of neat lavender or tea tree oil on the patches can stop anything developing. Anything more dramatic needs proper veterinary treatment. Though demodectic mange looks awful, and sarcoptic mange has the potential to become nasty, the right treatment can deal with it most successfully. A diet that includes plenty of raw fruit and vegetables will boost your dog's immune system while she is being treated; if the dog of your dreams is in the rescue kennels and they want her to stay there and be conventionally treated, try to persuade them at least to add an apple a day to her dried food diet. Dogs know what they need, and I recently saw a bitch with obvious demodectic mange which had been treated with chemical baths, pathetically trying to graze on the one tuft of grass that remained in the kennel yard.

Eczemas and Allergies

You will not find many lurchers suffering from these, but there is the odd one. Skin problems divide broadly into two categories: something on the outside trying to get in, or something inside that is trying to get out. The skin is the biggest organ in the body, and acts as a barrier and an eliminatory vehicle. Therefore, toxins which challenge the skin manifest themselves as eczemas and allergies. Internal problems are most usually food-related, and a simple change of diet can help enormously. Some dog food manufacturers even include a hypo-allergenic range of products. Common sensitising substances can be wheat gluten, maize, rape, soya, dairy products, chicken and turkey. Rice, fish and lamb are generally considered to be the least likely to cause allergies. Dyes, additives and even packaging can cause allergies in some animals. Holistic vets encourage a complete changeover to fresh foods, with a lot of pulverised fruit and vegetables, which often effects a complete cure.

Worms

Parasites can cause skin reactions: the protective mucus on internal worms can create sufficient toxins to cause problems, and on the outside, some dogs are sensitive to flea bites. Regular worming – three or four times a year – with a wormer such as Drontal-Plus, which tackles tape and roundworms, is essential. Good heavens, I hear you say, she is not advocating a natural product! This is because dogs and worms are designed to live in symbiosis, and therefore natural wormers are either so harsh as to be capable of damaging the dog (as in areca nut, tobacco or wormwood) or else only capable of removing part of the problem (for instance garlic and couchgrass). If a dog is fed garlic and fresh fruit, vegetables and herbs on a regular basis, she will develop resistance to worms but not eliminate them completely. In the season, she may choose to eat common hogweed, cleavers and various grasses, which will help her, but if you want your dog free from worms, you will have to use chemicals. There is anecdotal information that aloe vera given on a daily basis will eliminate worms, but I have no personal experience of just how good it is, which would have to be confirmed by a faecal worm count. Equally, I am told that half a dozen pumpkin seeds daily will create a sufficiently hostile intestinal environment that worms will be deterred. These are cheap and easy to feed, and I often give them to my own dogs, but I also worm them with chemicals three times every year.

There are two types of worm common to dogs in this country: tapeworms and roundworms, of which there are several sorts. Less common are various sorts of worm that live in the vital organs, such as heartworm, and hookworms that infest the pads. Now that dogs are travelling more freely to other countries, they are bringing back more parasites, so no doubt we will be seeing a greater variety before long. If your dog becomes out of sorts after a trip abroad, be sure to inform your vet that she has been away, and where, in case she has brought back a parasite with which the vet may be unfamiliar. Better still, leave your dog in the care of someone you trust, and go abroad without her.

As the name implies, roundworms are round, like earthworms, and tapeworms are flat and made up of segments. Sometimes you will see tapeworm segments wiggling around the anus of an infested animal; each segment is full of eggs so do not touch with a bare hand! Tapeworms need to go through the system of a carnivore and a herbivore to complete their life cycle, and some forms of tapeworm arrive vectored by courtesy of fleas. You may see no sign of roundworms in your dog, or she may pass or vomit some if she is carrying a significant worm burden. Dogs with a few worms may look quite well, but a heavy worm count will cause the dog to be hidebound – the skin tight on the body – pot-bellied but lean, with a dull coat. Appetite can be ravenous, but with a very big worm burden, the dog may seem to have little appetite, and vomit if she eats a normal-sized meal. If you have taken in a rescue, it is to be hoped that she has already been wormed before she came to you, but you will need to continue the work by worming her out a little more often than normal for the first year, perhaps every two months, but liaise with your vet. Always use wormers from a veterinary outlet, as the ones that you buy from the pet shops are not man enough for the job, and will not get rid of all the worms. Wormers should not be given in the same week as flea treatments or vaccinations, as all of these put an appreciable burden on the dog's immune system, and it is better for her if she has the chance to recover before the next barrage of chemicals. It might be more convenient for you but it is not good for your dog to have her system challenged like that. All animals get worms and there is no avoiding them, so be diligent with your worming programme and the situation will never get out of hand.

Fleas

Similarly, you can repel some fleas with a combination of natural feeding as above, plus the addition of brewer's yeast tablets to the food, but your dog will still get a proportion of fleas which in a bad year will necessitate the use of a chemical product. There are aromatic oils that will repel fleas, but take it from me, they don't repel them all, and lavender oil will actually kill them. I make up a potion in a vegetable gel base, which combines therapeutic quality lavender, yarrow and rosemary, and comb it into the hair with a fine-toothed comb, and you can see the fleas struggling out of the coat as soon as

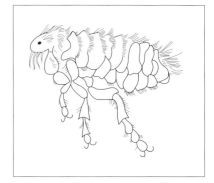

Flea

you start to apply it, from whence they are dumped without ceremony in a bowl of hot water. Even combing through using a comb dipped in warm water to which a few drops of lavender oil have been added will cause an appreciable flea exodus. I do not personally recommend the herbal flea collars and bandannas, having found them ineffective, and also I wonder on the humane aspect of having strong smells permanently on an animal which has such a terrific sense of smell as a dog.

Sometimes, about once every two years on average, we are driven to using a commercial, chemical flea killer, of which there is a wide choice. We use Frontline, which at the time of writing is considered to be safe enough to use on tiny puppies and kittens. I will not use any flea killer that involves the flea having to bite the dog before it dies, or anything that is added to the dog's food. I will not use organophosphates, or any substance that requires me to use protective clothing, not touch my dog after treatment, keep her in a separate room or away from naked flame! That is the best that I can do; for yourself, I suggest that you read and ask around as widely as possible, and make your decision based on the information that you receive, bearing in mind that the producers of chemical treatments will not be unbiased in their advice. Make your decision on what is healthy for your dog rather than what is easy and cheap for you, or easy and a good earner for your vet. Some dogs are very sensitive to flea bites, and so it is best in such cases to tackle the problem right at the start of the flea season (March to October) and to remember that if you use a product where the fleas have to bite the dog before they are killed, you are still going to get the flea allergy, because the dog is still having the flea saliva, which is the allergen, injected with each bite. Much is made of houses needing to be de-fleaed as well, and central heating and carpets being the culprits, but I can assure you that I have never seen a rabbit warren with either, and there are always plenty of fleas in those! Vigorous vacuuming with a powerful cleaner that is then emptied straight afterwards will help to avoid establishing indoor colonies, but the fleas come from outside as well, and every time your dog goes outside, she will come back with some more little pets. It might surprise you to know that dog fleas are quite rare, and the fleas that your dog suffers from are much more likely to be cat fleas. Cats are huge reservoirs of fleas, so if you have a cat as well, de-flea her with as much dedication and frequency as you treat your dog. Wash animal bedding on a hot cycle, and hang it out to air on sunny or windy days. Are you scratching yet? There is more to come!

Ticks

Ticks come from the spider family, and before they latch on to an animal and feed, they look like tiny spiders. They are surprisingly hard to kill at that stage as well. Once a tick finds a host, it buries its head under the skin and sucks blood, and its exposed abdomen inflates to the size of a small pea. Removal is easy and does not require the services of a vet: the tick breathes through its abdomen, so you simply cut off the supply by anointing it with something like butter, margarine, nail varnish, petroleum jelly or similar – we often use typewriter correction fluid, which has the added advantage of painting the tick white so you can find it afterwards as well! After five or ten minutes, the tick will usually back out, or at least loosen its grip so that it can be grasped and pulled out. An alternative is to dab on some sort of alcohol-based fluid – methylated spirits, after-shave, even vodka or gin if that is to hand, or else neat tea-tree or lavender oil, which will usually have an instant loosening effect. Do not, however, take any notice of people who recommend applying the lighted end of a cigarette to the tick – while it undoubtedly works, you

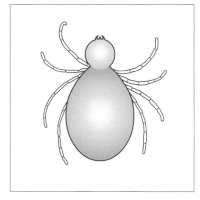

Tick before engorgement clearly showing membership of spider family

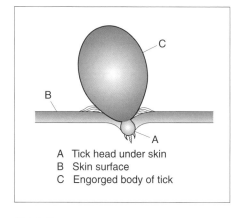

A Tick head under skin
B Skin surface
C Engorged body of tick

Tick feeding

183

need a steady hand and an animal that keeps absolutely still; most won't, when they feel the heat. Use one of the safer ways described here – after all, a bit of butter on the skin is not going to upset even the tiniest puppy.

When you grip the tick, do not squeeze the swollen abdomen, but grasp it between your nails as close to the skin as you can, give a quarter turn anti-clockwise (because they screw themselves in) and pull sharply. Then make sure that you kill it. Now brace yourselves for an enduring myth! Received wisdom ensures that many people who have never removed a tick in their lives will tell you that if the mouthparts of the tick are left in the body, there will be a terrible abscess, the mouthparts will have to be surgically removed, the animal will become dreadfully ill and it is all your fault for being an irresponsible owner. This is utter nonsense. I have been involved with rescued animals for many years, and have removed countless ticks from a great assortment of creatures, and there is only ever an abscess problem if the animal is already very ill. This quite often is the case with the ferrets that I take in, which are so covered in ticks that they resemble miniature armadillos, and are starving and dehydrated. In such a case, I simply dab the site of the tick with a drop of – you've guessed it – lavender or tea tree oil, and no further problem arises. However, a healthy dog, cat, ferret or whatever does not suffer if a tick's head is left under the skin – bodies just aren't that incompetent. What happens is that a tiny bump forms with a scab at the top, which you must leave alone – no picking or fiddling! – and in the scab are the mouth parts. When the scab drops off, the foreign matter has gone, expertly eliminated by that marvellous organ the skin. So do not panic if you do not get the tick's mouth out, because the dog can deal with it quite competently.

Ear Mites

If your dog starts to show that her ears are irritating her, ear mites could be the cause. These are very common, and extremely uncomfortable. There are several ear washes that you can get from your vet, or if you prefer, you can put a little olive oil with a few drops of lavender oil in, or some Thornit powder, which is marvellous for ear problems, or aloe vera gel. It is a good idea to get your dog checked for ear mites at her annual veterinary inspection.

Other Ear Problems

Ear mites irritate, but foreign bodies in ears really hurt, so if your dog cries and flinches when her ear is touched, or carries her head lopsided, expect a grass seed or similar in the ear, and get her to the vet. She will have to be lightly sedated while the offending material is extracted. Surprisingly large foreign objects can get into ears: one of my dogs once had a whole seed head in his ear. Keep dogs out of fields with crops in – as well as being considerate to the farmer, it is safer for the dog – and don't forget that hay is a crop as well. The flowering grass heads can be inhaled, get into ears or work right up between toes, and will cause a lot of distress.

Hormones

Skin problems can also be due to hormonal changes such as season, pregnancy or suckling in the bitch, neutering too young, which is rather a hot potato at the moment with some large animal rescue organisations neutering whelps that are still with the bitch, or a slight malfunction in the endocrine system. Even a neutered bitch can experience hormonal changes at the time when she would have had her season, as the sex hormones are made in small quantities in other areas than the ovaries, and the testes in the male. Lurchers in any case are seldom high in reproductive hormones even when entire, some bitches not coming into season for several years at a time. So you can see how important it is to get a correct diagnosis of any skin problem before commencing treatment, rather than going for the obvious and throwing chemicals at the problem which in some cases will make it very much worse. This is why homoeopathy has such good results with skin problems, because the whole animal has been treated, and why, by contrast, the application of steroid creams may result in an immediate improvement because the immune system which is trying to heal its dog is then suppressed, but ultimately and almost without exception, makes the situation much worse. A change in diet to fresh food, and a bit of attention to what is used to wash and clean doggy areas and accessories will improve most skin conditions right away, but in more complex cases, an accurate diagnosis is vital. I prefer to use homoeopathic medicines in tincture form on animals, because then the medication can be dripped onto the nose, from where it is licked off. It is important not to handle homoeopathic medication, so if you are giving tablets, tip out the required number into a sterile teaspoon, crush with the back of another, and then tip the fragmented tablets into the dog's mouth. Not all treatments work for all dogs, so be prepared to give a fair trial to whatever you use – at least a month – and if that is not the one, then back to your vet to try another.

Be sure to give homoeopathic medication correctly, on its own, with nothing in the mouth for twenty minutes before and afterwards: so often I hear homoeopathy dismissed with 'it didn't work' when the medication has either not been correctly given, or has not had long enough to prove itself. Homoeopathy works with the body's immune system, and heals 'from within to without, and from above to below' which can give the impression of the illness on occasion appearing to get worse before it gets better. This is called a 'healing crisis' and is perfectly correct, though sometimes a little dramatic. With conventional medicine, we are used to seeing symptoms treated rather than causes, and so a rapid improvement is what appears to result, but which is really just a 'papering over the cracks' of the underlying illness. By contrast, holistic healing takes longer, because it is stimulating the body's own defences rather than suppressing them. One of the statements I hear from time to time is that, 'the treatment didn't help, but it sort of got better on its own'. Well, yes, precisely, and that is how holistic treatments work. Whether you elect to use allopathic (conventional) medication, holistic treatment or both, remember a quote that came my way from a very old herbalist: 'When a treatment does not succeed, a good doctor changes the medicine: a bad doctor doubles the dose'.

Other Parasites

There is a variety of mites that your dog may encounter at certain times of year, so if you see a skin condition starting to develop, give your dog a good going-over with a flea-comb, and see if you can find anything. Usually mites will disperse with nothing more exacting than a comb-through with a few drops of lavender oil in water, or a bath with tea tree shampoo. Harvest mites in particular can cause very irritable paws, which feel more comfortable from being dipped in either salt water or water with a few drops of lavender oil added. They seldom stay for long, but susceptible dogs can find them very itchy. Irritable paws can also be caused by nettle stings, and again are easily soothed with a footbath. Please be very careful with the use of aromatic oils: I often find people who think if two drops is good, twenty must be better, and this is not a good idea at all. For instance, tea tree oil is extremely strong, and should only be used very sparingly and infrequently, for specific problems and not as a preventative.

General Grooming

Lurchers do not need professional grooming or stripping. Even those with a comparatively thick coat will give up dead hair readily at moulting time simply with regular brushing and a weekly going-through with a fine-toothed comb. As they are not bred for exaggerated hair growth, the hair that you see on the paws and ears is there for protection and should be left in situ. Nor do they need bathing, for they are naturally sweet-smelling; if a lurcher begins to smell musty or mousy, that is the skin telling you that there is an internal problem. If perchance your lurcher rolls in something that is delectable to her nose and unspeakably vile to yours, then it is better just to bathe the affected area. My American friends tell me that pure tomato juice is an excellent remover of skunk smell, and it certainly works for a dog that has rolled in fox or badger muck. Wearing rubber gloves, work the tomato juice right into the coat and then shampoo out with a mild shampoo designed for dogs or babies. Fortunately, most lurchers are far too dignified to roll in muck on a regular basis – each one of mine has done it once or twice in their entire life – as opposed to our terrier, who indulges on every possible occasion. Most lurchers have non-stick coats, from which mud is easily brushed off, and the clingier slurry from the bottom of ponds rinses out without too much difficulty. Any residue comes off easily on the furniture, I find.

Cuts and Tears

Lurchers are thin-skinned, and can be in trouble if they hit barbed wire or dumped rubbish. Most working dogs have spectacular scars, but a pet dog need not encounter these hazards if the owner is careful. Sadly, it seems to be impossible to stop people dumping rubbish, so it is best to avoid areas that you cannot see properly, such as thick undergrowth, and keep right away from places where you know there has been fly-tipping. If your dog is likely to encounter barbed wire, then it is best that she understands its qualities before she attempts to go between the strands at speed, so take her to wire fences where they cross the footpath; you go over the stile and take her carefully through the fence. Do not trespass! Sometimes old strands of barbed wire remain from defunct fences, or are hidden in hedges, so always be on the alert for it. Also be careful with ponds and brooks, because there is a certain sort of person who finds dumping rubbish in water to be irresistible, and such rubbish is often of the broken glass or metal type. If your dog does cut herself, a small nick will heal readily without any help, though you could, if you wanted, rinse it out with salt water or a few drops of lavender oil in water. If your dog is long-coated, carefully clip the hair away from the region of the wound. Let her lick the injury, for dog saliva is a great healer, even mentioned in the Bible when the dogs came to lick the beggar's sores. For large tears, which can look terrible, use your own judgement: would you go to a doctor if that injury was on you? If you are at all uneasy, go to the vet, but take comfort in that most cuts and tears look a lot worse than they really are, and will heal with a minimum of interference. Quite often, they are impossible to stitch, and your vet will simply provide some antibiotics and tell you to keep the injury clean. First aid for deep injuries is to sluice out with water, salt water or the lavender

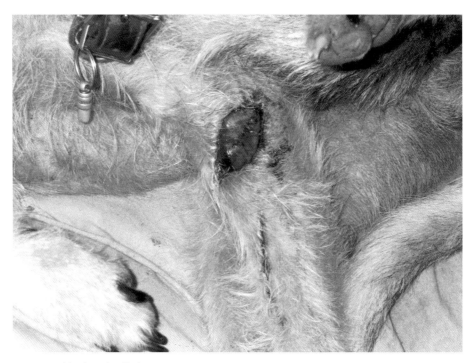

Injury caused by dumped rubbish…

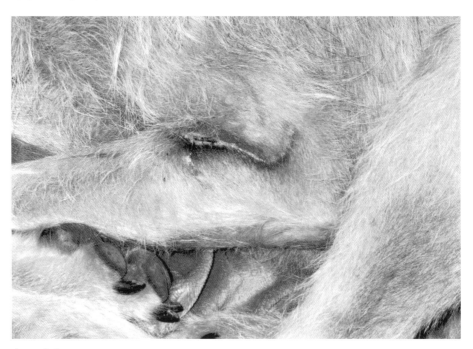

three weeks later

in water, clip the hair clear of the injury if you can, then off to the vet. Do not put any dressing on the injury, nor any substance such as purple spray, because your vet needs to see that it is properly clean, and dressings will stick, ointments and sprays need to be cleaned off, and it all makes for unnecessary hassle for dog and vet. It is perfectly legal for you to treat your own dogs, and I do mine for all but the severest injuries, but you must not cause 'unnecessary suffering' which can be rather fluid in interpretation. So, if you are happy with your level of competence in dealing with everyday injuries, then continue, but if in doubt, take your dog to the vet. There are some injuries which are always better dealt with in the surgery, such as snakebite, fractures and eye injuries, and foreign bodies in ears.

Shock

Shock after an accident is one of the biggest killers of humans and animals alike. While you are waiting for or en route to the vet, keep the animal warmly wrapped up, but do not give anything to eat or drink, not even the traditional reviver, the sip of brandy. In shock, the dog's eyes might be rolled back, or the third eyelid that comes across the eye from inner to outer corner, might be visible, the gums may be pale or blueish, the corners of the mouth turned back to expose the lining, and the dog might be deathly still or shivering uncontrollably. If you have to move the animal, get a blanket under her and carry or drag her in that. Homoeopathic arnica administered at ten-minute intervals while you wait is very helpful, as is Bach Rescue Remedy, and neither of these will interfere with any subsequent treatment. You too are likely to be suffering from shock if you have just seen your dog badly hurt, so get some down yourself as well. Above all, once you have committed your dog to veterinary care, do be careful with driving yourself home. We cope with emergencies and then the shock sets in with us: your dog needs you to nurse her when she comes back from treatment, and you must take care of yourself as well.

Feet

Second-hand lurchers often have some sort of foot injury, which may have caused their retirement from work but will hardly affect them in a pet environment. Splayed toes or a flattened profile to the paw denote tendon injuries, and quite often the nails have been knocked slightly askew. Your dog will still be able to run and play, and have good quality of life. Sometimes toe injuries are such that the toes are amputated; if this has happened before you acquired your lurcher then there is nothing to be done, but some vets are a bit quick to whip toes off when they are injured, so if this is an option offered to you when your dog injures a toe, try everything else before you agree to the removal of the toe. Even a badly injured toe can mend to a surprising degree, and the dog is always better for having a full complement of toes. Once they are gone, the remaining toes have to do extra work, and can result in shoulder and hip problems later on, because of the altered angles of use. A perfect foot will not need its nails trimming because they will wear naturally, but as the dog ages or the foot sustains injuries, so the nails will have to be attended to by you as they will no longer strike the ground at the right angles. Nails should be kept sufficiently short that they do not push the toe up and out of alignment, but not cut right back to the quick, which prevents their use as 'football studs' when the dog is running and especially cornering. If your dog has her dew claws left on, then these need trimming as well, because they only touch the ground on a fast turn. Always use the 'guillotine' style of clipper, not the ones that are like the human nail-clipper, and which can crush the nail rather than slice through it cleanly. Some lurchers have very strong, thick nails which take a strong hand to cut them. In a white nail, the correct length is easily seen because the pink quick is quite visible, but a black nail does not show this. The best modus operandi with black nails is to trim them back by small degrees each week until you reach a good working length. The week's grace between trimming allows the quick to shrink back from the nail tip. When you are getting near to what you judge to be the live area, half-closing the clippers will give the dog a chance to flinch and so tell you that you are too close before you do any damage. Some lurchers, however, flinch and cringe as soon as they see the clippers! If the worst happens, bathe the foot in salt water, which will stop the bleeding. Apologise profusely to the dog. It is the least that you can do.

Interdigital Cysts

These are first noticed when a dog starts niggling at her paw, or walking lopsided, and are small semi-transparent fluid-filled lumps between the toes. They are almost always the body's reaction to penetration from a thorn, grass seed or similar. Your vet will treat these, but if you prefer natural methods, tubbing the foot several times daily with salt water as warm as the dog will stand usually sorts cysts out within a few days, and if, like me, you are a homoeopathy user, then silica will push out the foreign body if it still in there. Continue the tubbing after the cyst has opened, to remove all the matter, and give echinacea for five days while it heals. If at all in doubt, do go to your vet, though.

Cut Pads

Pads have a rich blood supply, and bleed alarmingly when cut. The injury is quite a common one, and can be exasperating to treat because of the difficulty of keeping the dressing dry. You can buy special boots to put over the injured foot when taking the dog outside to empty herself, but these will not stay on through any kind of real exercise. Unfortunately, a dog with a cut pad has the other three legs still raring to go, and may not take kindly to being confined until the foot heals. Most vets like to bandage the injury completely, and check it on a weekly basis, along with a course of antibiotics, which system works well. I like a wound to be open to the air if possible, so I only bandage while the dog goes out, or else put the little boot on. This works well, too, but I'd suggest that unless you are very confident of what you are doing, you follow your vet's system rather than mine. If you have access to a homoeopathic vet you have the best of both worlds, for there are very effective homoeopathic remedies for dealing with wounds of all sorts.

Healing

Let us look briefly at what happens when a wound heals. Initially, the wound should be cleaned, but over-vigorous cleaning can have a detrimental effect. For instance, strong disinfectants can kill off the tissue at the edges of the wound, which will delay healing, and too vigorous washing might drive dirt into the wound instead of flushing it out. Salt water is a safe and effective first aid for any wound, after which the dog's natural immunity should take over. If the wound is deep, warm salt water can be gently syringed into it. If unstitched, which all but the worst wounds should be, the inside begins to granulate while the surface remains open. Across this open surface, a very pale yellow sticky liquid will form. This is normal and correct. The dog, left to her own devices, will lick at the wound, which is also normal and correct – it is most unusual to find a dog that worries at a wound to the point of damaging it. The injury itself must heal from the inside to the outside, because if the top scabs over, it may trap bacteria within, and start an infection; the dog's licking therefore helps to keep the wound open. The skin at the wound surface may die back, and the dog will nibble it off: don't panic as this is again quite normal. It is quite amazing how quickly a healthy dog can heal, if the wound is sensibly treated. A stitched and bandaged wound, however, may have dirt and bacteria trapped within, which necessitates a precautionary course of antibiotics. Antibiotics kill good bacteria as well as bad, it can't be helped, so if this is how your dog's wound has been treated, give her a tablespoonful of natural yoghurt in her food until the antibiotics have all been taken. This will at least maintain the 'good' bacteria in her intestines, the 'intestinal flora' and save her getting an upset stomach, which is a frequent side-effect of antibiotics. Stitched wounds itch like mad, and many dogs worry at them constantly, some taking the stitches out.

The 'lampshade' type of head cover that prevents dogs chewing at their wounds is not suitable for most lurchers and terrifies some; there is a much more humane arrangement that consists of a thick wide collar reaching from jaw to chest, which should be obtainable from your vet, or is easily made if not. It is rather like a horse's anti-cribbing device. Best, in my opinion, is to leave the wound unstitched and unbandaged, but some vets won't have that at all. However, I include some photographs of the stages of a wound healing which was monitored and approved by my own vet: the dog received no antibiotics but had homoeopathic treatment, and healed beautifully, as they always do. What if dirt that you cannot see gets into the wound? You will be surprised at how efficiently the body deals with this. As long as the wound surface stays open, the healing tissue will carry any dirt to the surface and seal it into the scab. When the scab drops off, so any dirt is ejected.

Stopper Pads

At the back of each forefoot, in line with the wrist, is a fat pad known as a 'stopper pad'. These pads aid braking, especially at extreme angles, and consequently get grazed as often as a small boy's knees. Sometimes these pads can sustain quite a bit of damage, or even slice through, and believe me, they bleed! All dogs have stopper pads, but the running dog gives hers much more work than a slower animal. If she is a rescue, she might even have one or both pads missing through accident. Unless the injury is dramatic, stopper pads need no more than bathing in salt water – much kinder than disinfectant – if they get grazed, and they heal very quickly.

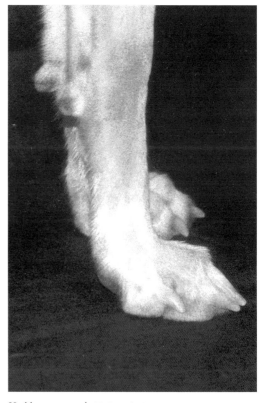

Healthy stopper pads (E. Dearden)

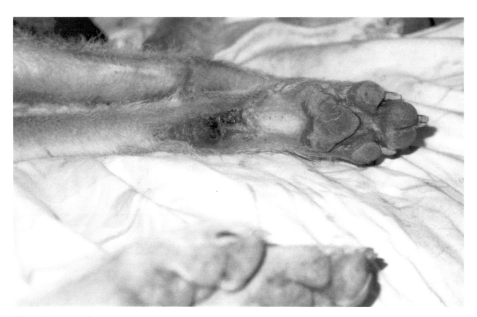

Typical stopper pad injury

Cruciate Ligament

A damaged cruciate ligament can happen to any dog, and is a fairly serious injury. The cruciate ligament holds the stifle joint in place on the hindleg, and is so called because it crosses at the joint. The dog will be very lame, and in a lot of pain. There are several options for treatment, all of which rely on stabilising the joint until it can adjust, because the ligament does not regenerate, and a dog with damage to the cruciate will never be completely sound again, though she will still have good mobility and quality of life. One option is surgery, which effects a temporary repair lasting three or four months, by which time the joint will have strengthened; another is an injection into the joint, or you can try homoeopathy and acupuncture which is what I used on one of my bitches. This was very successful, and avoided the use of anaesthetic, which is always a risk with any animal and more so with running dogs because they carry so little body fat in comparison with other breeds. A careful rehabilitation programme is necessary after a cruciate injury, with very short, frequent exercise periods. The other hindleg will take a lot of stress during this time, and the other cruciate ligament may be at risk. Also, I found with my bitch that the diagonally opposite foreleg sustained a lot of wear. She snapped her cruciate at eight years old, and is now twelve, still able to run and go for long walks, but she has to have a top-up acupuncture treatment about twice a year, and takes a nutritional supplement for her joints.

Tails

Lurchers have very long tails, which they need for cornering at speed, and being generally happy dogs, they wag their tails a lot. Their tails are thin-skinned, unlike, for instance, Labrador tails, and can be injured by enthusiastic wagging against walls, kennel sides or furniture; in addition, a lurcher can clear a coffee table with a swipe of her rudder, and scald her tail. Tails have been caught in doors and car boots, sometimes broken, sometimes sliced right off. This is nearly as terrible an injury as losing a leg to a running dog. Prevention is a big issue here: always be aware of that long tail before you shut a door, especially a car door, and if you have just come home, greet your dog somewhere that gives her enough room to wag without slamming her tail into a hard surface. Don't make her happy anywhere near the coffee table! But what if, despite your best efforts, she has injured her tail?

Tails bleed desperately when the skin is broken, and are almost impossible to bandage successfully. If the tail has been sliced off or broken, you may have no choice but to agree to an operation which shortens it further. If, however, the tail has an injury that has ulcerated or otherwise become infected, there is quite a lot you can do before an amputation becomes inevitable. If you have access to a holistic vet, you are streets ahead, because there is a lot in the

Failed tail amputation showing swollen infected tip and protruding bone

After homoeopathic treatment, bone expelled, tailtip still showing slight infection

Healing well

world of natural medicine that can help an injured tail. I was recently involved in a case where a friend's dog had injured her tail-end, and the vet had elected to amputate. The amputation did not heal, and so more tail was taken. When this refused to heal, despite quantities of antibiotics and the best of care, it was proposed to remove the remainder of the tail, at which point I was contacted because, as the owner said, the treatment had failed twice and what was to stop it failing a third time?

Put in touch with an excellent holistic vet, the treatment took a radical change. It was explained that normally the initial amputation is successful, but with a skinny lurcher tail, the risks are increased. As there was a protruding vertebra at the end of the tail now, and swelling indicative of infection, the vet did not propose to operate for two weeks, because as it stood, he would have to take four inches off the remaining tail, but if the infection could be cleared up first, he could probably reduce that to two inches. A full general health check of the dog was given, because in holistic medicine, the whole animal is treated and not just the affected part. She was then taken off the antibiotics as she had been given quite enough and her digestion was suffering, which of course was going to affect her powers of recuperation. The owner was told to bathe the tail in warm salt water for a full five minutes twice daily, and in addition give homoeopathic silica; the operation was booked for a fortnight hence. The style of the operation would be slightly different in that, instead of cutting between two vertebra, the cut would be through one of the vertebra, which would stimulate healing again. After a fortnight, the dog was brought in for her pre-surgery inspection: the silica had caused the ejection of the protruding bone, the salt water treatment had cured the infection, and the tail had begun to heal over. No operation was necessary! The tail healed over very rapidly, and though much shorter than desirable, still has three quarters of its length rather than being reduced, as originally mooted, to a mere stump. I must stress that you do need a good vet for this, as every dog is assessed individually, and what suits one may not suit another.

Sexual development

Just like us, dogs go through an adolescent phase in which most of them become just as 'Kevin' as a human teenager. Once they have put that behind them, they will revert to the nice dog that you used to know before someone stole it and replaced it with a hooligan. As with any other adolescent you have ever met, teenage dogs will question your authority, be bone idle and manic by turns, and be obsessed with sex. With bitches, this culminates in the first season, after which she will be noticeably more grown up. Some lurchers, however, do not have early seasons but wait until a year old or more, and with these, you will notice the behavioural patterns and sometimes the physical hormone changes. Bitches may go through a phase of mounting while their hormones are surging, which is usually sexual but occasionally testing pack hierarchy. Firmly dissuade any attempt at mounting humans, but leave other dogs to sort her out, which they most assuredly will. Dogs telling off other dogs can seem violent, but is usually nothing more than noise and spit. Young male dogs almost always go through a spell of mounting behaviour, but they grow out of it very quickly, and it should be ignored unless attempts are made to mount humans. Many adolescent male dogs are taken to be castrated at this time, which is a pity, for they are not going to be like this for ever. It is a temporary developmental phase just like the chewing brought on by teething. A few dogs will always chew, a few dogs will always mount, but lurchers in general are not very randy dogs, and few will continue to be troublesome. A dog that knows its place will never attempt to mount people, but a few will test their status, particularly with children, whom they assume to be lower in the pack hierarchy. Children are moreover a handy size, and more usually to be found on the floor. Such behaviour must not be tolerated. However, if your adolescent forms an attachment to (say) a cushion or similar, just let him get on with it, and console yourself with the thought that dogs grow out of adolescence a great deal more quickly than people.

Seasons

Because most bitches are spayed nowadays, relatively few people have experience of keeping a bitch during her season. There is enormous pressure to have dogs neutered by the rescue organisations, which is understandable given the huge numbers of unwanted dogs that come their way, but you may wish to keep your bitch as nature intended, which is not difficult given that most sighthounds only come on heat once a year or less. It is useful therefore to understand the mechanics of the season.

Two or three weeks before your bitch comes on heat, she will start scent-marking more than usual, i.e. stop to void urine at frequent intervals during her walk. This is to advise entire dogs in the area that she will be in an interesting condition very soon. Sometimes this frequency is mistaken for cystitis, but there is no pain with it, and if you are worried, a simple urine test will confirm whether or not infection is present. Her coat will soften due to the upsurge in hormones, and will become very shiny. The bitch's nipples will stand proud, and she may become intolerant of other dogs sniffing round her flanks and back end. She may suffer quite distinct PMT; this is not anthropomorphism but a fact that I have often observed. Your bitch may have quite a character change, becoming cranky and clingy by turns. Ignore this behaviour: she cannot help it, and she will be back to her normal sweet self before long. The season proper starts with 'showing colour' when a blood-coloured discharge issues from the vulva. Sometimes this is scanty and barely noticeable; at others, especially with a first season, there can be quite a lot of it. Some bitches keep themselves scrupulously clean, and clean up any splashes they have made around the house, and others don't make any attempt to tidy up, but even so, there is very little mess.

Over the next few days, the vulva begins to swell until it is large and soft enough for mating to take place. Usually the bitch is receptive to males between the tenth and fifteenth days, but they can vary markedly. Text books state that the discharge becomes much reduced and changes in hue until it is straw-coloured, but my own observations are that the colour stays red throughout the season. When the bitch is receptive, she will turn her rear end to any approaching males, and 'flag' her tail; that is, turn it to one side in a graceful movement that invites mating. She will be very coquettish at this time. A very few bitches are never receptive, and will attack any male that approaches them during their season. Most male dogs are very chivalrous and do not attempt to force their attentions on an unco-operative bitch, but some will. After the receptive period has finished, the vulva will gradually return to its normal state over a week or so, and for a further week to ten days, although the bitch cannot physically be mated, she will smell enticing to male dogs and may be attacked by them. The season proper lasts for three weeks, but great care must be taken not to expose your bitch to the attentions of male dogs for the remaining week or so, because during this time, she may be injured by frustrated male suitors. Once this time has passed, the season has finished, and you can relax until the next one.

If you intend to keep your bitch whole, you should plan ahead how you are going to house and exercise her during her seasons. If, for instance, you want to keep her kennelled during her season, it is cruel to wait until the season has started and she is in a turmoil of hormones, and then shut her away. Instead, see that she is accustomed to staying in her kennel, and regards it as a pleasant place to be. She will need plenty of your company if this is your choice, as it is unwise to kennel a hot bitch with another dog: a spayed bitch or one that is not on heat may well cause fighting, and a male dog will cause a pregnancy. Often, castrated males will attempt to mount an on-heat bitch, especially if they have had experience of mating prior to their castration. And do not think that a very small dog cannot mate a very tall bitch; believe me, if they want to mate, they can. The best sort of company is in an adjacent kennel where your bitch can see the other dog but they cannot reach each other; under no circumstances have an entire male next door, however, because this is very stressful for both, and you will be amazed just what strength either or both will demonstrate in order to couple. Personally, I keep my bitches in the house, and they stay in the house during their season; it is not the choice of everybody, but it works well with us. Some people choose to send their bitch away to a professional kennels for the duration of her heat, and in that case, again you owe it to your bitch to have thoroughly familiarised her with her change of home well before her season commences. I would add that nobody is more conscientious about keeping your in-season bitch away from prospective mates than you are, and many a litter has followed a spell in boarding kennels! Greyhound kennels sometimes take boarders, and usually have a separate block housing hot bitches; I find greyhound people much better at keeping lurchers than conventional kennels simply because they are much more used to handling that calibre of dog.

The most testing issue with the in-season bitch is exercising her. It is sheer cruelty to keep a bitch shut away for four weeks when she is used to being exercised. This means that you will be scanning the horizon at all times for other dogs, and may have to time your exercise periods very precisely to avoid meeting dog walkers at peak traffic times. You may live in an area where most people have bitches or castrated dogs, in which case exercising is much easier, but it only takes one dog to cause puppies, and some male dogs are adept at finding their way to an on-heat bitch. It is wise to drive your dog to a walk destination, and carry her out to the car from your home if you can (not always possible if she is a big lurcher) to avoid leaving a scent trail which could lead a dog to your house. If you live in a rural area, straying male dogs can be a real penance, which is why you get so many crossbred collies and Labradors in rescue centres! If this is the case, then whenever you leave your bitch, have her absolutely secure in a roofed pen with a concrete base if you do not have her in the house. Given these precautions, you should not have too many problems with your bitch, and if there are one or two persistent strays hanging around, a chat to the dog warden can sometimes be helpful, though beware the zealot who thinks all dogs should be unsexed! That is your decision alone, for you have to live with the results of it. However if other people are irresponsible in the way they keep their dogs, yours should not have to suffer for it, and it is amazing how many dogs that 'can't be kept in' suddenly finding their care is improved once the owners have to pay to get their animal out of the pound.

False Pregnancy

After the season comes the false pregnancy, which can be so minor that only the most astute owner notices, or a full-blown and very convincing changing of shape and coming into milk. Most animals, especially ones that litter rather than have single births, experience false pregnancy, and it is really not a matter of concern. Hormones affect all of us, and they are better accepted than fought. Some bitches will put on weight and become lethargic, most will have prominent nipples, and some will come into milk to a greater or lesser degree. Do not squeeze milk out of the mammaries, as that will stimulate production of more, may introduce infection, or else get you growled at because they can be sore. Homoeopathic pulsatilla can be very good at ending milk production in severe cases; if it is only minor, just let it run its course.

Bitches may develop nesting behaviour, even pre-birth tearing up of bedding and digging; just let it happen. We have a bitch who digs an 'earth' at the bottom of the garden where she keeps her phantom cubs. She visits them periodically, the intervals becoming less frequent as they become weaned, finally losing interest when they are about three to four weeks old. Some bitches take a fluffy toy or a slipper into their bed, and guard it against all comers. Some dog behaviourists get amazingly exercised about this, and tell owners to remove the toy and not allow the bitch to indulge her instincts. This will cause great distress. Just let her mother her toy or phantom pups, and once they are 'weaned' you will have your bitch back to her normal cheery self. There is really no need to do anything radical or preventative; just go with the flow. Not all bitches display this behaviour to any marked degree or even at all, especially working breeds which want to get out and about as soon as possible. Some bitches have a false pregnancy with some seasons and not with others, some get one every time, some never do. All you need to do is make sure that nobody teases her or tries to take her 'puppies' away, particularly children, and keep a cautious eye on her mammaries in case of congestion or infection – which should not happen as long as they are not touched by interfering humans. If you feel that she would be more comfortable with some sympathetic help, then a good holistic vet will be able to offer a range of homoeopathic and flower remedies. This is certainly not a matter for drugs. A very few bitches have such massive false pregnancies that their lives and yours are made unhappy over them, in which case spaying is quite justified. Be aware, however, that around 20 per cent of spayed bitches develop incontinence as a direct result, which is also very hard to live with.

Myths

There are several interesting myths associated with the bitch's season which will be quoted to you by people who are otherwise normal and ought to know better. One is that the bitch will not stand to be mated by a close relative. She most certainly will: brothers, father, it does not matter, if the bitch is in season she will stand for an entire dog. Another story is that known as 'telegony' where, if a purebred bitch is mis-mated and bears a litter of mongrel pups, she will never breed pure to a purebred sire again. It is hard to believe that people still believe this tosh but they do, and my mother once acquired a beautiful German Shepherd bitch free of charge that was going to be put down for that reason. Bitches do not go through a menopause and will have seasons all their lives, so it is just as important to watch an old bitch as a young one. Elderly bitches bear smaller litters and, just as with humans, there is a higher risk of weak or malformed young than with a bitch in her prime. There is also more risk to the mother, especially during the birth. Finally, it is useful to know that a bitch ovulates many eggs at a time, and will stand for a succession of dogs if she has the opportunity. She will hold service to them as well, which can make for an interesting litter! This has just happened not far from me, where a chocolate Labrador bitch was allowed to wander while on heat because the owner thought she would only stand for another Labrador. Having been courted by a collie, a lurcher (not mine!) a corgi and several mongrels, she then went off to be mated by a pedigree Labrador. The resultant litter is so varied that the stud dog's owner is refusing to have her dog's name on the pedigree papers. The moral is that if your bitch is on heat, keep her away from all male dogs unless you want puppies.

Pyometra

A regular scare story from those who are aggressively pro-spaying is that your bitch will develop an infection of the uterus called pyometra, and die, should she remain intact and unmated. In fact, this is a rare occurrence with a healthy animal, though it is indeed extremely serious when it does happen. To remove a uterus on the off-chance that it will become infected is rather like removing any other organ in case it becomes cancerous. You can, however, take the precaution of giving them echinacea daily for six weeks starting from the onset of the season, or raspberry leaf tablets similarly. Bach Remedy crab apple in the water every time you change it is also a good precaution, or you can use all three of these without harm, if you are a belt-and-braces sort of person. A bitch fed on natural raw food and properly kept is very unlikely to develop pyometra; as lurchers don't come into season all that often, there is a correspondingly reduced chance of infection. However, it is wise to be aware that pyometra exists, and if your bitch becomes lethargic, has a temperature, and drinks excessively after a season, seek the right sort of professional help at once. Older bitches whose immune systems are less effective are more at risk, as the ageing are more at risk from any illness, but even so, the likelihood of her developing it is much more remote than some would have you believe.

Mammary Tumours

Another reason regularly put forward in recent years is that spaying lessens the risk of mammary tumours. The research on which this was based proved to be a single piece of work on a small number of bitches, and is now something of an embarrassment to those in the know, but nevertheless has passed into the legend of 'received wisdom'. The truth is that susceptible bitches will develop mammary tumours whether they are spayed or unspayed, and the others will not. It has been suggested that suckling a litter helps to prevent mammary tumours, but the nature of the ailment means that nobody could ever know whether the animal would have developed or not developed tumours if a different course of action had been taken. The prevention of possible mammary tumours is not a good reason to breed a litter, nor to have a bitch spayed.

Testicular and Prostate Cancer

This is the corresponding scare story for the male dog. Again, these cancers cannot occur in a castrated male, though you do not see human males beating a path to the surgeon's door begging to be castrated as a preventative treatment. Frankly, everybody has to die of something, and the avoidance of testicular and prostate cancer is a pretty flimsy reason to have a dog castrated. Dogs are no more or less likely to develop these cancers than they are any other, and my vet tells me that sighthounds in general very seldom get prostate problems. There are, however, very good reasons for having dogs castrated: if they are oversexed (not puppies developing their sexuality, but as mature adults) if they are aggressive or dominant, and this behaviour is hormone-based, if there is a retained testicle, or if you can't be bothered to keep them on your own property. Lurchers are very seldom oversexed, aggressive or dominant, but you do get the odd one, and it is better for a dog to be castrated and live a happy life with you than to keep him entire and be miserable together. If you have your dog from the dog rescue, he or she will probably have been neutered already, so you do not have that decision to make. If you take on a pup, or a bitch that has not or may not have been spayed, some rescue homes will put you under intense pressure to do so. They deal with so many unwanted dogs that it is wholly understandable that they take this stance; however you have to live with the consequences. I would suggest that you see how you get on with the complete animal; you can always have him or her 'done' if you have difficulties, but you may, like me, have no problems at all. Providing you are confident that your dog(s) will never be responsible for unwanted puppies, and are happy in their entire state, there should be no compulsion to neuter.

Anaesthetics and Sedatives

Lurchers and other sighthounds are very sensitive to the effects of anaesthetics and sedatives, and the old-fashioned anaesthetics were quite dangerous to them because of their lack of body fat in comparison with more pedestrian dogs. More modern anaesthetics are a lot safer, but there is still a greater risk to a lurcher than to another type of dog – and all anaesthetics carry a small risk. This leaves the lurcher owner in something of a dilemma, for no-one wants to seem to be teaching a vet how to suck eggs, but nor do we want our lurcher to be the victim of that small risk. I once had a healthy, fit young lurcher almost die following the correct use of a popular sedative; it was nobody's fault and he had to be sedated in order to remove a grass spray that had gone right inside his ear. Nobody can foresee that. It is therefore, in my opinion, better to voice your concerns as tactfully as possible and risk upsetting your vet, than to lose your lurcher and risk upsetting all three of you. If there is a bad reaction in your dog to any medication, but especially to anaesthetic or sedative, your vet must know, and the details must go onto your dog's notes. If your dog has to be treated by a different practice for any reason, you must communicate your knowledge to that vet – if he or she does not know, then nothing can be done to prevent something similar happening to your or someone else's dog. Feedback is very important; even the best vets are only human, and the more information they can have, the better – after all, they can always ignore what they do not need. Some anaesthesia is unavoidable, but it is best to keep the use of anaesthetics to a minimum, and avoid, for instance, the practice that some veterinary surgeons encourage of having the dog's teeth cleaned under anaesthetic every year. That can add up to a lot of anaesthesia in a dog's lifetime, and the risks increase each time.

Better to have the teeth cleaned by other methods, a variety of which are suggested in this chapter.

Vaccination

Following on from that, vaccination is a very hot subject of debate between different health experts. It is customary to give puppies two injections of multiple vaccine at times which vary from vet practice to vet practice, but are generally at nine and twelve weeks of age. These vaccines cover distemper, parvovirus and canine hepatitis, sometimes leptospirosis as well. After that, annual boosters are recommended by the vaccine manufacturers. Additionally, most boarding kennels insist that all dogs have been vaccinated against kennel cough within the preceding six months, and some vets encourage six-monthly leptospirosis (Weil's Disease) vaccinations. Along with some serious doubts raised in the field of children's vaccination, there is considerable dispute now whether this level of vaccination is correct, or if it is contributing to the increased levels of disease being seen in animals and children, such as asthma, eczema, arthritis and autism in children, skin diseases, epilepsy, leukaemia, diabetes and cancers in animals. Concentrating on the dog side of things, as this is a book about dogs, your vet is between a rock and a hard place when asked for advice. The only research into vaccine damage is done by the vaccine manufacturers themselves. The vets are compelled by their governing body to recommend the full course of puppy vaccinations using live vaccine, and annual boosters thereafter. Boarding kennels and most training establishments insist on this as well, and their insurance companies will not insure them otherwise. Most pet insurance companies will not insure dogs that are not vaccinated to this programme either. As for taking dogs abroad and bringing them back in, well, that is asking for a massive chemical overload of flea treatments, wormers and vaccinations all in one go. Those of us who study holistic health and animal management, including many vets, find cause for concern here.

In the blue corner are the radicals who believe that all forms of vaccination are damaging, and prefer to feed a natural, healthy diet and use drug-free methods of boosting the immune system when necessary, believing that only unhealthy dogs become ill. Then there are people like me who remember the ravages of distemper and in later years parvovirus. There are homoeopathic nosodes available as an alternative to conventional vaccine, but their use is very complicated, and there have been no scientific tests (because these are done by the vaccine manufacturers!) to prove their efficacy. Let us be clear that nobody, particularly not vets, whose hands are tied by the system, is able to advise you what to do about vaccination. The best any of us can do is research the available options as much as possible, and take an informed decision. Nor am I going to suggest what you do. I will tell you what I do, and why I do it, but I am not recommending any course of action over any other: you must assess the information and make up your own minds.

My puppies receive two injections of killed vaccine (not live vaccine) at nine and twelve weeks. This vaccine is not easily available, and sometimes the veterinary practice that I use has difficulty in obtaining it, so that a decent period of notice has to be given. Thereafter, my dogs are blood tested to check their levels of antibodies. We used to test annually, but the recommendation now is to test every three years. This is called the 'titre test' and costs the same as the annual booster vaccination; there is little saving in money but a considerable saving in health. After their twelfth year, I do not have them tested any more, as I consider the risks of the vaccination in an elderly dog equal the risk of contracting the disease. This is purely my opinion and not backed by any scientific study. Out of interest, I have yet to need to have a dog re-vaccinated after the puppy vaccinations. Every year there are outbreaks of kennel cough in the area, always from dogs that have been in boarding kennels and often which have been vaccinated. Unfortunately, despite the extremely infectious nature of this illness (sputum remains infectious for several days) people will walk their dogs where the rest of us exercise. At these times, I use a homoeopathic remedy in my dogs' drinking water until the epidemic has died down.

Regarding leptospirosis, well, here is a very interesting subject. Leptospirosis (often erroneously referred to as 'rat bite fever') is spread in rat urine, and is supposedly rife anywhere that there are rats – which is everywhere – and especially where there is water as well, such as brooks and ditches. There are many strains of lepto just as there are many strains of human influenza, and it is impossible to vaccinate against all of them; just as with human 'flu vaccination, only the common or most prevalent ones are covered. Furthermore, protection only lasts for three to six months. Now, there is no doubt that leptospirosis can kill, and not just dogs either: it used to be known as 'rat catcher's yellows' and was an occupational and rather permanent aspect of the rodent controller's job in days gone by. All of my life I have been constantly exposed to leptospirosis, for I have hung around farmyards and stables, fields and streams, since I was tiny. Likewise for my dogs, as we hunt these areas and they frequently catch rats. Yet I have asked many doctors about the wisdom of protection against leptospirosis, and always been told that it is extremely rare and not worth bothering about! So who is mistaken – the vets who insist on a six-monthly or yearly booster for this disease that is everywhere, or the doctors who have not come across it at all? Unable to find the answer to this, I continue to keep my dogs as fit and healthy as I can with proper fresh food and plenty of exercise, and do the same for myself, while taking sensible precautions such as washing my hands very thoroughly before I eat, never drinking stream water, and not letting my dogs lick my face just after they have caught a rat. As far as vaccination as a whole is concerned, the jury is still out, and there are more questions than answers. I do know a lot of people who never have their dogs vaccinated at all, and who rely on keeping them really healthy instead; this could be all that is needed, or else they could be riding on the coat-tails of those who do vaccinate, in that the old killer diseases are not that prevalent any more.

Stomach Problems – D and V

Diarrhoea and vomiting will be encountered with the healthiest dog, and in many ways, it is a sign of good health that foreign matter can be ejected so swiftly. D and V can be a sign that your dog has ingested something that even a powerful canine digestion has rejected, or else that she has an infection of some sort. Sometimes, dogs will vomit up worms, showing you exactly what the problem is. It is also perfectly normal for a dog to vomit bile – frothy thick yellow liquid – at any time, and most dogs will eat greenery, especially couch grass, as an emetic if they have over-produced bile. Dogs that are fed large amounts of pulverised vegetables and fruit tend to vomit bile less often; instead it is carried through the system and passed in the faeces, discernable by its sulphur-yellow colour. Faeces-watching is a dark art practised by most dog owners, and it is possible to have a very good idea of your dog's inner health purely from observing what is produced. Non-dog owners tend not to understand this, though, so it is definitely not a subject for polite company.

Dogs can produce diarrhoea out of sheer excitement, or fear, from chill and damp, from drinking dubious water to scavenging decomposing food, and still be perfectly healthy. Prolonged D and/or V is a different matter, and your dog may need veterinary help. How do you decide when this is required? Rather the same as you would for yourself. If an otherwise bright and active dog has produced one or both of these symptoms, the stool or vomit does not contain blood (bright red is fresh blood and rarely a cause for concern – dark red or black is old blood, possibly from a growth, and should be investigated) and the condition lasts for 24 hours or less, simply withhold food until the stomach settles, then offer a small amount of bland food on the following day. If, however, the symptoms persist for several days, or the dog is lethargic with dull eyes and dry nose, and no appetite, then veterinary investigation is needed. Puppies and older dogs should have help sooner rather than later, as they can dehydrate very quickly, and also their immune systems will not be fully functional. An active dog with no appetite may well have swallowed a foreign object which is partially or completely blocking the gut. If X-ray proves this, then surgery will be needed.

It is also perfectly normal for a dog to bolt its food, vomit it up, and then eat it again. This is extremely unpleasant for humans to witness, but not at all indicative of a problem with the dog. It is a relic of the behaviour of the pack at a kill, where as much meat has to be eaten as quickly as possible and carried away in the stomach, to be disgorged and re-ingested in a safer place, the pack around the kill being vulnerable to other predators. Best look away until she has finished.

Prolonged D and V definitely warrants a trip to the vet, but if you are quite sure that the situation is the result of inappropriate eating or drinking of something fairly trivial, then provided the dog is taking in enough fluid, just let Nature take its course. D and V should be allowed to happen and not be suppressed, because if it is, then the ejection of the undesirable matter may not be completed. Afterwards, useful first meals should be on the lines of scrambled egg with live yoghurt and honey, which will settle and soothe the gut, and help the 'friendly' intestinal flora to reach the correct levels. Give very small quantities at first.

First Aid Kit

I cannot emphasise strongly enough that, if in doubt with any condition, a trusted vet should be your first port of call, and it is important to find someone who suits your way of thinking before you need them. Especially check emergency cover out of hours, and do a 'dummy run' if necessary so that you know the quickest way to the surgery, remembering that it may be the middle of the night and you may be very stressed when you need to go there for real. Meanwhile, a first aid kit for the dog is an important addition to your dog care cupboard. What should you have? Take a look at mine, and adapt it to suit yourself.

I have two remedies for shock always to hand: homoeopathic arnica, and Bach Rescue Remedy. For wounds, I have a little container of salt, so that I can make salt water for bathing wounds at once, very sharp scissors for trimming the hair from around the wound, and a syringe so that I can syringe salt water right into the wound if it is deep or a puncture. A warning about scissors: families and scissors have a magnetic attraction for each other. When you

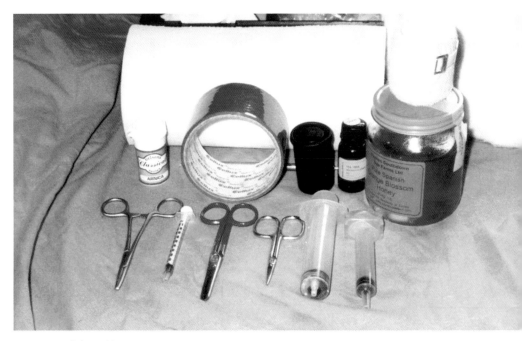

A simple first aid kit

need these scissors, it will be at once, and they need to be clean and sharp, not blunted and coated in glue from cutting-out or other hobby projects. Therefore, lock them away. Otherwise, you can bet your old sea boots that when you have a genuine emergency, your scissors will either be far away and no-one knows where, or else they will be unusable.

I don't have much in the way of bandages, preferring to leave wounds open if at all possible, but I do have a couple of sheets of clean gamgee, which is cotton wool in a gauze covering, obtainable from saddlers, a horse elasticated tail bandage from the same source, a couple of orphan socks, clean of course, some strong kitchen paper, and a roll of parcel tape.

If going to the vet, don't put anything on the wound after the salt-water bathing, as the vet. needs a clean wound to work with. If you are quite satisfied that you can cope without the need for a vet, then I suggest a generous dollop of thick honey on a folded piece of kitchen paper, right against and into the wound. Honey is strongly antiseptic, and a wonderful healer. So, honeyed or not, against the wound is the folded kitchen paper. Next, the gamgee pad, and keep that in place with the tail bandage, being sure not to bandage too tightly. Then secure the bandage with the parcel tape. This is a cheap and very efficient way of securing a wound until it either stops bleeding or you have arrived at the veterinary surgery. Again, I'd recommend that you practise this before you need to do it.

I also have a 'boot' to put over the foot in case of a cut pad, so that the dog can go out to empty herself without getting the injury dirty. If you are only going a short way, a couple of socks pulled over the paw and covered with a pair of supermarket carrier bags taped against the leg will suffice.

I keep therapeutic quality lavender oil and tea tree oil to hand, in case of a wound that is 'dirty' such as a bite, or a gash from rusty metal, and add a few drops of one or the other to the salt water. Please don't keep aromatic oils near homoeopathic remedies, though, as they will destroy their clinical usefulness – the two types of treatment must be stored and used separately.

That is it. There is very little in a first-aid situation that cannot be helped with salt water bathing, arnica, and maybe a bandage. Any more treatment is best accomplished by a professional. Let us hope that you never have to use any of it at all, but it is a comfort to know it is available.

The Older Lurcher

Old age comes to most of us, and though lurchers tend to age gracefully, it is a time when extra care is needed. Sight and/or hearing deteriorates, though the sense of smell seems to be as good as ever. Joints and backs lose their cunning,

Sixteen and still enjoying life

become stiff and sometimes painful. Coats change texture, become thicker or scantier, and each moult takes longer than the last. She will not be able to get as much goodness out of her food, and her digestion will slow down; she may also not be able to eat as much in one sitting, and benefit from more frequent, smaller meals. Cold and heat will affect her more, and damp weather may make her old bones ache, so that she does not want to leave her bed. She will still enjoy her walks, but will tend to potter and sniff, wanting to stop frequently, instead of the eager forging-ahead that you remember from her early days. Other dogs are quick to detect weakness, and long before your dog shows any sign of illness detectable to a human, they will be aware of it. Strange dogs may attack her without provocation: to them, her infirmity is provocation enough. If you have several dogs of your own, she may start to lose her status in the pack. I witnessed a desperately sad incident when an old dog was going downhill, and a small dog that we met out walking ran past the others without a glance to attack my old girl with every intention of killing her. My other dogs made no attempt to defend her; clearly as she was near the end, it was fitting in the dog world if not in our society, for her to die. The other dog's owner did nothing helpful to the situation, instead screaming as if she was the one being attacked. Before I could reach the mêlée, the old dog rallied, bit the other one hard and flung it up in the air. The owner's shrieking merely served to excite her dog further, and it dashed in to the attack once more, to get another hard bite and a further flying lesson. Having exhausted her energy, the old dog then collapsed into shock, leaving me dealing on the one hand with a dangerously ill hound and on the other trying to ignore a woman in a fit of terminal hysterics. It was not the best walk I had ever been on, and a graphic illustration of how dogs will sense weakness in other dogs. My old girl did survive the attack, more thanks to a lifetime of good food and regular exercise than any human intervention; I still see the other little dog and the owner has never said a word to me, though for some reason she always walks the other way when our paths are due to cross.

Bear this in mind, though, if you have an elderly dog that is in failing health, and see that when you are not at home, she is safely away from other dogs, even ones that she has lived with for years. It is not uncommon for illness in one dog to trigger an attack, and though there is plenty of warning for those with eyes to see, people often ignore the signs. If your old dog is slipping down the pack status, or worse, has become a 'non-dog' in that her presence is no longer acknowledged by the others, if other dogs mount her that have hitherto not done so, if they push her away from her food, her bed, and you, beware tragedy. This behaviour is common to all dogs, not just lurchers; in fact, such is the sweet nature of most lurcher types that an old, sick dog can still live in harmony with others, but be very watchful of other breeds. I once was left to look after an elderly lurcher who, unbeknown to his owner, had an aggressive cancer. At the last minute, I also had another dog to care for, with which the lurcher had always got on well. The warning that everybody ignored before I arrived was that the weimaraner was scent-marking the door of the house – claiming the lurcher's territory as his own. I had a terrible few days trying to keep them apart, for the weimaraner was determined to kill the lurcher, the house did not possess a single door that shut or an outbuilding in which a dog could safely be left, and in the end I had to leave the lurcher with a neighbour. Sadly, kind though the neighbour was, he then became so upset at having to leave his home (regrettably, she would not take the weimaraner instead) that he went into a decline from which he never recovered. This preying of the healthy upon the infirm is the nature of the animal world, and indeed is not unknown with humans, being the source of bullying, persecution, and crimes against the elderly.

Medication

This will be a time in her life where medication is needed to keep her comfortable. Food supplements may help her joints, a copper or magnetic collar might be useful for some aches and pains, or she may have to go onto veterinary drugs to help her. An early sign of all not being well can be a change in her body scent, for lurchers are usually sweet-smelling hounds. If this is accompanied by staining of the skin, it might mean that a major eliminatory organ such as the kidneys is under stress, and so the body is trying to remove toxins through the skin. Heart medicine puts a significant strain upon the kidneys too, which should also be boosted if such is being given. My old dog has homoeopathic support for her kidneys for this very reason; as she also has tremors in her hindquarters, she has a natural source of potassium such as half a banana daily, given last thing at night, and a squirt of organic tomato purée in her dinner. Such little extras, simple and inexpensive, all add to her quality of life, thanks to the help of a holistic vet.

Lumps

The elderly are prone to lumps appearing here and there, most of which are benign. Any lump should, however, be investigated as soon as it is noticed. A few cancers are very aggressive, and will kill in a matter of weeks; others are slow-growing and do not cause trouble for years. Sometimes a dog will worry at a lump until she has chewed it off, which is common animal behaviour: I have seen my ferrets do this as well. Once you know whether the lump is dangerous or not, you can decide what treatment, if any, should be used. Mostly, lumps are better left alone, but follow your vet's advice, and be sure to balance any proposed treatment against the subsequent quality of life on offer.

Comfort

Lurchers are legendary for enjoying their home comforts, and this does not diminish with age! Your old dog might appreciate a warm coat at night – but check that she does not overheat, especially if you have central heating on at night. Despite the popular habit of putting coats on dogs, lurchers do not normally need to be coated on walks, and they do need fresh air, sun and wind on their hides. Old dogs, however, will appreciate a coat on bitter days, or in the rain, and a good towelling to dry them afterwards. If you go off to work and the heating goes off too, then put a coat on her during the day at chilly times of year. A lurcher is healthier with a coat on and plenty of fresh air than in a stuffy heated room. Make sure that she has lots of bedding to snuggle into: another advantage of the older dog is that she has outgrown any tendency to shred duvets or beanbags, and so can be bedded more luxuriously than a youngster. Keep a check on her nails, which may need trimming more often, and her teeth.

Lurchers can stand any amount of comfort

A proper diet with plenty of bones and hard biscuits to chew will keep teeth healthy, but as she gets older, she may need a little help with tartar at the roots of the canine teeth. I have never had a lot of success with dog toothpastes, which might be due more to my ineptitude than the system, but instead have two useful natural remedies in my quiver. The first is homoeopathic fragaria, which needs to be given orally for about three weeks before it shows results, and the other is aloe vera gel, which can be rubbed onto the affected areas with a fingertip, and again takes some time to loosen the tartar. Use the best quality aloe vera gel that you can get, with the aloe vera content up in the 90 per cent range, which will be quite expensive. Cheap products do not contain enough of the herb. Results are usually very good, and once loosened, the tartar can be gently rubbed off with a piece of kitchen paper. Quite badly neglected teeth can be cleaned this way, and it is a lot safer than subjecting an elderly dog to an anaesthetic just for a 'scrape'. Before I found out about these two methods, I would clean the affected teeth with a dentist's scraper padded with kitchen paper (what would I do without kitchen paper?). It is important to pad the scraper if you use it, as otherwise you might put small grooves in the tooth which will then provide a 'key' for further tartar to stick onto. If it is a double-ended scraper, be sure to pad the other end as you do not want to prong your long-suffering dog if she wriggles.

None of this should be taken to mean that owning an elderly dog is a penance: indeed it can be a joy. You can enjoy the world at a gentler pace, and though you will not be taking those long walks, neither will you have to go out in inclement weather – as soon as she has seen to her hygiene needs, she will be happy to return home to her bed. She will enjoy gentle grooming and a little bit of spoiling, and you will not need to worry about undermining her training, because she understands you so well that you hardly have to think about where she is. On sunny days, you can sit in the grass and take time out to relax while she mooches about enjoying the smells and the warmth on her back, presently to lie beside you and share the glorious intimacy between you: a dog who has been part of your life for so long that it is difficult to say where she stops and you begin. As her face whitens, every day together becomes the more precious. What if her sight is growing dim, or she does not hear so well? It comes to us all in the end; for sure, she will still be able to read your mind with crystal clarity.

The Last Goodbye

When I was a child, a dog past its eighth year was an old dog indeed, but nowadays dogs can achieve twice that lifespan. However, it is not a growing-older competition but a quality of life experience; I once encountered a dog in her twenty-seventh year and found her a heartbreaking sight. She was blind, deaf, incontinent and senile, and spent all her time in her bed. Once an incredibly beautiful dog, she had been old for twice as long as she had been vital. Did she have quality of life? I cannot answer that question, but I hope that she did; she died shortly after I saw her, in a bitter winter, though her owner had done his best for her and put a heat-lamp over her.

One question that haunts all owners who love their animals is how to know when the time has come, and whether to gently help their pet into the next world, or to let nature take its course. There is no easy answer to this, though I am inclined to think better a week too soon than a day too late. When you see an animal every day, it is easy to miss the signs of deterioration, or to kid yourself that she is 'happy'. I have seen some truly awful sights of animals that have been kept going for the benefit of their owners or unscrupulous vets, when they are long past dignity, never mind pleasure. But it is a very, very hard decision to make, and you are the one who should make it, for if you shuck the responsibility off onto anyone else, you may also unfairly blame them too. It is also your responsibility to be with your animal at the end rather than have her spend her last moments with strangers. If you have other dogs, they need to know what has happened, or else the pack hierarchy will descend into anarchy. If it is not possible for them to see their friend's remains, then be sure to tell them; you would be astonished what they can pick up from your mind, even if they don't understand your words. When the deed is done, do not make a guilt-stick to hit yourself with for ever after, for you will have done your best, and your animal will depart loving you for it. Nor should you feel bad about getting another dog once you have had your period of mourning: although nothing will ever replace a lost loved one, the new dog will give you plenty of occupation, and help you to grieve. She should, for all your sakes, be quite different from the dog that you have lost, otherwise you may be tempted to make comparisons. How long do you leave it before getting another dog? The same length as a piece of string. When you are ready, get another dog. It is not a betrayal: it is the supreme compliment to your previous hound.

Useful Addresses

Thornit Ear Treatment – contact Miss P. Betts, Thornham, Hunstanton, Norfolk, PE36 6NB

Ainsworth's Homoeopathic Pharmacy 36 New Cavendish Street, London W1M 7LH

Canine Natural Cures 49 Beaumont Road Purley Surrey CR8 2EJ

British Homoeopathic Association (for a list of homoeopathic vets) 020 7566 7800

Canine Health Concern P.O.Box 6943, Forfar DD8 3WG

Contented bitch and puppy

11 BREEDING LURCHERS

If you were considering breeding from your lurcher, most people, myself included, would do their best to dissuade you. There are a few commercial lurcher breeders who struggle to make a living, the market for lurchers is relatively small, and the rescue homes are stuffed with them. Why add more lurchers, when instead you could be giving a home to a lovely hound that is in dire need of one? But indeed, that may be a simplistic view – why should you not be every bit as responsible a breeder as any breeder of KC registered dogs? If there are going to be lurchers, why not carefully bred, carefully reared and carefully placed with the right type of owners? If you have a dog or bitch that has been a dear friend to you, why not carry on the line? Dogs of good temperament and good health should be bred for future generations to enjoy. There are immeasurable joys and considerable pitfalls to breeding lurchers; if, after reading this chapter, you decide not to breed after all, then you will still be equipped to choose the very best puppy from all the options that are open to you. If you are still determined to breed, I hope that I can help you through the minefield before you.

Type

The lurcher, being a specialist type of mongrel, offers considerable challenge to the breeder. Most commercial breeders concentrate on either the show or working market. Show dogs are bred very 'typey' ie greyhoundy in shape, sometimes with just enough other blood to give a broken coat, if that is the current fashion. This is most usually deerhound, which retains the beautiful sighthound shape. As lurcher shows are judged by working dog people who are looking for a working type, the show dog has to be the right build, so the greyhound side will always be from a working, not a KC registered greyhound. As with pedigree dogs, sometimes much is sacrificed on the altar of physical perfection, and the winner of many championships might not be so easy to live with as a companion dog. Working dog people breed worker to worker, trying to add to each generation what they perceive to be lacking in the previous one. The committed working lurcher owner, though he or she

Deerhound cross to deerhound cross — almost pure deerhound to look at, and one of the most ancient colours

may only breed one litter every few years, will breed from stock that has been tested to the inch to be sound, biddable, game, fast and agile. Looks come a long way after these criteria have been fulfilled. Commercial breeders do not always have the time or inclination to field-test their stock, and sometimes bad behavioural faults can creep in. These faults would usually be of no consequence to the pet owner, who will never need a dog that is soft-mouthed, or silent when running hard, but would be of great concern to the working dog owner. Some commercial breeders do test their stock very thoroughly, some 'backyard' breeders may not: it is up to the buyer to ascertain what has been done if this is of importance to them. So before you ever bring dog and bitch together, consider what you want from the finished article, whether you would improve on what you have, and if so, how, or whether you would like something exactly the same. If the last, then you need to find a canine partner for yours which is as much like him or her as possible, and preferably bred similarly. Which brings me to a small lesson in genetics: be brave and read it, because it is necessary, and I'll make it as quick and painless as possible.

If you have a first cross collie greyhound where c=collie and g=greyhound, every pup will be genetically cg and the litter will look, colour apart, very much the same, and grow into the same type of dog, smooth-coated and strongly built. If, however, you breed one cg to another cg, the pups will turn out as three specific types: some will look very like collies, some very like greyhounds, and some like the cg parents i.e. c x g= cg, cg, cg but cg x cg =cc (like a collie), gg (like a greyhound), cg (like a first cross collie/greyhound). Therefore a collie/greyhound first cross litter will look different from a collie/greyhound x collie/greyhound, though a proportion of the pups will look the same. Add another breed, and the variations will continue, so that you can have pups from the same litter growing into very different dogs. Some will be rough, some smooth, some light, some heavy (known as 'cloddy'), some favouring the sighthound temperament and some the base blood. Some breeds of dog are very prepotent i.e. they stamp their breed characteristics into their pups so strongly that the effect is unmistakeable for generations after the cross has been made. Bedlington blood, for instance, is very prepotent. Therefore, if dog and bitch each with Bedlington blood a long way back are used, there may be a pup in the litter that comes out very bedlington-like in size, shape and manner. I once crossed dogs with deerhound in the background of both, but well mixed with other breeds, and produced a magnificent dog that was almost pure working deerhound to look at, and furthermore was one of the ancient colours that is all but lost in the modern show deerhound. Sadly, his owner never bred from him.

Why I am telling you this is to prepare you for a wide divergence in the litter that you breed. This is not a bad thing. The people who come to buy your pups may each want different dogs: large, smaller, rough or smooth. Or maybe they won't mind at all. But what they will want to know is what breeds are in your pups. So often I get asked if I know anyone who wants a lurcher pup, but when I query the breeding, it is not known. While some people will be happy with any old lurcher, the knowledgeable homes want to know what is in the melting pot. Perhaps they want to avoid a particular type, or they have a favourite cross. Maybe they want a big or a small dog. If you cannot answer a prospective buyer who asks 'how are they bred?' I submit that you should think very carefully about breeding at all.

Colour Breeding

Tempting though it is, I do not intend to go into great lengths about the fascinating subject of colour breeding. As lurchers are crossbreds, you can get any colour occurring in the litter. Some, however are more dominant than others, which can be useful to know.

Differences in littermates

If a dog is pied, that is, mainly white with flecks or patches of another colour, (sometimes known as 'gay pied') then the other colour is the dominant one that it will pass on. However, you will probably get one or more pied pups. Black is a very dominant colour, as its dilute, which is blue. Liver is another black dilute, but not so often seen in the lurcher. Black and tan is extremely dominant, slightly less so is black and white. Very ancient colours in lurchers, which will pop up unexpectedly in many litters, are brindle, black-masked fawn, oatmeal, and white with red ears. These colours have been prized for hundreds of years, and mention of them can be found in many ancient texts.

The attractive merle colouring is very popular in the modern lurcher, but to it is attached an important health warning. If a merle is bred to another merle, a proportion of the puppies will be deaf and/or blind. I therefore strongly recommend that you do not do this. A merle bred to a whole-coloured parent will still produce some merle pups.

Generally, pups are born dark and get lighter as they get older. Sometimes a little of the dark remains: it is common to see a fawn dog with enough black hairs in its tail to make it look black. Pups born white can acquire flecks and spots when they change their puppy coats. Black brindles can become a lighter shade of brindle. The mud-coloured ones can become beautiful fawns and creams. Puppy colour, unless a true black, is seldom kept into adulthood.

When to Breed

A dog may be bred from before his first year or well into his dotage, but there are caveats for both. A very young dog can physically sire pups, but if immature and unproven, may have undesirable characteristics that have not yet developed, and which should not be passed on. An old stud will have fewer viable sperm, and so be less fertile, but you have the advantage of knowing all about him. Lurchers as a rule are not very highly-sexed dogs, and one that has been dissuaded from mating for all of his life might take some encouraging, or refuse to perform at all. The ideal is a hound in his prime, between three and six years old, which should produce strong sperm and have no genetic secrets. If he has been used successfully at stud before, and produced live pups, this is even better. If you have the chance to see some of his progeny, take it: the more knowledge you have, the better. I did once take a chance and used a yearling dog on my bitch: he was a little shy to mate, but managed in the end, and threw a stunning litter. I knew him well before I used him, having seen him being trained and starting to work, and he certainly fulfilled his early promise. I also knew exactly how he was bred.

A bitch should be at least two years old before she produces a litter. Any younger, and she has not finished growing. At the other end of her life, I'd say be careful about breeding a bitch that is over seven years old, particularly a first litter. Carrying and raising young is a considerable strain on an immature or elderly system. Sometimes older bitches have borne and raised litters with no trouble at all, especially if they have had a litter early in life, but statistically, there are more likely to be complications with the pregnancy and/or birth, sometimes life-threatening ones, and there is a higher risk of deformed pups. If, however, you have one of those bitches that only comes into season occasionally – I know several that did not show a season until they were four –then you must breed when you can. It makes sense if one dog is old to use a young, healthy mate rather than another older dog.

There are sighthounds in India from which the bitches are not bred until they retire from working, at around eight years old. These dogs are exceptionally tough, have been thoroughly field-tested, and seem to breed without problems, or perhaps problems are taken as normal and as only the survivors carry the line on, gradually reducing over the generations. But for our dogs, there is quite a risk attached to breeding from older bitches, and though many bitches and pups do survive, many do not. Ask yourself whether it is worth the gamble.

Summer or Winter

Assuming that you have the choice, do you breed a summer or a winter litter? Winter litters need a lot of extra warmth, and are a little more difficult to house train, plus need a lot more clearing up after the inevitable wet muddy days leading to wet muddy bedding. Christmas falls in the middle of things, meaning a lot of extra work at an already busy time – rearing a litter of puppies properly is a lot of work – or else pups ready to go to their new homes at a time when no conscientious breeder would dream of moving them on. Christmas is emphatically not a time for a puppy to change homes. Summer is Nature's time to rear young things, but summer brings wasps, flies and fleas and requires ruthless cleanliness if you are to avoid tummy bugs. Ideally, I'd say a late winter mating for a spring litter, or a late summer mating for an autumn one; many bitches come on heat at one or other of these times.

The Stud Fee

Expect to pay the set price if using a commercial stud, or the price of one pup, or the pick of the litter after you have had your choice if not. If a financial transaction, you will agree this and pay in advance. Personally, I find it better to pay money and then have the stud owner pay the going rate for a pup if they want one, because that way no offence is caused if they don't after all like any of the pups, or their circumstances change so that they can't have one. They might only like one pup, and that is the one that you have chosen for yourself, or they might take a pup and promptly sell it. Out of such arrangements can a lot of bitterness result. But money is wonderfully consistent, and one example is very like another. Sometimes people don't want anything, especially if the dog has not been bred from before and is therefore an unknown quantity, in which case a bottle of something is appropriate. Some people offer a refund if the bitch does not conceive, but if she aborts the pups for whatever reason, a repeat mating may or may not be offered, depending on the stud dog owner's wishes. After abortion, it is important to have the bitch swabbed and checked for infection by a vet, and most stud dog owners will refuse to let their dog/s be used until the bitch is proven clear. Not doing so is a waste of money as well as irresponsible, for if infection lingers, your bitch may abort again, may infect the stud dog which could then pass infection to other bitches, or may sustain internal damage which renders her sterile or even kills her. The responsibility for the litter rests squarely on the shoulders of the bitch owner, and though many stud dog owners take a paternal interest in the litters their dog sires, it is quite in order if they do not. If you have problems rearing or homing the pups, those problems are yours; don't expect the stud dog owner to bail you out.

Size Matters

There should not be a great discrepancy between the size of dog and bitch, and it is downright cruelty to attempt to mate a large dog to a small bitch. A slightly smaller dog can be helped by either standing the bitch in a hollow, or providing a platform for the dog: if the latter, it must be absolutely firm and steady. The dog should not be expected to stretch as he might damage himself.

Before the Deed

Your bitch should be let down a little if she is fit, and if you have her vaccinated and a vaccination is due, this is better brought forward than given during the pregnancy; alternatively, you might prefer her to miss being vaccinated this time. She should be wormed before the service with a wormer such as Drontal-Plus. All puppies are born with worms because during the pregnancy, encysted worms in the bitch activate and travel down the placenta to infest the unborn pups. Some of these worms encyst in the pups' bodies in turn. In dog pups and bitches that do not breed, they then go no further, but with breeding bitches, they infest the puppies during pregnancy again, and so the parasitic cycle continues. This worm burden cannot be totally avoided, but by worming the bitch before she is served, and then worming during the pregnancy at intervals and with a specific product recommended by your vet, you can reduce it.

The Mating

It is usual for the bitch to be brought to the dog. Many dogs refuse to mate away from their own surroundings, and it is foolish to let a dog out of your sight to mate an unknown bitch. Anything can happen to him: he can be used to mate several bitches, taken out poaching, or even sold. Similarly with the bitch: if you want to be sure that the right dog has covered your bitch, be there when he does it. It is by no means unknown for another dog to be brought forward if your chosen stud is reluctant to cover, and not just with dogs either. Years ago, I was involved with a Thoroughbred stud where a purebred mare produced a skewbald (brown and white patches) foal. It is genetically impossible for two Thoroughbred horses to do this, and they settled out of court. However, if that foal had been whole-coloured, nobody would have known that the wrong stallion had covered the mare.

The mechanics of the bitch's season have been covered in Chapter 10. At around the tenth day, she will be ready to stand for the dog, and demonstrate her willingness by 'flagging' her tail (lifting and angling it to the side) and turning her quarters towards a touch on the haunches. Some bitches are ready to stand earlier, some later. There are expensive temperature-detecting devices for testing when a bitch is ready, but none can beat the accurate nose of a male dog. Males that are kept all the time with bitches will show little interest in an on-heat bitch until the time is right. If you have chosen the stud dog some time previously, the mating will be

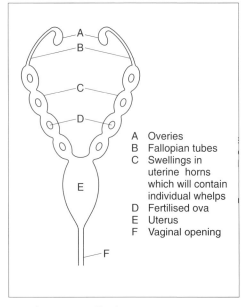

A Overies
B Fallopian tubes
C Swellings in uterine horns which will contain individual whelps
D Fertilised ova
E Uterus
F Vaginal opening

Reproductive system of bitch

Soft cloth muzzle

Plastic 'box' muzzle should not be used

easier if they have been allowed to get acquainted long before season time. This is not anthropomorphism but fact: dogs have their likes and dislikes just as we do. Some dogs will mate anything, some are very fussy. If they already know each other, you are ahead of the game. When stud dog meets in-season bitch, and she is ready, there will follow a spell of flirtatious play which must be allowed to happen as it releases hormones in the bitch that make her ovulate better. However, all matings must be supervised: leaving them in a shed while you go and have a cup of tea is a recipe for disaster, especially if one or both of the star players is a maiden. If the bitch snaps at the dog, then she is not ready: try again tomorrow. If she stands with head down and tail flagged as the dog prepares to mount, then the time is right, and she should then be gently restrained by a supporting arm round her chest. Be aware that some bitches find the act of penetration painful; most scream and some snap. For that reason, a soft muzzle is appropriate, either a bandage tied around her muzzle and then fastened at the back of her head, or one of the cloth muzzles that you can buy at a pet shop. Do not use a plastic or wire muzzle as this can injure you or her if she swings her head and clouts you with it. If the position of the dogs needs adjusting, move the bitch's vulva to meet the dog rather than the dog's penis. Be aware that the dog may not be fully erect until he achieves penetration. The dog needs tact at this time, and may refuse to mate if handled, especially by his owner, to whom he has learned to defer.

After penetration, the dog will show signs of wanting to turn so that he is back to back with the bitch. At this time, the ring of muscle round the bitch's vagina will have contracted around the swollen base of the dog's penis, and this is known as the 'tie'. The tie cannot be broken until the bitch relaxes, which may be ten minutes or fifty minutes after penetration. During the tie, the dogs should be gently held in the back-to-back position, and they normally become progressively more relaxed until the bitch releases the dog. Then the bitch should be put safely into your car and you can go and have that tea.

What Happens Inside

Immediately after penetration, the bulk of the fertile ejaculate passes from dog to bitch. This is why a bitch can become pregnant even if the mating does not tie. However, during the tie, the seminal fluid is washed deep into the bitch's uterine horns as the dog continues to ejaculate. Bitches produce ova throughout the fertile period, and so can hold service to a number of different dogs if they mate with them. Some people get very exercised about fluid running out of the bitch after mating, and try cold water, or even, heaven help us, nettles, to try and stop this, but just ignore it and let dog and bitch clean up themselves and each other if they want. The fertile ejaculate is long gone, and the other fluid has done its job of washing it far inside the bitch. The fertilised ova will float for a few days before implanting into the uterine horns, which is where the pups will develop. This system allows multiple-birth animals to carry on with their lives without being hampered by the pregnancy. The pups will be carried high up and either side of the bitch until almost ready for delivery.

What Goes Wrong

If dog and bitch are left to mate unsupervised, much can go wrong. The bitch can attack the dog and bite him severely at the moment of penetration. If she struggles during the tie, she can rupture the dog, and damage herself. Previously unmated dogs might not have much idea of what to do, because they have never seen other dogs mate; sometimes instinct takes over and sometimes it does not. The result of the latter event is two exhausted and miserable dogs, neither of which will be keen to try another time. Injury can occur with even a slight size discrepancy if one dog lifts the other off its hindlegs during the tie. Dogs can attack each other as they separate. It is just another manifestation of Sod's Law that it can be quite tricky organising a mating between two dogs that you want to get together, whereas the accident with the cur-dog down the road seems to go off without a hitch.

Early Pregnancy

There is no need to do much that is different during the early stages of the pregnancy, which lasts 63 days on average. The bitch should be kept well away from other male dogs until she has completely finished her season, and remember that animals do not have an incest taboo – she will happily stand for father, sons, brothers, any male dog that takes her fancy. She does not need extra food yet, and in fact may well go off her food or even develop 'morning sickness' due to the extra hormones circulating at this time. Bitches that are overfed during pregnancy may produce pups that are too big for easy birth, and bitches will be heavy enough at the end of the nine weeks without being fat on their own account as well. Save the extra rations for when she is lactating – then she will need a lot of food, and of the best quality.

Having a bitch scanned for pregnancy is a waste of money. The scan will not make her any more pregnant if she is, nor will it create pregnancy if she is not. She cannot in any case be mated if she 'misses' until her next season. The scan will only tell if she is pregnant at the time it is taken, and she may later

Pregnancy just beginning to show at six weeks

abort or re-absorb some or all of the foeti. So save your money, watch and wait. Her nipples will become larger and more prominent, her coat soft and shiny, and her demeanour may alter. Up to five weeks, you will notice little change in her shape, but from six weeks onwards, her normal streamlined look will begin to change.

The Whelping Area

During the first part of her pregnancy, she should become familiar with the place that you would like her to have her puppies. Don't expect a house dog to be enamoured of suddenly becoming relegated to the garden shed; if possible pick a place where she can still be in the house and of her human family, but private from other animals, dark and peaceful. For your own convenience, it should have a floor that is easily cleaned, not too warm or cold, and be well ventilated without being draughty. There should be power for light and heat, and water with a sink, while not essential, is a great help. If you are using an overhead heat lamp, it should be high enough that the bitch can stand up and not be uncomfortably close to it. Ideally, there should be easy access to outside. The room should be big enough for a very big whelping box, plus allow the bitch to get out and away from her pups when she needs. If you have a kennel and run earmarked for raising the puppies, it is still beneficial to have them close by you in the house while they are very new. Feed her in this place, and sit with her there from time to time, so that she finds it a relaxing place to be. Lurchers tend to have very large litters – twelve is not uncommon – the pups grow big very quickly, and unless you have a sizeable room available, you should plan to have somewhere ready to move them to once they become more mobile.

The Whelping Box

This is important. It should be large enough to let the bitch lie at full length, which is very large for a lurcher, tall enough at the sides that big puppies cannot fall out, slightly raised but not so high that a puppy could become stuck underneath, with a sliding door so that pups can be confined while the bitch can come and go, and they can be let out when you are there to watch them, and with bitch rails all around the insides. Bitch rails are there to allow pups to squirm out of mother's way when she lies down, and cut down the risk of their being lain on. Some bitches are clumsy and squash puppies, some are very careful and never do, but the bitch rails will save lives if you have one of the former kind. Bitch rails should stand sufficiently out and high to allow a sizeable puppy to shelter underneath. Of course, these will cut down the floor space of your whelping box, and you must take this into account when deciding on the size. The whelping box should not be made of or coated in any substance that could be toxic if chewed. There are now disposable whelping boxes on the market, which are a very good idea if you have limited storage space or only intend to breed an occasional litter. If you can persuade the bitch to sleep in the whelping box, this will be a help, but if she is used to sleeping with you, beside your bed or even on it, she is likely not to even consider such a demotion. Perhaps you can compromise and treat it as a day bed for her, leaving her there when she is tired after her walk and perhaps with a bone to chew.

Bedding

Now is the time to start saving newspaper. You will need far more than you could ever imagine. Additionally, I recommend a product called VetBed, which is a fleece pad that can be cut to any size. It is expensive, but it will save you a great deal of time and work, is so easy to wash and dry, and is much safer than other bedding. Whelps can get trapped or lost under straw, hay, blankets or shredded paper, straw and hay is dusty and can harbour parasites, shredded paper can wind itself round tiny limbs and cause damage, and all of it can be ingested by accident. Put a thick layer – a really thick layer – of newspaper down first, and lay the VetBed on top of it so that there is a bedded side and a newspaper side to the whelping box. You will need three VetBeds so that you always have a clean one to hand. Invest in some stout bin-liners and some rubber gloves as well.

Later Pregnancy

From six weeks to birth, she will become progressively larger along each side, and the neat tuck-up of her belly will disappear. Now there is less room for food inside her, and so she will need several smaller meals instead of one large one daily; she will also need to empty herself more often. Please arrange the facility for her to go outside at night rather than trying to 'hold on', and make sure that she has constant access during the day as well. Always have plenty of clean water available. She will need her rations increased now, using appetite as your guide. She will still enjoy her walks, but will not be able to go so far, and may appreciate a rest or two en route. It can be very pleasant on a nice day to sit with your expectant lady and enjoy the scenery. She will enjoy a

Eight weeks pregnant and feeling the strain

gentle back rub, and may spend a lot more time upside down, with her vast belly exposed. If you gently place your hands there, you will be able to feel the pups moving, and see them as well. This response of the unborn to contact is very moving. Tiny newborns will make great efforts to squirm into your hands as well. Do the pups remember, when they are born, that they snuggled their tiny bodies against your hands before birth? Perhaps it is just fancy. Or perhaps, one day we will know more about what makes our domesticated wolves so desiring of human contact.

During the last week of pregnancy, she will become more uncomfortable, and may seem preoccupied or even grouchy. She will be testing areas for dens, and you should tactfully return her to where you would like her to bear her litter. Physically, her belly will have dropped down, and she will look very heavy. She may go off her food in the last few days, or vomit a lot, or show increased need for greenstuff, and she will certainly need to empty herself very frequently.

The Birth

This is a nerve-wracking time for the novice owner. Be sure that you have done your homework and know what to expect: if you have been able to talk to an experienced dog breeder, so much the better. The first signs of labour come when the bitch starts to nest-build, which usually involves frantic digging and scraping at the place where she wants to give birth. Lots of newspapers and perhaps some paper sacking are good things for her to scrape at, as you do not want her to damage her feet, and she must be allowed to dig. Leave her where you want her to birth, and check her at intervals. She will like to be in the dark. Some bitches prefer to be alone when they give birth, some like company; they have a certain amount of control over things and will wait until they have the circumstances that they prefer. Labour is preceded by a drop in temperature, though it has to be said that at times like this a bitch does not need an owner fussing about with a thermometer. Many bitches vomit before they go into labour as well – the stomach needs to be empty. When the time comes, you may see her sides ripple with the labour pains, she may cry or gasp or arch her back. Then a bag of jelly is thrust out of the vulva to lubricate the way, and a puppy should follow in its own time, which may be quite a while later.

You may find that all this has happened while you were out, and there may be another puppy every time you reappear. Or she may be desperate for your company, and try to produce puppies on your lap. Last time I bred a litter, the bitch lay with her head on my lap while I sat on the floor, which suited both of us. Let her do whatever she wants, within reason; you may baulk at whelps being born on your bed, but other than that, the main issue is to get them born and suckling. Birth is a very private time, just for you and your bitch: please do not invite anyone else over to see this happening, as the bitch may well panic and try to hold on to her pups until she is 'safe'. She needs quietness and near dark. Obviously you will need enough light to see what is happening, but no more than that.

Each whelp is born in its own bag and has its own afterbirth, and the bitch's task is to tear open the bag so that the puppy can breathe, nip through the umbilicus, lick the puppy clean (this is the origin of the phrase 'to lick into shape') and present it to the milk bar. Some bitches go at this with such vigour that you think they are going to eat the whole puppy, but try not to panic. Some breeders say that the bitch should not be allowed to eat the afterbirth, but I say she should, not only because it is full of nutrients, and because it is a natural behaviour, but because the afterbirth will loosen her bowels, which is very important for her comfort when she is sore after giving birth. There are those who insist on weighing and measuring newborns, but again, I feel this is unnecessary stress to bitch and pups. Let them be dried by her tongue and nestled up against her belly to suckle. You may be desperate to know the sex and colour, but they will be the same sex and colour in a few hours, and the bitch will be much happier for the minimum of interference.

Pups can be born at intervals of a few minutes, or an hour or more. When you get to a lull in the proceedings, offer your bitch a warm drink that has a very little milk* and some honey dissolved in it, and then offer her the chance to go out and empty herself. Most are really grateful for this. Make sure that she does not fire out a puppy while she is outside! Then back in to nuzzle her babies, settle, and carry on. When she seems to have produced every puppy, clean up the worst of the mess and leave her in peace but with plenty of water to drink where the pups cannot crawl into the bowl. Even newborns are surprisingly active, and can squirm a long way. This is why you need a box for the whelps, otherwise they will crawl under furniture and in all sorts of places, particularly behind the door so that you cannot open it. Go and have some much-needed rest, and don't be surprised if there is an extra puppy or more when you see her later.

What Can Go Wrong

Generally speaking, lurchers are healthy beasts, and not given to birthing

---

*I do not normally advise giving milk to dogs, but they do enjoy it, and this is one occasion when a very little milk, well diluted, will encourage her to drink.

problems the way some breeds with huge heads and narrow pelvises can be. However, there can be exceptions, and my advice is to have your vet ready primed in advance of the due date, yourself making sure that you are au fait with all telephone numbers. Your bitch may suffer from uterine inertia, which means that the contractions stop without any pups arriving. This can be due to a big litter, or one large pup holding all the others up: there is often one pup significantly larger than the others in a lurcher litter. No matter what the time of day or night, vets would rather be called too soon than too late, so if contractions cease, go and get help. The drive to the vet might shake things loose, and you won't be the first person to arrive with more dogs than you left with, but otherwise the most usual treatment is oxytocin, the 'feelgood' hormone, which should start her off again. I have twice had hounds with uterine inertia, and the difference in veterinary treatment was profound. The first practice insisted that I left the bitch, who was a very nervous, clingy animal, and the result was that she had to have an emergency caesarian. Complications followed, and I ended up hand-rearing the litter, not a process I would recommend to anyone. The second practice was much more sensible, and left me, the bitch, a pot of coffee and some reading material all tucked away in a side room, with the result that she relaxed and eventually produced the first pup – a whopper – naturally, after which I took her home for the others. Try to find a veterinary practice like the second one! Of course a bitch isn't going to want to produce her pups in a strange place full of bright lights and noise, with her owner far away.

If your bitch has to have a caesarian, she will be shaved, sore and sorry when she comes out. It is likely that her milk will not come down, or that she will refuse to feed the pups, which will deprive them of the first milk, the vital colostrum, which contains all the antibodies that the pups need for protection against infection. Should this be the case, you can buy replacement colostrum, and your vet should be able to provide some for you.

Hand Rearing

This is very hard work. New whelps need feeding every two hours, and their bowels and bladders need stimulating in order to function. The bitch does this with her tongue, and clears up the resulting mess (never let a nursing bitch lick your face!) but you will need the corner of a soft cloth dipped in warm water. Again, get your vet or an experienced dog breeder to show you how to do this. Feed and clean each pup in turn, so that you do not spread germs. Your vet will be able to supply puppy milk substitute and proper feeders. Hold the puppies upright to feed, so that they do not choke, do not overfeed them, and be sure to wipe up all dribbles, because they don't have the bitch to do that for them. The puppies should be kept in a warm, humid atmosphere: remember they cannot regulate their own body temperature, so aim for a constant room temperature. Humidity can be created by having a bowl of water in the puppy room, and a damp towel either in or over the puppy box. A heat lamp will be needed even in summer, but high over the puppy box, or to one side of it, so that they do not get too hot. You will not be able to lead a normal life during the first two weeks of this unless you have help. Believe me, it is bliss when they go on to four-hourly feeds. If, in addition, you are caring for a post-caesarian bitch, you will learn what it is to feel like a zombie. At around three weeks, you will be able to wean them, and the worst of the job is over. Except, that is, for parting with the pups, because you and they will have bonded incredibly strongly during the rearing process.

Milk Fever

Otherwise known as eclampsia, this is a condition which is relatively rare but extremely serious. The cause is a malfunction in the metabolism which upsets the calcium levels in the bitch's bloodstream while she is producing milk. It is not a lack of calcium, but a breakdown in the ability to process it, so a well-nourished bitch with a small litter is every bit as likely to develop it as an underfed bitch with a large litter. Simply feeding extra calcium will not prevent it, because the calcium is not metabolised in isolation, but in ratio to other important minerals.

The symptoms come on very quickly. The bitch will tremble, stagger and pant uncontrollably, and will progress to a stiff-legged tottering gait before collapse and death. This is a veterinary emergency, and you do not have a lot of time, so call the vet out straight away. The condition is quickly treated with an injection of calcium borogluconate, after which the bitch must be closely watched in case of a recurrence. The first three weeks are the danger period for milk fever, and some bitches are much more prone to it than others. Bitches fed a diet which includes plenty of raw meaty bones will be taking in lots of minerals balanced in exactly the way their system needs, and will therefore be far less likely to develop eclampsia. Some research points to a link with an iodine deficiency, and a few kelp tablets daily would help to balance this in bitches known to be susceptible, but iodine is extremely toxic and should not be given in any other form.

Mastitis

This is a painful condition where one or more of the mammary glands becomes inflamed. The area is purplish-red and hot, and will become hardened if untreated. The bitch may have a raised temperature. Initial treatment is by local application of a warm, wet cloth, but if this does not result in a rapid improvement, antibiotics will be needed. The bitch may be so distressed that she may snap at a puppy that tries to suckle from the affected teat, or even at you when you touch it. A suckling bitch on antibiotics means that the litter will get them as well via the milk, which will make them scour, but over a short spell of time this should not be detrimental. If pups are partly weaned, a teaspoonful of plain yoghurt each twice a day will guard against this. Untreated mastitis can ulcerate, so keep a close watch on the teats and try not to let the condition develop.

Fading Puppy Syndrome

This very distressing condition shows when puppies succumb to one of several infections, weaken and die. It is sometimes known as 'flat puppy syndrome' because they go from round, vigorous whelps to flat lethargic ones in a matter of hours, sometimes with vomiting, diarrhoea or both. Clearly, this is a matter for the vet, for the whole litter can be lost. Prevention includes keeping people and dogs away from the litter for the first three weeks, and then insisting that visitors wash their hands with antibacterial soap, and change their shoes, before going near the puppies. Occasionally, the infection can be brought in or carried by the bitch, in which case there is nothing at all that can be done. Puppies from the best-reared litters can be unlucky enough to get one of these infections; however it is obvious that those litters raised with great attention to cleanliness and good feeding will have stronger powers of recuperation than those raised in dirty conditions.

Week One

Assuming that all goes well, with a normal birth and a healthy litter, the first week should pass fairly calmly. It is sensible to have the bitch checked over by the vet to ensure that she has passed all the puppies and all the afterbirths, as it is by no means uncommon for one or the other to be retained. Sometimes a puppy has died in utero, and is just a jelly blob, but it still has to come out; this is usually achieved by an injection of oxytocin or similar, but in some cases, surgery will be needed. Equally, it is necessary to ensure that the puppies can all suckle, and they each have the usual complement of toes, eyes etc. Sometimes pups are born that cannot suckle due to a cleft palate, crooked jaw or similar malformation. Harden your heart and have deformed puppies humanely put down. Lurchers have big litters, and it is far better to rear

Two-day-old whelps

healthy pups than sick ones. Although there is quite a fashion at the moment for life at all costs, the truth is that a malformed dog has a miserable life, and it is quite indefensible to rear such a creature just to appease human conscience.

You may find that the bitch may reject one or two puppies, and she knows what she is doing: they may look all right, but there will be something wrong with them. If she is persistent about this, and she is caring for the rest of the litter, remove the unwanted pup/s and have them put down as well. If, however, she seems to think that motherhood is not for her and is not at all motivated to care for any of her young, then you will have to help out, either by assisting her with the feeding, just giving her a couple of pups to tend at a time, or by hand-rearing. Sometimes the maternal instinct kicks in after a couple of days of this, sometimes the bitch does not bond with the litter at all. If she can, with your input, just feed and clean the pups, that is an enormous help to them and to you.

Foster Mothers

Sometimes when there are rearing problems, your vet may know of a bitch that has lost her litter and who could be a foster mother. This is not the easy answer it seems. Either the bitch must live with you or the pups must go to her, which means that in both cases, the bitch's owner must be an exceptional and wonderful person to either lose a beloved pet for several weeks or endure all the work and upheaval associated with raising a litter. You will have to be on trust to look after the bitch as your own, or the other person must be equally responsible with the puppies. Of course, you cannot automatically expect the bitch to fall in with these plans either: she might hate the puppies and refuse to nurse them, or worse, kill them. Sometimes, however, the plan works well, as some bitches are so exceptionally maternal that they will raise any young animal. I saw a remarkable example of this years ago at an animal sanctuary, where a maiden bitch came into milk and raised a litter of kittens. As the kittens matured, a baby otter came into the premises, and she suckled that as well. Having found her vocation in life, she was thereafter often called upon to foster orphaned babies, but she was a rarity.

During the first week, the bitch will be reluctant to leave her litter except to go out and empty herself. It is wise if you insist that she takes regular trips outside, otherwise she will hang on as long as possible. Because she is clearing up after her puppies, she will probably have loose bowels, and she will certainly have truly horrendous wind. I once reared a litter in my bedroom for the first three weeks, and may have sustained permanent brain damage from the noxious fumes. It was a bitter winter, and I could not even open the window. I still feel queasy thinking about it.

The bitch will be cleansing internally, and so a copious vaginal discharge is quite normal. This is usually brownish-red, sometimes green, and while not exactly attar of roses, smells inoffensive. If, however, she produces a foul-smelling discharge of an unusual colour, do have her checked by the vet. At the cleansing time, raspberry leaf tablets will help, as will Bach Remedy Crab Apple in her water.

Protectiveness

It is common for bitches to be very 'puppy proud' in the first couple of weeks. Some may only tolerate their owner near their babies, and this should be respected. A bitch protective of her puppies may not even growl a warning before she snaps in defence of them; she should not be put into such a position. Even the sweetest bitch can attack, and it is her right to do so: she is obeying a deep instinct. Treat her with understanding, and do not allow people or other dogs near her. This is a sensible hygiene precaution as well. She will be pleased enough to get away from her litter before long, and then anyone can play with them! Bitches should be left in peace as much as possible, because stress can make them carry puppies around in an effort to find a safer place for them, or even, in desperation, eat them.

She might, of course, be so attached to you that she gives you equal status in puppy-rearing, and expects you to take your turn. I have often had whelps thrust into my hands or onto my lap – 'here, just take these a minute, will you?' while the dam got on with some personal dog task. I have even had very unhygienic but rather touching snuggles with a bitch leaking milk, birth fluid and hideous wind, and the pups tucked between us. Just as well someone invented the washing machine, I feel.

The Nursing Bitch

While she is suckling, she will need an enormous amount of food, no different from her normal rations, but a lot more of it. As a guide, around four times her normal intake, split into four feeds, but if she looks for more, let her have more. Don't forget that she will need to empty out more often as well. She needs a constant supply of fresh water, but she should not have milk. It surprises me how often people think a lactating bitch needs cow milk. Cow milk is for calves, dog milk is for puppies, and lactating bitches need grown-up dog food, which her system is perfectly designed for turning into milk for her own young. Please do not economise by feeding cheap food. Your bitch needs the very best if she is to rear a strong litter.

Puppies for the first week are blind and deaf, but live in a world of smell and touch. They are surprisingly mobile, and often rather vocal as well. The squawk of a tiny pup in extremis is very loud, as it needs to be, but otherwise you will find a low hum of chatter in the nursery quite normal. They will dream, twitching and yipping, but of what, I wonder? Although they cannot walk, they can wriggle surprisingly far, and you will get into the way of counting them every time you see them, to ensure that no-one has trapped itself somewhere out of sight. At this age, they look like small plush bags with snub noses, and you might wonder if these are indeed lurchers, or if someone swopped them in the night? Don't panic: they will look like many things before they become lurchers, but one day they will look like the real article. Unless of course your bitch knows something that you do not.

Dew Claws

Some working dogs have their dew claws removed to prevent injury. Personally, I prefer front dew claws to be left on, as I feel that their function outweighs risk of injury – after all, a dog can be injured anywhere. However, this is a matter of personal choice. Rear dew claws are another matter, however, being vestigial where they appear, and serving no purpose, and if your pups have these I would recommend that you ask the vet to remove them as soon as possible and certainly within the first two or three days, when the pups' nervous systems are not fully formed and the dew claws mere flaps of gristle.

Week Two

The second week progresses much as the first, except that the whelps will be bigger, noisier and more mobile. They will begin to empty themselves independently of the bitch, but she will still clear up after them. Though they can only crawl, they will make tremendous efforts to squirm off their bed and empty themselves on the newspaper. Their front legs will be much stronger than their hindlegs, which are not much more than flippers at this stage. At around ten days, eyes will start to open, first with slits, then right open, one eye at a time or else you might find someone looking right back at you one morning. They can tell light and dark and movement, but not really focus at first. The eyes will be blue, and not take on their adult colour for some time. It is extremely important to have the puppy room in semi-darkness, because it is so easy to damage eyesight at this time. If you are using a heat-lamp, and it is the kind that gives out light as well as heat, I would advise changing to a nursery heater or similar while the eyes are so vulnerable. Always welcome and so difficult to find nowadays, is the stone hot-water bottle. I scour junk shops for these, as they have a high mortality rate, but nothing is better for puppies. They cannot chew them, there is no trailing flex, and no danger if they get wet. Would someone invent a modern version, please? Make sure that the rubber seal works, and wrap it well in cloth, and you will find the hot-water bottle in great demand, particularly in later weeks when the bitch is out and about again.

By the end of the second week, the puppies' nails will need cutting. They are soft and easily trimmed with a sharp scissors – blunt-ended if you can manage – but it is easier if you can have someone hold the pup while you trim it. They can't half wriggle, and some of them will complain very loudly as well. Their mother will appreciate this kindness very much, as all those little hooks scraping along her mammaries are most uncomfortable. Check her nails as well, as she won't have been getting much exercise.

Your bitch may want to leave her puppies and come out with you now. It will refresh her to be away from maternal responsibilities for a spell, but balanced with that is the fact that you do not want her to be carrying infections back to the puppies. As an uneasy compromise, I take the bitch where there are not many dogs exercised; you must decide for yourself if you find that acceptable.

As the pups' eyes unseal, so do the ears, and the little ones will become even rowdier. They will squirm towards your hands when you put them in the puppy box, and seem to enjoy being stroked. I don't pick up puppies, even quite old ones, unless it is unavoidable, nor do I allow others to. It frightens the puppies, and if people hold them carelessly, it may injure them. If the bitch is amenable, tell visitors to sit on the floor with the puppies, and then no-one can be hurt.

Week Three

This is when tiny teeth arrive. They are pointed and extremely sharp, and the puppies will seek to relieve the discomfort of their growing by chewing on anything they can reach – the bitch, your hands, each other, anything. At the same time, the hindlegs begin to take some form and strength to match the front legs, and the infants will be toddling. There will be many sudden

Three weeks old

givings-way and unplanned flops to begin with, but as this week develops so will their strength grow. Eyes can focus much better now, and pups will turn their heads towards sound. This is when weaning commences, and the bitch will become increasingly reluctant to suckle as the needle teeth and infant jaws get stronger. To accommodate these new teeth, noses must grow, but snouts will by no means have the sighthound profile just yet.

Weaning

This is a natural process, and does not have to be as stressful as some breeders, even very experienced ones, make it for themselves. Left to Nature, the bitch would eat and then carry food home in her stomach to regurgitate it for the pups. The resultant semi-digested mess is ideal for weaning, but the process is unpleasant to humans. As long as you make sure that the bitch is keeping enough food down for her own needs, just let her get on with it: it will soon stop. If she is taking all her food to her pups, then feed her separately and keep her confined for an hour or so afterwards, by which time her food will be too far down to fetch up again. Many bitches do not do this at all, and lots of puppies are self-weaning. I remember the first time I came across this when putting the bitch's food bowl down and then watching the litter pile into it and start eating. Good mother that she was, she made no attempt to eat her own food, or to threaten them. Thereafter I fed them separately, and the job was done with absolutely no effort on my part, though she voluntarily topped them up with milk afterwards. This is the ideal way to dry a bitch off: just feed the puppies more solid food, feed it first, and they take less milk each time. Allow the bitch to feed them for as many weeks as she wishes; I have had a bitch quit cold at three weeks, and another that continued to feed until the pups left home at twelve weeks. They did not take much milk by then, but the process was clearly a source of comfort to both the pups and the dam, notwithstanding those very sharp teeth.

What food do you give weanlings? Very much the same as you would give their mother, for you will be surprised at how efficient those baby jaws and teeth are. I favour minced raw meat with puréed fruit and vegetables, with the liquid from cooked rabbit or chicken and a little of the cooked meat as well. Plain yoghurt is very good for maintaining bowel health, but do not feed cow milk. Serve the food with the chill taken off, as they are used to mother's warm milk. Like tiny children, whelps are messy eaters, and need a big shallow dish to begin with. Make sure that you feed them outside their sleeping quarters! They will paddle in, walk through and get covered in their food, and at times seem to do everything except eat it, but though some will learn faster than others, they will all work it out in the end. Some of them will complain bitterly and at length about the fall in catering standards, but let them get on with it at their own pace and eventually they will learn. Raw chicken wings and breast of lamb, the latter cut into chunks, are very good for teething, and the pups will eat the lot. Feed four times a day, and clear up uneaten food immediately afterwards so that it does not attract flies and wasps. If the bitch is amenable, a big beef bone is good gnawing material for pups. Mine have never threatened their pups over food or bones, but I have heard of it happening, so if there is a hint of possessiveness over either, feed the bitch separately and remove any bones that you have left for the puppies before she returns. I suspect that any bitch who growls her puppies away from food is not getting enough herself, unless she is that rare beast, a food-oriented lurcher.

As with feeding the bitch during pregnancy and lactation, please feed good quality food. It is the worst of false economies to feed 'cheap' food where cheap means inferior, and yet how many times I hear breeders boasting of the latest, cheapest way they have found of feeding their pups. You will only ever get rubbish through feeding rubbish. I have seen pups reared on bread, rice pudding, pasta and the like, cut-price low-quality dog meal, tins of soup, broken biscuits and cake, and all manner of other unsuitable trash. Don't breed if you can't feed. Growing pups need proper meat, raw bones, fruit and vegetables if you want strong, straight limbs, good teeth and good health. Pups fed properly are much more resistant to germs, and develop strong immune systems.

While the pups are feeding, you have time to clean out their bed, and then they can all be licked clean by Mum and put back to sleep while you clear up the carnage on the floor of the puppy room. That sliding door to the puppy box is now justifying its existence in damage limitation, and enabling you to work without a mêlée of pups around your ankles. For dogs that are silent adults, lurchers are amazingly noisy puppies, and you will be creeping around your own house trying not to wake them and start another round of feeding and cleaning up. It is time to think about extending their quarters.

By the end of the third week, they will be needing a lot more freedom. As they are eating solids, what comes out of the other end is solid too, and the bitch will be more reluctant to clear up after them. Pups that are given the chance to be clean and empty themselves away from the nest will do so, but now they need more space. This could mean leaving the puppy box open all the time so that they have the run of the puppy room, or you might be moving them into a kennel and run. Whichever you choose, the bitch must be able to get away from the puppies whenever she wants to, and you must be able to attend to them without the risk of them either being trapped behind a door or escaping through it. The baby gate is very useful here, and you can also buy dog-gates which are a little taller. Whatever you use as a barrier, ensure that bars are screened off so that heads and paws cannot be trapped. I once had a puppy trap himself in a wrought-iron gate in his owner's garden, and he had to be freed with bolt-croppers. You now need to worm your puppies for the first time.

Worming Puppies

Your vet will recommend a wormer suitable for puppies – I use Panacur – and make sure that you get it in liquid form. If you can possibly get help, do so, for inserting the right amount of wormer in the right number of puppies is a lot easier with two of you. Use a syringe, and measure out the amount carefully. Despite your care with the worming of the bitch, your puppies will have worms, and they will demonstrate this within the next 24 hours. In an adult dog, the wormer destroys the protective mucus around the worm, which is killed and digested so that you will not see worms in the faeces. Puppy digestions are not so strong, and (if you are eating while you are reading this, please stop now) the result is the expulsion of knots of lively worms. These must be cleared up without delay and burned, and I suggest you wear rubber gloves and don't let any other dogs near until you have done so. Roundworms and especially their eggs can survive for a long time away from their host, and you do not want to infest the soil in your garden. You will, in any case, be faced with a waste disposal problem if you are not able to have a bonfire, as the puppies are producing vast quantities of what is effectively clinical waste, and the general haggard demeanour of the new puppy breeder will acquire deeper stress lines as you strive to dispose of it responsibly.

Your puppies must be wormed fortnightly until they are 13 weeks old, which is a lot of wormer, so buy in bulk if you can. After that, they should be wormed between two and four times a year, depending on their lifestyle. Wormer is quite hard on the system, so do not worm them the same week as you take them to be vaccinated, or if you suffer a flea outbreak and need to treat them for that. Worm at longer intervals rather than shorter if you have to adjust your programme. Immature immune systems should not be subjected to too much stress in one go. Your vet will recommend a flea treatment that is safe for young puppies, but remember that they lick each other and the bitch licks them, so steer clear of any substance that is going to cause problems in this event. Keeping the bitch flea-free will go a long way to helping the puppies. She will need to be wormed when you worm the pups, because she will have taken quantities of worms in from clearing up after them when they were tiny.

Week Four

Your puppies enter week four newly wormed, well on the way to being weaned, and needing their nails cut again. If you thought they wriggled last time, that is nothing to how they will be this time. The bitch is content to visit them at intervals during the day, and may well spend all night away from them, just as a wild mother canid would. They are active and rowdy, and beside themselves with joy to see you. Now is the time for them to meet as many people as possible, both sexes, and as many children as you can find. Everyone must be cautioned to wash hands before and after handling the puppies, to have disinfected footwear, and not to let the puppies lick their faces, as these pups will still have worms. Puppies should not be picked up; instead, visitors should be prepared to sit with them and let the puppies come to them. Milk teeth nips are painful, and the pups should be distracted from chewing on fingers by being given a carrot or

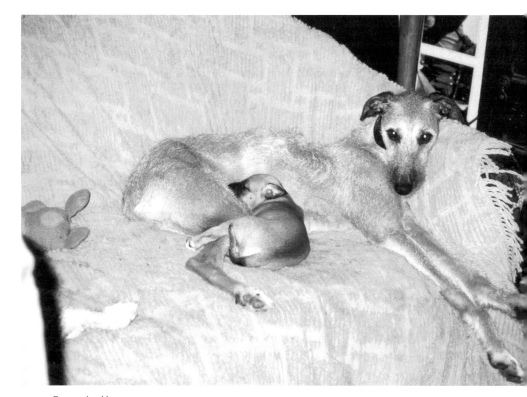

Four weeks old

Four weeks – noses beginning to lengthen

similar vegetable to chew – anything except potato. I don't like puppies having pet shop toys to chew because these do not have any safety checks, and if a lump is bitten off and swallowed, it may be curtains for your puppy. Likewise, do not let your puppies chew sticks. As well as people, puppies should be exposed to low-level noise, such as a radio. Pups in the house can get used to washing machine and vacuum cleaner noise, but if yours are in a kennel and run, as mine are, then you will have to take the noise to them. Clap your hands, talk loudly, sing, drop things in the garden and generally clatter about: the more noise they hear now, the less they will be fazed by it in future. Being a quiet person, I find this part of their education difficult, but it must be done. Never leave children and puppies unsupervised, and to be honest, there are few adults that I leave alone with puppies. It is easy for a little pup to be hurt, albeit unintentionally, and you only seem to have to turn your back for a second to find a puppy being picked up when you look round. Responsible children are so important to have around puppies, but don't allow the other sort, even if it risks a friendship. I vividly remember seeing a litter, not mine thank goodness, carried about by their heads or a limb, by the breeder's small children. They were sold as 'raised with children', this apparently being a good point; not surprisingly all developed skeletal disorders while very young. But children and puppies are made for each other, and providing attention is paid to hygiene, and the children are gentle with the puppies, each will be enchanted by the other. Puppies play hard and sleep often, and the cycle of sleep-play-eat-sleep is how they will occupy the next few weeks, getting ever bigger, noisier, more destructive and more enchanting.

Care of the Bitch

By now, your bitch will likely be back in her normal life apart from short visits to suckle her pups. She may, despite your best care, be looking a bit rough by now. The huge flood of hormones makes some bitch's hair fall out, and she might be as hollow-hipped as an old milch cow – 'milking off her back' as one of my dairy farmer friends puts it. Keep on feeding her as much good-quality food as she needs, until she is properly built up again. Gentle exercise will tighten up her muscles inside and out; keep an eye on her for any signs of discharge, excessive panting, or drinking more than usual. Groom out that old, dead coat to make her comfortable. Don't worry about drying her milk up; let it follow its own schedule. Some bitches will be almost dry by now and others

Five weeks, being separated from the rest of the litter for short spells

Seven weeks, happy and confident – as long as Mum is there

in full flow; either way, don't interfere.

Finding Homes

Now is the time to start seeking homes for your puppies. You may have a few prospective owners lined up, though sadly it is amazing how often people want a puppy until it is on the ground and raring to go, and then the excuses start. Or there is a change of circumstance that cannot fit a puppy in, such as a work contract abroad, a new baby or a house move. Advertising is expensive, but if word-of-mouth is not sufficient, then advertise you must. This has security implications, because if you have strangers coming into your house you might find that they would like to return later, having had a look at your belongings and being of a mind to re-home some of them. It is not unknown for prospective puppy buyers to return and steal the whole litter, and sometimes the bitch as well. There is no easy answer to this problem; please be careful, and if you have a friend who will offer a halfway house for people to view the puppies, this can be a good compromise. Buyers like to see the

Fourteen weeks old and in a loving new home (B. Hurley)

pups with their mother – I would as well – but they will have to be content with photographs or a video of the sire, unless you own both or he is well-known. Beware of the buyer who wants to see your bitch run – no sensible person would ask that of a lactating bitch. As far as price goes, you can judge the going rate for lurchers from advertisements in such specialist papers as *The Countryman's Weekly*. Bitches generally fetch more than dogs. You may be tempted to give the pups away, but it has to be said that people place more value on what they pay for. If you know that the home is good, you might choose to give your puppy to it, and that is your decision, but nice people offer you money anyway, knowing how expensive it is to rear good puppies. Finding homes for your puppies is very time-consuming; many people treat it as a social exercise and keep visiting to tell you their life story, and then decide at the last minute not to have a pup, and you will get telephone calls at unsocial hours. I never mind genuine people visiting several times, as it is important to pick the right puppy. One family even videoed a litter, which was eminently sensible, and helped them to decide which puppy wanted them. If people are genuine, they won't mind at all paying a deposit on their chosen puppy: for the rest, the first person to come up with the full price takes the puppy home. People will try and give you the run-around; just don't have it. You have reared these pups with every care and don't need to home them with people who bid you on the price or press you to keep a certain puppy for them and then let you down. I do stress to people that if it doesn't work out, I must have the puppy back, because I don't want them to go from owner to owner and end up goodness knows how badly off. This is unenforceable even if you ask them to sign an agreement, and I'm afraid the odd puppy will nevertheless get moved on, but it is a partial safety net.

Psychology Testing

This became popular in the 1990s when a scientific test was devised which claimed to grade each puppy for dominance. Prospective owners were advised to separate a pup from its littermates and perform certain tests on it, such as rolling it on its back and holding it there, the puppy's reaction then determining how dominant it was – canine dominance was a fashionable issue in dog training circles at that time. Should any of your puppy customers show signs of trying this, stop them at once. It is not that the tests are not accurate; it is all about puppy welfare. Imagine the effect of every puppy viewer carrying out these tests on every puppy. The shy ones would be well on the way to nervous breakdowns, and the tough guys would be getting very cross indeed. Instead of welcoming the human hand, they would have learned to detest it. If anyone wants to know how dominant or shy a puppy is, they can either ask the breeder, who should know each puppy to the inch, or just sit and watch them for a spell. Any breeder who has not figured out each puppy's character by the end of six weeks raises the question of how much time has been spent with the litter. Buyer beware!

Keeping a Puppy

If you are keeping a puppy for yourself, now is the time to separate her from the others for a short time, or several short times, each day, so that she will bond with you. She can have a soft collar on, and be played with, fed from your hand, and allowed to sleep on your lap. I know several men who carry their puppy around in their shirt. The more that your lurcher pup is with you, the more she will bond with you, and will subsequently be easier to train. But she needs to be a dog as well, so she will need to be returned to her siblings for the greater part of the day. Take her collar off before you do so, or else they will get hold of it and pull her about. She will undergo a status change upon her return, and may well have to do a bit of growling and posturing as she re-assumes her order in the litter. This is all part of dog politics, and should be allowed to happen.

Changing Homes

However carefully this is done, it is a traumatic time for a pup, and often for the new owners. I give a 'puppy starter kit' with dietary advice for those who want it, and if they are local, a recommended vet and dog training classes. A little piece of soft cloth that smells of the puppy bed will aid as a comforter, and if the worming programme is still under way, I list when the puppy has been wormed, with what, and when the next worming is due. If I have enough, I will often include the next worming dose. I am always available if the new owner wants to ask about anything; I believe that I am responsible for the whole of a pup's lifetime, having brought it into the world.

In my youth, puppies changed homes at six weeks old, and if I were buying a puppy in, that is the oldest I would want mine. However, it is now illegal for them to change homes so young, unless, strangely enough, it is to a pet shop or other retail outlet! The law, as so often, is an ass, for a puppy seemingly cannot change homes from one loving, knowledgeable person to another, but can go and spend one of the most critical periods of its development in a shop window.

Most people like to take their puppy after it has completed its initial vaccinations, which is twelve weeks old. Believe me, no matter how much you love your puppies, you will find them exhausting by then. The garden is too small for them and they need to be out and about, but of course cannot until they have been vaccinated, if you follow a vaccination programme. As various puppies leave, other puppies that have been dominated by them come into their own. Puppy squabbles at this age can be noisy and violent, and just as in a playground, some can gang up on an individual and make its life a misery. Plenty of space to get away is the answer, until the various monsters have gone to their new homes.

Aftermath

The season after a bitch has bred might well be heavier than normal, and some bitches take two or three seasons to get back into a regular cycle. If she has had a caesarian, do not breed from her again. If she was a lousy mother, there is no reason to believe another litter will change her mind. If she was a good mother, her subsequent post-season false pregnancies might be more involved than when she was a maiden bitch. If you want to breed from her again, wait until she has had at least one normal season in between. You will probably need that much time yourself, to get over the whole experience and then just remember the good parts.

Now re-read the chapter. Are you *sure* you want to do this?

Further Reading

All About Mating, Whelping and Weaning David Cavill, Pelham Books Ltd. first published 1981

The Mating and Whelping of Dogs R. Portman-Graham, Popular Dogs Publishing Co. Ltd first published 1954, regularly revised and reprinted

Practical Lurcher Breeding D.B. Plummer, Huddlesford Publications, first published 1985

The above books are out of print and if you can find secondhand copies I strongly recommend that you buy them

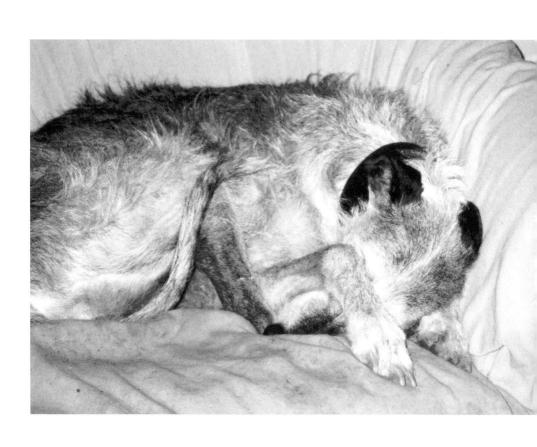

POSTSCRIPT

Like many other good things, lurchers slip sweetly into your life leaving you wondering how you ever managed without them. They make new friends for you, extend your social life and add a whole new dimension to going for a walk. You will catch yourself looking for lurchers when you are out, finding them in the flesh as well as in antique shops and art galleries. You will search out information on them, probably coming to the same conclusion that I have, which is that the more you learn, the less you know. Lurchers have caused many people to examine long-held prejudices about hunting, and to relax and understand its role in the natural world. They cause us to look inside ourselves because of the penetrating way that they see into us, and perhaps some of their numerous virtues will rub off on us and refine us as well. They are most character building, being incapable of an ignoble deed. They are dogs and yet so much more than just dogs: they are graceful, silent sons and daughters of the elements, ethereal, mysterious, spiritual. Yet on occasion, they will bring us down to earth with a well-aimed nose, a grin and a pair of laughing eyes. They are never importunate, yet they make their wishes known with subtle dignity. Lurchers are devoid of pretension: what you see is what you get. Their sensitivity makes us more sensitive, their quietness makes us peaceful, their unbounded joy and energy makes us forget our earthly shackles, our appointments, workload and deadlines. They have roamed the forests and plains of the earth with us since time began, they have shared our lives, our hearths and our inmost secrets, and given freely of their speed and cunning. Ownership of a lurcher transforms the humblest dwelling into a chieftain's tent or a lord's castle. By the very act of allowing you to love them, they have raised you to nobility. They will teach you joy and despair, often in the same ten minutes, they will teach you to stop and think, to see the world through other eyes, to pause and look back through thousands upon thousands of years. See, there is a long head laid in your lap: look into those fathomless eyes, and speak with history. Long may our special relationship with them continue.

Running free (E. Dearden)

INDEX